WITHDRAWN

SILKO

American Indian Literature and Critical Studies Series
Gerald Vizenor, General Editor

SILKO

Writing Storyteller and Medicine Woman

BREWSTER E. FITZ

UNIVERSITY OF OKLAHOMA PRESS : NORMAN

A version of part of chapter 1 appeared in *The Postmodern Short Story: Forms and Issues,* eds. Farhat Iftekharrudin et al. (Westport, Conn.: Greenwood, 2003). A version of chapter 5 appeared in *MELUS* 27.3 (2002): 75–91.

Library of Congress Cataloging-in-Publication Data

Fitz, Brewster E. (Brewster Edmunds), 1941–
    Silko : writing storyteller and medicine woman / Brewster E. Fitz.
        p.   cm. — (American Indian literature and critical studies
    series ; v. 47)
    Includes bibliographical references and index.
    ISBN 0-8061-3584-0 (hc : alk. paper)
        1. Silko, Leslie, 1948– —Criticism and interpretation. 2. Women
    and literature—United States—History—20th century. 3. Western
    stories—History and criticism. 4. Pueblo Indians—Intellectual
    life. 5. West (U.S.)—In literature. 6. Oral tradition—West (U.S.)
    7. Indians in literature.   I. Title.   II. Series.

PS3569.I44Z66 2004
813'.54—dc22

                                                                2003061308

Silko: Writing Storyteller and Medicine Woman is Volume 47 in the American Indian Literature and Critical Studies Series.

1   2   3   4   5   6   7   8   9   10

*The god of writing is thus a god of medicine. Of "medicine":
both science and occult drug. Of remedy and of poison. The
god of writing is the god of the pharmakon.*

—JACQUES DERRIDA,
"La pharmacie de Platon"

*The imperfection of languages consists in their plurality, the
supreme one is lacking: thinking is writing without accessories
or even whispering, the immortal word still remains silent; the
diversity of idioms on earth prevents everybody from uttering
the words which otherwise, at one single stroke, would mate-
rialize as truth.*

—MALLARMÉ,
"Variations sur un sujet"

Contents

Preface and Acknowledgments

In 1992 I took up and read Leslie Marmon Silko's *Storyteller.* I was particularly interested in Silko's depiction of the importance of books for her mixed-blood Laguna Pueblo family. Although I had begun to branch out into cross-cultural literature after having lived and taught in the People's Republic of China in the early 1980s, American Indian literature was a new area for me. My previous teaching and research interests lay in literary theory, French medieval narrative, and the short story. I had been a graduate student at Yale during the rise of deconstruction. The aesthetic, ethical, linguistic, and formal problems posed by the interaction between literacy and orality in a writer like Silko attracted me. From the beginning I saw signs that Silko was not an oral storyteller, that the cultural construct of a writing storyteller was part of the tradition that was passed on to her by literate family members. It struck me that many of the questions Jacques Derrida had raised, especially in "La pharmacie de Platon," about Western culture's tendency to privilege the live voice over writing might be raised in regard to Silko's texts. Also, I found that Roland Barthes' concept of the writerly, in contrast to the readerly, text lent itself to a theoretical understanding of the stories and longer narratives produced by the writing storyteller. Eventually I perceived, though quite obscurely at first, that Silko and her writing storyteller, from the time she first started to write in grade school, had been yearning for something like a perfect language that would heal the cultural wounds embodied in her own mixed-blood ancestry.

I conceived this book as a project after I had begun to teach Silko and other American writers as part of a course on Southwestern literature. The eight interrelated essays about textuality, or secondary orality, and the writing storyteller in the writings of Leslie Marmon Silko that make up this book were written and revised over a period of five years. In these essays I offer readings of passages from *Almanac of the Dead, Gardens in the Dunes,* and of stories and passages from *Ceremony* and *Storyteller. Storyteller* is a book written and assembled by a writer who sees books and writing as central to her upbringing, to her family, to Laguna Pueblo tradition, and to all Indians. I argue that writing was already interiorized in the Laguna Pueblo tradition that Silko received from members of the Marmon family. Nevertheless, she finds herself conflicted between a writerly acceptance of Laguna culture as literate and a desire to live and paradoxically to write in a culture that is primarily oral. This conflicted desire for both orality and literacy evolves in Silko's writing and becomes a yearning for a written orality that is ontologically and epistemologically privileged and different from Anglo-European literature. In some ways this written orality resembles a pure language, the concept of which is found in Walter Benjamin's essay "The Task of the Translator," or the mythic perfect language about which Umberto Eco's wonderful book *The Search for the Perfect Language* provides a wealth of learning.

In the introduction I take a look at two theoretical tendencies in criticism on Silko's writing, before turning to passages in *Storyteller* and in Silko's essay "Books: Notes on Mixtec and Maya Screenfolds, Picture Books of Preconquest Mexico," in which Silko tells the story of a quarrel about a book between Aunt Susie, on whom the writing storyteller is modeled, and Maria Anaya Marmon. In chapter 1 I take up and read scenes involving bears in *Humaweepi, Warrior Priest, Storyteller,* and *Ceremony.* Silko's adolescent vision of a giant bear becomes a trope relating writing, the unspoken, and madness in these texts. In chapter 2 I offer a reading of "Lullaby." In this story, writing is both the instrument that destroys the Navajo protagonist's oral, maternal, religious, aesthetic, and economic culture and the remedy administered by the writing storyteller who takes the place of the Navajo medicine man. Writing is figured in the unraveling U.S. Army blanket in which Ayah wraps herself and her husband as they are freezing to death at the end of the story. Writing as remedy and natural universal language is metaphorically depicted by the brightly colored, finely woven Navajo blankets that Ayah remembers from her childhood and to which Silko's text likens itself. In chapter 3 I compare Austin N. Leiby's historical narrative about the role of the Laguna scouts in the Apache campaign of 1885 with Silko's "A Geronimo Story." In this superb story, Silko paradoxically construes the aphorism *traduttore/traditore* (translator/traitor) as a cross-cultural trope for writing and narration. In chapter 4 I compare the yellow-journalistic narrative of the murder of Nash Garcia by two Acoma brothers with Silko's "Tony's Story." Silko's story, I argue, portrays Tony's murder of the state cop as a continuation of the Pueblo Revolt of 1680. Written Pueblo law is contrasted with Tony's conception of the oral tradition in which he finds his right to kill and burn the deadly witchlike arm of Western law. In chapter 5 I take up Coyote as a ribald and outrageous narrative force that enters into the anonymous protagonist of "Coyote Holds a Full House in His Hand." I describe how Silko's special version of the so-called free indirect discourse (*style indirect libre*) produces a warm, equalizing, maternal or matronizing (rather than cold, condescending, and patronizing) irony. In chapter 6 I examine the tropes of writing and reading as cannibalism and of scientific writing as absence in *Almanac of the Dead.* In chapter 7 I take up and read Silko's paradoxical treatment of the perfect language of love and the language of flowers in *Gardens in the Dunes.* This language of love is contrasted with the dry, allegedly objective discourse of Western science and with the patristic language of orthodox Christian exegesis. I argue that the language of love takes on the form of an ontologically and epistemologically privileged written orality, which evolves from the dominant voice of the Pueblo that is central to

Storyteller. Silko finds traces of this language of love that subverts orthodox patristic exegesis in passages that she collects and cites from Elaine Pagels's *The Gnostic Gospels*. In *Gardens* there are passages in which the writing storyteller merges metaphorically with the perfect language, becoming a kind of mystic simultaneous translator, communing with non-Christians and so-called heretics. Babel and the Pentecostal gift of tongues are glossed in the scenes of the Ghost Dance and in the account of an apparition of the Holy Mother on a schoolhouse wall in Corsica. For Hattie this apparition is the turning point in her "conversion" to the matriarchal spiritual principle on which she had intended to write her thesis. Syncretically conflated in the Holy Mother are snake mothers from pre-Christian Europe and the Americas. As the novel closes, the Indian adolescent protagonist, Indigo, and the Anglo protagonist, Hattie, are geographically separated. The perfect written orality, the cosmic womb, is still a luminous dream, ever deferred, ever interrupted, ever respun. Hattie and Indigo will communicate in writing. Silko's yearning for the perfect language of written orality has resulted in her becoming not only a well-known Laguna Pueblo poet and storyteller but also an internationally acclaimed writer and postmodern medicine woman.

I would like to thank my students at Oklahoma State University for their enthusiastic interpretive insight into "Coyote Holds a Full House in His Hand," a wonderful story, which I teach every chance I get. I would especially like to thank my spouse, Carol Lynn Moder, whose astute reading skills and tactful suggestions helped me untangle many an overlong sentence for which I have a baroque fondness. I would also like to thank Andrea Dodge of Albuquerque, New Mexico, for opening to me the private archives of her mother, Florence Hawley Ellis. Finally, I would like to thank the late Louis Owens who generously shared with me some of his thoughts about the interaction of literary theory and American Indian writing. His death is a great loss to our profession.

SILKO

INTRODUCTION

The Writing Storyteller

*So we went to school to copy, to imitate; not to exchange
language and ideas, and not to develop the best traits that
had come out of uncountable experiences of hundreds and
thousands of years living upon this continent. Our annals,
all-happenings of human import, were stored in our song and
dance rituals, our history differing in that it was not stored
in books, but in the living memory. So, while the white people
had much to teach us, we had much to teach them, and what
a school could have been established upon that idea!*

—LUTHER STANDING BEAR,
My People the Sioux

S*toryteller* has been read and celebrated as a work intended
by Leslie Marmon Silko to foreground and continue the live
voice of Pueblo oral tradition. Linda Danielson and Bernard
Hirsch have both devoted studies to *Storyteller* in which they emphasize the importance of oral tradition for Silko in her writings and
the need for critics to read Silko's texts as informed by living orality.
The studies of these scholars of American Indian literature have
much to recommend them. They have contributed to a rethinking
of what American literature is and its role in contemporary literary

studies at universities in the United States and abroad. Occasionally, however, there emerge in these critics signs of a tendency to distrust writing and a desire to purge themselves of Western cultural concepts and thought. Paradoxically, in their effort to escape Western culture these critics have in some instances more or less unwittingly allied themselves theoretically with the logic of exclusion and hierarchy that informs ethnocentric Western critical discourse. In so doing they have blinded themselves to some of the most interesting cross-cultural intellectual seedings of the florescence of Indian writings to which Leslie Marmon Silko's work belongs. Of course, these tendencies are not discernible only in the critics. At times Silko herself has taken vehemently anti-Western stances in some of her essays, interviews, and notably in the plot of *Almanac of the Dead.* In her short stories, however, and in *Ceremony,* in *Gardens in the Dunes,* and even in *Almanac,* there is a sensitivity to language, both oral and written, that raises questions that cannot be answered by simply anathematizing and excluding Western culture. Silko's vision, though conflicted, I shall argue, is profoundly syncretic, cosmopolitan, and at times almost postmodern, rather than exclusionary, regional, and essentialist.

What Hirsch and some other scholars of American Indian literature have not adequately considered is the possibility that the written text does not necessarily keep the story from growing and changing, that it does not freeze the words in space and time and rob stories of their meaning, as Hirsch has claimed,[1] but that it can be conceived to enhance the growth and the change of the story. The enhanced growth and change, however, come at a price that repeatedly shows itself in a multitude of tropes for writing. One of the oldest of these tropes is found in Plato, who likens writing to a *pharmakon,* an ambiguous term that designates both remedy and poison: Writing is a paradoxical gift from the god of medicine. It serves to both poison and supplement memory. It both wounds and heals. It is a curse and a blessing. These and similar tropes show up in Silko's texts, in which there is nearly always a tension between orality and writing in the content and in the narration. In this book I attempt to explore some of the philosophical questions that arise owing to Silko's having constructed her narratives around these and other tropes that interweave writing and orality with the practice of medicine. Silko, I shall argue, is a writing medicine woman.

Writing from a theoretical position that is somewhat different from that of Hirsch and Danielson, critics such as Arnold Krupat, Susan Perez-Castillo, David L. Moore, Helen Jaskoski, Janet St. Clair, Robert Nelson, Ellen Arnold, and critics/creative writers like Gerald Vizenor and Louis Owens have set out to incorporate poststructuralist and postmodernist theoretical perspectives into their understanding of writing and orality in the work of American Indian writers.[2] Krupat, employing the vertiginous logic (and rhetoric) of deconstruction in a thumbnail reference to research on formulaic diction in oral cultures, suggests that what many poststructuralists (who reject "a signified-based theory of meaning") laud under the label of textuality could just as appropriately be called secondary orality:

> So far as research has been able to determine, the audiences for oral performances—Native American or Yugoslav, a hundred years ago or today—are very little concerned with interpretative uniformity or agreement of any exactitude as to what a word or passage *meant*. These are the worries of manuscript and book cultures, pretty exclusively. Thus, it is probably not accidental, as Walter Ong has pointed out, that the post-structuralist insistence on interpretative openness and undecidable meaning coincides with the first moments of—this is Ong's phrase—"secondary orality" in the West, with a technological shift away from print to electronic information retrieval systems that are not exclusively or inviolably text based. . . . That post-structuralists in fact call this openness textuality rather than orality is a confusion bred of their relative lack of interest in historical detail. ("Post-Structuralism and Oral Literature" 118)

To this deconstructionist theoretical strategy, which appears partly intended to effect a rapprochement between poststructuralist literary theorists and critics of American Indian literature, Krupat adds Bakhtinian dialogic in his reading of *Storyteller:*

> *Storyteller* is open to a plurality of voices. What keeps it from entering the poststructuralist, postmodernist, or schizophrenic heteroglossic domain is its commitment to the equivalent of a normative voice. For all the polyvocal openness of Silko's work, there is always the unabashed commitment to Pueblo ways as a reference point. This may be modified, updated, playfully construed: but its authority is always to be reckoned with. Whatever one understands from any speaker is to be understood in reference to that. Here we find dialogic as dialectic (not, it seems, the case in Bakhtin!), meaning as the interaction of any voiced value whatever and the centered voice of the Pueblo. ("Dialogic of Silko's *Storyteller*" 65)

Espousing and elaborating on this modified poststructuralist theoretical direction signaled by Krupat, I shall argue that in *Storyteller,* as well as in Silko's novels, essays, and critical presentations, the written word and books—both literally and metaphorically—repeatedly show up interiorized and prioritized in the "normative" Pueblo voice. This Pueblo voice, I shall attempt to demonstrate, is part of the Marmon tradition of the writing storyteller. I will elaborate on the writing storyteller in a reading of Silko's story of a quarrel between her great-grandmother A'mooh and her great-aunt Susie. This writing storyteller insinuates herself into all of the American Indian voices that Silko's writing presents, Navajo ("Lullaby"), Yupik ("Storyteller"), Maya, and Yaqui (*Almanac of the Dead*), as well as into the fictional Sand Lizard language and the non-American aboriginal voices that figure in *Gardens in the Dunes.* I contend that in Silko's work, what Krupat (referring to *Storyteller*) calls "the centered voice of the Pueblo" evolves, taking on characteristics of a universal perfect language, for which Silko yearns in her earlier texts and which is explicitly part of the plot in *Gardens.* Thus, within the fundamental orality, to which many of Silko's academic readers and at times Silko herself want to give ontological and epistemological priority, writing turns out to be always already there, not as the curse of a Babelian library full of infinite combinations of dead written signifiers, but as a cosmic womb, the matrix of diversity and being itself. In her writings and interviews Silko seems to shuttle back and forth between, on the one hand, a desire to reclaim primary orality by purging herself, her worldview, and her work of Western thought (in which writing is conceived of as mendacious, desiccating, and semiotically larcenous) and, on the other, a *writerly* dream of grounding the oral tradition and her texts in an ontologically privileged kind of universal language in which writing and orality are organically one, life-affirming, all-embracing, and motherly.

In order to describe this privileged kind of textual orality in Silko, I have borrowed the concept of the writerly text from Roland Barthes, whose highly influential and controversial writings spanning French existentialism, structuralism, and poststructuralism are not often mentioned by critics of Native American literature.[3] Barthes' description of the writerly text in *S/Z* calls to mind in many ways the semiotic and temporal strategy adopted by the writing storyteller. For Barthes the writerly text does not freeze words or rob meanings. It is not a dead letter, a desiccated, mummified representation of speech or of acts; rather, it is the text as difference rewriting itself:

> [T]he writerly text is not a thing, we would have a hard time finding it in a bookstore. Further, its model being a productive (and no longer a representative) one, it demolishes any criticism which, once produced, would mix with it: to rewrite the writerly text would consist only in disseminating it, in dispersing it within the field of infinite difference. The writerly text is a perpetual present, upon which no *consequent* language (which would inevitably make it past) can be superimposed; the writerly text is *ourselves writing*, before the infinite play of the world (the world as function) is traversed, intersected, stopped, plasticized by some singular system (Ideology, Genus, Criticism) which reduces the plurality of entrances, the opening of networks, the infinity of languages.

> The writerly is the novelistic without the novel, poetry with-
> out the poem, the essay without the dissertation, writing
> without style, production without product, structuration
> without structure. (5)

Barthes' writerly text might be described as written glossolalia, as
text in the perfect language that is open to readers of all languages.

In the chapters of this book that offer readings of stories and
passages from *Storyteller,* I will expound on and support by close
readings the hypothesis that in Silko's worldview the conflict
between the oral and the written resolves itself dialectically in a web
of cultural syncretism, interweaving the Western and the Indian.
This web centripetally gathers toward a syncretic and ancestral
figure: the writing storyteller. She makes her Pueblo appearance in
Storyteller both as Aunt Susie and as Grandmother Spider, a natural
spinner and weaver of verbal creation from Pueblo culture, whose
storytelling is metaphorically a written web in which nature cannot be conceived without culture and the oral cannot be unraveled
from the written. In this guise she is clearly helpful and life affirming.
She also makes her appearance in *Almanac of the Dead* as the cannibalistic spiderlike woman whom the four children carrying the old
almanac encounter at the village called "The Mouth." Here the
downside of writing appears in the trope of reading and writing as
cannibalism. She also makes her appearance as the Holy Mother of
the Messiah (*Gardens in the Dunes*). Most often, however, the writing
storyteller is the anonymous third-person narrator of the free indirect
discourse that is dominant in Silko's novels and in most of her short
stories. In interviews that have been collected by Ellen Arnold, Silko
has implicitly linked this third-person narrator with a spiritual narrator and with the voices of many spirits for whom she is the scribe.

Silko's vacillation between "primary orality" and "secondary
orality" (aka textuality) shows up in passages from *Storyteller,* in
critical essays, and in passages from her novels. Some of the theoretical problems, which arise from her writerly dream of grounding
the oral tradition in an ontologically privileged kind of writing, are

figured in Silko's essay about precontact Mesoamerican writing. In the remainder of this introduction I would like examine this essay, a passage from the opening of *Storyteller,* and passages from several essays in which orality and writing figure in order to initiate a description of the writing storyteller and her relation to the special kind of writing in which Silko's text grounds itself.

In the opening pages of *Storyteller,* Silko portrays herself as the literary heir of her father's aunt, Susie Reyes Marmon, or Mrs. Walter K. Marmon, usually referred to as Aunt Susie. The relationship that Silko explicitly portrays between her great-aunt and herself can be used to construct a potential interpretive model for reading *Storyteller* and Silko's novels. The didactic relationship between Aunt Susie and Silko should help the reader to understand her/his relation in Silko's text to the oral storyteller, to the audience, and to the writing storyteller. This potential interpretive model, which belongs to reader response theory, is not, however, without problems, for an ambivalence concerning the relation between orality and writing shows up in the brief portrait of Aunt Susie:

> She [Aunt Susie] was already in her mid-sixties
> when I discovered that she would listen to me
> to all my questions and speculations.
> I was only seven or eight years old then
> but I remember she would put down her fountain pen
> and lift her glasses to wipe her eyes with her handkerchief
> before she spoke.
> It seems extraordinary now
> that she took time from her studies and writing
> to answer my questions
> and to tell me all that she knew on a subject,
> but she did.
>
> (4)

Aunt Susie's gesture, putting down her fountain pen in order to *tell* "all that she knew on a subject" to the young Leslie, both figures Silko's desire to reclaim the oral tradition's epistemological and

ontological superiority to writing and prefigures her realization of
the irrevocable need to take up the pen to rewrite a new vision, of
which *Storyteller* is the embodiment. Silko makes clear that the
writing that Aunt Susie defers as she takes off her glasses and
wipes her failing eyes is intended to supplement the interruption
of the oral tradition, which many persons, apparently including
Aunt Susie herself, once thought imminent:

> She had come to believe very much in books
> and in schooling.
> She was of a generation,
> the last generation here at Laguna,
> that passed down an entire culture
> by word of mouth
> an entire history
> an entire vision of the world
> which depended upon memory
> and retelling by subsequent generations.
>
> She must have realized
> that the atmosphere and conditions
> which had maintained this oral tradition in Laguna culture
> had been irrevocably altered by the European intrusion—
> principally by the practice of taking the children
> away from Laguna to Indian schools,
> taking the children away from the tellers who had
> in all past generations
> told the children
> an entire culture, an entire identity of a people.
>
> (4–5)

As a graduate of Carlisle Indian School and of Dickinson College
(3) and as a schoolteacher (3–4), Aunt Susie embodies this irrevocable alteration, this intrusion of European education and literacy
into Pueblo tribal and family life. As scholar, bibliophile, schoolteacher, and storyteller, this remarkable woman spoke and wrote
from the perspectives of two generations, of two pedagogies, of

two cultures—one oral, the other literate, one Laguna Keresan, the other Euro-American. Understanding how these two perspectives interrelate in Silko's portrayal of Aunt Susie is crucial to understanding Silko's rewritten and writerly vision of Laguna culture.

Despite her obvious respect for Aunt Susie's scholarly concern with the irrevocable alteration that literacy and Western education had brought to oral Pueblo tradition, Silko portrays her great-aunt's legacy as almost entirely oral and explicitly chooses to emphasize the oral part of that legacy:

> And yet her writing went painfully slow
> because of her failing eyesight
> and because of her considerable family duties.
> What she is leaving with us—
> the stories and remembered accounts—
> is primarily what she was able to tell
> and what we are able to remember.
>
> And with any generation
> the oral tradition depends upon each person
> listening and remembering a portion
> and it is together—
> all of us remembering what we have heard together—
> that creates the whole story
> the long story of the people.
>
> I remember only a small part.
> But this is what I remember.
>
> (6–7)

Thus, where Aunt Susie puts down her pen and defers her writing in order to respond *orally* to the young Leslie's questions, Silko, the writer, takes up the pen to *write* the first story in the book while still *hearing* the now-silent writer's voice:

> This is the way Aunt Susie told the story.
> She had certain phrases, certain distinctive words
> she used in her telling.

I write when I still hear
her voice as she tells the story.

(7; my emphasis)

Silko then recounts the story of Waithea, as *told*—not as written—
by Aunt Susie. Nowhere in *Storyteller* is Aunt Susie's writing quoted
literally. From what I have been able to ascertain, Aunt Susie's
writings are not presently accessible.[4] Judging from the reasons
Silko gives for her great-aunt's having "come very much to believe
in books," namely that the European intrusion had irrevocably
altered the Pueblo oral tradition, it is possible to speculate that
these writings may have been at least partially informed by what
Edward Bruner, in an article treating ethnography as storytelling,
has posited as "the dominant story." Bruner contends that it was
according to this story that ethnographers writing about Native
American cultures from the nineteenth century into the 1940s "saw
the present as disorganization, the past as glorious, and the future
as assimilation" (139). If this is the case, the current inaccessibility
of Aunt Susie's writings would conveniently allow Silko to portray
the progressive and literate perspective in her great-aunt's worldview as certain *audible* traces, "certain phrases, certain distinctive
words" (*Storyteller* 7), rather than to enter into an exegetical apology
or justification for elements in Aunt Susie's writings that may run
counter to the currently dominant narrative that views "the present
. . . as a resistance movement, the past as exploitation, and the
future as ethnic resurgence" (Bruner 139). In their absence, Aunt
Susie's writings function like a writerly oral tradition, which Silko
not only glosses but also rewrites, much in the manner of the oral
storyteller retelling ancient stories. In being rewritten the stories
change; they grow—to use Hirsch's term—textually. In rewriting
the absent writings, Silko portrays her great-aunt as a writing storyteller who *defers* her writing in such a way that her now-silent
writerly voice informs *Storyteller*.[5] Likewise, in foregrounding orality,
Silko defers a literal meaning in a writerly voice that informs the
written interpretations of *Storyteller* by critics such as Hirsch and

Danielson. In taking up the pen to write a revision of Pueblo culture that is compatible with the currently dominant narrative of ethnic resurgence, Silko may be revising both literally and figuratively an ancestral vision that Aunt Susie herself realized was failing. The themes of vision, insight, and blindness, which recur at specular turning points in "Tony's Story," "Coyote Holds a Full House in His Hand," as well as in Silko's rewriting of Robert G. Marmon's "Story of Coyote and Lark," provide the occasion for close readings to explicate the way in which the ancestral vision is rewritten in *Storyteller* by a special kind of writing.

An inkling of the metaphysical status of this special kind of writing is found in a letter from Silko to James Wright.[6] Writing at the time that she was putting *Storyteller* together, Silko portrays her beloved great-aunt looking forward to being finally able to take up her pen again and complete her writings, once she has joined her ancestors at Cliff House: "Aunt Susie is 106 and she talks about getting out of there soon (the nursing home her children, my cousins, have put her in). She'll get around to writing out the stories then, she says, in far greater detail than she's ever been able to tell them— over at Cliff House, she says, with Tsa'na'di, her mother's sister, an aunt who was only a few years older than she" (48). Here Aunt Susie is portrayed as viewing her writings not only as surpassing in detail her oral tellings, but also as aspiring to a totality that would encompass "an entire history / an entire vision of the world" (*Storyteller* 6). As such, this special kind of "posthumous" writing would not only resolve the irrevocable alteration that Protestant education and literacy effected at Laguna, it would also revise and ground the conditions of memory among the ancestors in writing. In this bookish revision of storytelling, Silko takes up the pen not only where Aunt Susie put it down to tell her orally all she knew on a subject, but also where her great-aunt would take it up again at Cliff House to write out the oral tradition. In such a vision Laguna culture becomes a text, a weaving together of the oral and the written, which is grounded in the writerly voice of literate ancestors like Aunt Susie at Cliff House.

Without a doubt, Aunt Susie was an extraordinary person, whose roles included storyteller, mother, devoted and hardworking partner in a ranching operation, as well as schoolteacher, historian, interpreter, informant, and ethnographer. She was both friend of and collaborator with the late Florence Hawley Ellis, an anthropologist whose writings are still an excellent source of information on Laguna. These writings contain footnoted references to conversations with and texts written by Aunt Susie.[7] Keeping in mind this composite figure, as well as Aunt Susie's vision of herself at Cliff House "writing out the stories . . . in far greater detail than she's ever been able to tell them," let us return briefly to Bernard Hirsch's reading of Aunt Susie's story of Waithea as exemplary of Silko's attempt to portray textually and texturally in writing some of the distinctive traits of oral storytelling. After having quoted from *Storyteller* and having stated that "Silko uses poetic form with varying line-lengths, stresses, and enjambment to provide some of the movement and drama of oral storytelling" (7), Hirsch comments that the italicized expository passages are used by Silko "to evoke the digressive mode of traditional storytellers and the conversational texture of their speech" (7). He quotes the italicized passage in which Aunt Susie glosses *"yashtoah"* and quotes Silko's comment that being able to "stop the storyteller and ask questions and have things explained" is the "beauty of the old way" (7). What Hirsch does not mention, which Anthony Mattina has pointed out (146–47), however, is that the "italicized expository passages," rather than evoking the "digressive mode of traditional storytelling," function like glosses in footnotes in an ethnologist's text. Not only are they written in the concise style most editors prefer, they also provide crucial linguistic and cultural information both to young Leslie and to the reader. In so doing they signal the irrevocable alteration to the oral tradition, the difference between the linguistic and cultural worlds into which Aunt Susie was born and her great-niece was born. Paradoxically, the attempt to make writing serve the oral tradition, on which Hirsch insists, underlines the "primary" oral-aural gap between generations while bridging it "secondarily" in a special type of print that signals itself as the self-translating and writerly voice of the interpreter-informant, the figure on whom the ethnologist's cross-cultural project depends. Aunt Susie's expository remarks belong to the tradition of ethnological writing, of glossing "foreign" words and concepts.

In an interview with Larry Evers and Denny Carr, Silko makes a disparaging remark about Elsie Clew Parsons while unfavorably assessing the songs and stories collected from Indian informants and translated by ethnologists.[8] She also talks of her disdain for contemporary poets who use these ethnological texts as sources and of her belief that the contemporary Laguna oral tradition—which is principally in English rather than Keresan—conveys a vitality that is lost in the written recordings of the interpreter's voice. Given that Silko also suggests in this interview that she was "sort of self-conscious about not knowing the Laguna language better" ("Conversation with Leslie Marmon Silko" 30) and that she admits elsewhere that she knows very little Keresan,[9] it would appear that she contends that the contemporary Laguna oral tradition in English successfully "translates" from Keresan into English some ancient, Laguna vitality. Silko states that she can hear this ancient vitality even through rumors and gossip about a "trash fight" (30), whereas the nearly literal translations made by Elsie Clews Parsons and other anthropologists are, she implies, like mummified stories preserved in the dry, written English that killed them in literal translation. In other words, Parsons's translations exemplify the Italian adage: *traduttore/traditore* (translator/traitor), whereas Silko's written storytelling in English does not. Central to this reasoning and anthropology-bashing is the desire to believe that what matters is not not knowing Keresan as well as Aunt Susie, or even as well as Elsie Clews Parsons, for that matter. Instead, what matters is knowing a special kind of English as well as Aunt Susie and better than Elsie Clews Parsons. I will argue that not only is this special kind of English part of the Marmon bibliophilic tradition at Laguna, but it is a writerly step toward a perfect language of love that unites orality and literacy. Silko's Ghost Dancers in *Gardens in the Dunes* literally attain this goal when they are visited by the Messiah and the Holy Mother (see ch. 7).

A paradox similar to the one that was signaled in Hirsch's reading of the story of Waithea—that is, that the passage printed in italics intended to evoke the direct conversational contact of speaker and audience characteristic of orality actually signals the temporal and cultural barriers between them—is found in one of Silko's best-known critical pieces, "Language and Literature from a Pueblo Indian Perspective." In this presentation, which Silko made in 1979 at Harvard to the English Institute, the story of Waithea, the little girl who ran away, shows up *not* as an oral storytelling performance, but as a written text read aloud. In reading this text aloud Silko interrupted the extemporaneous mode of presentation that she had insisted was crucial to her audience experiencing the authentic Pueblo orality of her discourse:

> Where I come from, the words that are most highly valued are those which are spoken from the heart, unpremeditated and unrehearsed. Among the Pueblo people, a written speech or statement is highly suspect because the true feelings of the speaker remain hidden as he reads words that are detached from the occasion and the audience. I have intentionally not written a formal paper to read to this session because of this and because I want you to hear and to experience English in a nontraditional structure, a structure that follows patterns from oral tradition. For those of you accustomed to a structure that moves from point A to point B to point C, this presentation may be somewhat difficult to follow because the structure of Pueblo expression resembles something like a spider's web—with many little threads radiating from a center, criss-crossing each other. As with the web, the structure will emerge as it is made and you must simply listen and trust, as the Pueblo people do, that meaning will be made. (54)

This oft-quoted and somewhat troubling admonishment, in which signs of defensiveness and condescension can be detected, was delivered to an audience many of whom were probably familiar with avant-garde writers such as Borges, Pynchon, and Gass, some of whom probably had read Barthes' *S/Z*, the translation of which was published in 1974 to much fanfare in part of the Eastern literary community, and most of whom in their literary upbringing must have been nurtured on Joyce and Proust, whose texts are temporally and semiotically informed by concepts of nonlinearity. Thus, the audience of this emphatically extemporaneous, unrehearsed, from the heart, nonlinear presentation might indeed have been surprised when Silko, having arrived at the point where she could finally *tell* a story from her family's Laguna oral tradition, produced a prewritten, premeditated text and admonished her audience to listen for, among other things, the marks of Aunt Susie's literacy in a special kind of English:

> I would like to read that story to you now, and while I am reading it to you, try to listen on a couple of levels at once. I want you to listen to the usage of English. I come from a family which has been doing something that isn't exactly standard English for a while. I come from a family which, basically, is intent on getting the stories told; and we *will* get those stories told, and language *will* work for us. It is imperative to tell and not to worry over a specific language. The imperative is the telling. This is an old story from Aunt Suzie [*sic*]. She is one of the first generations of persons at Laguna who began experimenting with our notion of English—who began working to make English speak for us—that is, to speak from the heart. As I read the story to you, you will hear some words that came from Carlisle. (61)

What follows is the story of Waithea, printed not in verse as in *Storyteller*, but in indented paragraphs, with some of the cultural and linguistic gloss included, but not italicized, and accompanied by a footnote that signals the contractual, written relation of this story to the world of publishing and all that it entails: "Copyright © by L. M. Silko in *Storyteller*, a Richard Seaver Book" (63).

Why, if she "deliberately did not read from a prepared paper so that the audience could experience firsthand one dimension of the oral tradition—non-linear structure" (54 n), did Silko read from a written text a story that could have been told orally in order for her audience to experience more than just one dimension of the oral tradition?[10] After having disparaged prewritten discourse as not being from the heart, as being "highly suspect" to the Pueblo people "because the true feelings of the speaker remain hidden as he reads words that are detached from the occasion and the audience," did Silko choose to "speak" from this written text in order to hide her true feelings? Of course, this is a rhetorical question that I will answer by hypothesizing that the story of Waithea as told by Aunt Susie and written by Leslie Marmon Silko belongs to a tradition in which the oral and the written are already linguistically and culturally irrevocably interwoven, that it is a story informed by a consciousness of the alteration that writing and education in the English language had already brought to Laguna Pueblo culture before Leslie Marmon was born, before her father was born, before her Grandpa Hank was born. It is a writing storyteller's story. Furthermore, I would like to speculate that the "great family or personal loss"(61) that occasioned the telling of this story to Leslie is both figuratively and literally a maternal loss, about which Silko has feelings she would like to *hide from herself.* In telling this story, which Silko specifies "is sometimes given to you when there has been a great loss" (61), Aunt Susie was offering comfort to her great-niece both for the loss of the mother tongue brought about by the European intrusion and the loss of direct Pueblo matrilineal descent that resulted from Silko's mother not being Laguna and not at Laguna to take care of her.[11]

Patricia Jones has noted the absence of Silko's mother in *Storyteller* (Jones 213–32).[12] Indeed, Aunt Susie's story about a little girl feeling hurt and neglected because her mother deferred making *yashtoah* for her is one of a cluster of stories about surrogate mothering ("Storyteller" 17–32; "It was a long time before" 33–35), apparent maternal neglect ("*The Laguna people*" 38–42; "Lullaby" 43–51), and loss of the maternal tongue in which storytelling and mothering are both explicitly and implicitly equated. Given that there are no photographs of the young Leslie's mother in *Storyteller*, and that the only mention of her is en passant and concerns her not being around because she worked (33), one can infer that Leslie and her sisters may have felt neglected, owing to—among many things— their mother not being there to tell and read stories aloud.

However we may interpret Leslie's mother's not being portrayed as a storyteller in *Storyteller*, she did tell at least one story to Silko, which is recounted in an essay entitled "Books: Notes on Mixtec and Maya Screenfolds" (*Yellow Woman* 155–65). This essay comprises two parts: first, a section on the surviving Mixtec and Maya pictographic writings, in which Silko scathingly indicts the Spaniards for having burnt most of the precontact Mesoamerican "texts," the remnants of which are usually referred to as codices by European librarians,[13] and second, a section on the role books played in the Marmon household, which closes with the story of a quarrel about a book between Grandma A'mooh and Aunt Susie. This intriguing family story, which was apparently kept secret by many of the Marmon storytellers, was told to Silko's mother by Grandma A'mooh; it nearly ends in a book-burning. It is to this essay with its two stories about book-burning that I turn now in continuing the examination of the special kind of writing embodied in *Storyteller*.

In her description of the existing Mesoamerican screenfolds,[14] Silko touches on nonlinear thought and speculates about how these texts were read:

> The screenfolds, complementing non-Western, nonlinear thought, store information so that several pages may be viewed simultaneously. When folded out, the screenfold served as a mural. . . .
>
> The writing must be read like a painting, that is, the colors and lines and figures within give the reader the clue of how to read the painting, which *area was meant to be read first,* and so forth. *Sometimes red lines indicated the directions.* Page layout, the scale of the symbols, the position they occupy in relation to one another, and the way they are grouped together are all elements that determine *which direction the writing is to be read*

and its ultimate meaning. The colors filling the spaces made by
these regular strokes constituted chromatic variations, which
influence meaning. (156; my emphasis)

Here I am not so much concerned with the philological accuracy
of Silko's remarks as with the remarkable role that linear progression plays in her abecedarian description of how meaning was read
in these texts. What emerges is a description of a pictographic and
ideographic text, which Silko wants to differentiate from linear
Western writing and thought, and yet the "ultimate meaning" of
which paradoxically seems to be determined by a narrative that
puts images and words into a linear order: "The Mixtec and Maya
combined painting and writing, two activities that European culture considers distinct. People probably talked about the images as
the books were unfolded, so that while the eye scanned the images,
the ear heard the words of the narrative. Both concrete and abstract
ideas could be expressed in picture writing" (157). Silko not only
opposes the Mixtec and Maya combination of painting and writing
to the alleged Western distinction between the visual and the scrip-
toral arts, she also attributes to this Mesoamerican combination a
divine ontological efficacy: "For the people, these images were
more than images are for Europeans. Certain aspects of the divine
world were actually present, at least for a while, in these images.
Thus the people ritually fed the books with sacrificial blood. The
universe of the gods came to life through the coupling of the brush
to the bark paper" (157). In other words, Silko is reasoning that the
Mixtec and Maya screenfolds were not just what the friars and the
conquistadors would have considered to be nugatory idols or occult
painted images, but were living receptacles that were ritually viewed,
narrated, and fed sacrificial blood in order to replenish their divine
life and meaning. They were "idols" or icons that really worked.

Silko does not take up the thorny historical question of the Spaniards' inquisitorial tendency in the New World to see and burn
another culture's sacred metaphysical and poetic constructions as
manifestations of satanic and pagan witchcraft, just as in the Old

World they had burned heretics, witches, and Jews and their writings. Instead, she soars into an ideological flight of the postcolonial imagination, flaying the scheming conquistadors for their illiterate and racist cunning aimed at defying international law and enslaving the indigenous population:

> In 1540, the great libraries of the Americas were burned by the European invaders, most of whom were illiterate but not stupid. They burned the great libraries because they wished to foster the notion that the New World was populated by savages. Savages could be slaughtered and enslaved; savages were no better than wild beasts and thus had no property rights. International law regulated the fate of conquered nations but not of savages or beasts. (157)

But Silko, despite her political commentary, which she may have conceived at least partially as darkly ironic since it inverts the usual tale of literate Europeans arriving to instruct illiterate Indians, is not really interested in the law, international or other. She is interested in something beyond law, beyond the practice of venal and squabbling lawyers and judges whose scribbled chicaneries are usually unreadable. For her what the European invaders burned were exemplars of a special non-Western form of writing that through a sacrificial, specular, and narrative act rendered the gods immanent in the book as in the world. In such an act orality and writing combine in a performance that makes divine words into flesh and spirit. Seen from the point of view of the Western religions of the Book—a Jewish, or Christian, or Islamic point of view—what the Spaniards did in Mexico was the equivalent of an invading army occupying Europe and the Holy Land in the pre-Gutenberg era and burning nearly every manuscript of the Torah, the Old and New Testaments, the Koran, and all of the exegetical writings attached thereto. (Of course, the Spaniards could not *burn* the glyphic writings of pre-Columbian Mesoamerica.) Keeping this in mind, let us turn to the second part of the essay, which concerns some of the books that were present as well as two books that were absent in the Marmon household, and a story of a near book-burning.

The second part of this essay begins and ends with the story of a book that was absent from the bibliophilic Marmon household: "Books have always been important for my family. As a child I remember the old lament the family had about the signed first edition of *Ben-Hur* that had disappeared. Local legend had it that Lew Wallace had written a portion of *Ben-Hur* in the priests' quarters at the mission church" (158). Given the subject matter of this novel, even had it been present in the Marmon family library, it is not likely that Leslie would have developed a fondness for it. It might have been the kind of narrative of conversion—a story of Evangelical acculturation—that the devoutly Presbyterian Grandma A'mooh enjoyed reading. Judging, however, from Silko's description of her reading habits, her family spent much time nourishing themselves with books that construed flesh and the word quite differently from the missing *Tale of the Christ* that a chariot-driving Charleton Heston immortalized for many moviegoers:

> My great-grandmother's house had a tall bookcase full of my great-grandfather's books. My grandparents' house also had rooms with shelves of books. We had books. My parents kept books at their bedsides. My father used to read at the table at lunchtime, and we did too. It was years before I realized it is considered impolite to read at the table. I remember waiting until I was alone in the house, and then I'd go find *Lolita* or *Lady Chatterley's Lover* half hidden under my dad's side of the bed. (158–59)

Perhaps Silko is enjoying her own private joke here by implicitly contrasting her father's and her own reading preferences to those of the book-burning Spaniards. The friars certainly would have added to the fire these two notorious books over which quarrels were stirred up between the powers of censorship and the avant-garde literati, some of whom championed the return to pagan sensuality and "blood consciousness" as embodied in Lawrence's prurient gamekeeper. However that may be, Silko makes a point of contrasting her family's love of books with what she clearly takes to be the bibliophobic attitude typical of the Anglo-American cowboy invaders who replaced the book-burning Spanish in New Mexico: "I have a friend who grew up in a house without books. There was a Bible and there were cattle growers' magazines, but he was in the sixth or seventh grade before a cousin going off to war gave him the first books he ever owned. My friend still suffers with insatiable lust for books" (159).[15] Not only may Silko once again be indulging her irreverent sense of humor in suggesting that the Bible and "cattle growers' magazines" are worthy of being grouped together as nonbooks, but she is also using language that implies that oppressed bibliophilic offspring of cowboy illiterati are all the more likely to entertain a powerful erotic attraction to writing. Such an attraction often produces great writers. What follows is an implicit subversion of the Hollywood cowboys and Indians topos in which the cowboys lose owing to books:

> Stampedes, storms, angry Indians, and bandits never did get to that great old cowboy Charles Goodnight, but lawyers and their books laid old Goodnight low. No wonder the cowboys distrusted books. They must have distrusted my friend too, when they sensed his passion for books. They clung to their old life, the old cowboy culture with its devotion to livestock and to the land long after the heyday of the cowboys had passed. These cowboys believed in action, not words, certainly not the printed word. (159)

These bibliophobic, illiterate, scofflaw cowboys lust not after books, but after riches that they plunder from the land and its people as they irreverently whoop it up: "In the Americas, the printed word, like the spoken word, had to be ignored if the settlers were to reap the riches they all desired. If you could not read the king's or the pope's edict, then you could not be held accountable" (159).

Meanwhile back at the ranch, Aunt Susie and Grandma A'mooh are empowering themselves and their descendants with books to defend their people and loved ones from the hoards of plundering bovine illiterati:

> My great-grandmother and Aunt Susie had been sent to Carlisle Indian School in Pennsylvania, and both women had returned with a profound sense of the power of books. The laws were in books. The king of Spain had granted the Laguna Pueblo people their land. The Laguna Pueblo people knew their land was protected by a land grant document from the king of Spain. The Anglo-Americans who swarmed into the New Mexico Territory after 1848 carried with them no such documents. The Pueblo people fared better than other tribes simply because of these documents. The land grant documents alerted the Pueblo people to the value of the written word; the old books of international law favored the holders of royal land grants. So, very early, the Pueblo people realized the power of written words and books to secure legitimate title to tribal land. No wonder the older folks used to tell us kids to study: learn to read and to write for your own protection. (159–60)

At Laguna the Marmons knew that the written word is mightier than the six-gun.

Reading aloud, it seems, was part of the storytelling at Grandma A'mooh's place. Not only did Silko's great-grandmother read to her from the Bible (17), she also read from children's books: "Grandma A'mooh used to read to me and my sisters over and over from a tattered little book called *Brownie the Bear*. My father and my uncles also remember *Brownie the Bear*. People told stories constantly, but Grandma A'mooh made a point of reading to us from a book too, perhaps because she feared we'd prefer listening to reading (who wouldn't?)" (160). Thus interwoven in the oral storytelling is the didactic intention to accustom at an early age the grandchildren and great-grandchildren to associate the written word with the oral tradition. In this tradition books become a surrogate maternal comfort to the young Leslie when she is away from grand-maternal care: "But when I got to school and there were no beloved grandmas or aunts to tell me stories, I remembered that books tell stories too, and whenever I felt alienated and lonely in school, I would begin to read a story, and immediately I felt that happy secure feeling come over me as it did whenever Grandma A'mooh began telling me a story" (160). The logical progression is predictable. Young Leslie goes from hearing stories told and read, to reading stories, to telling stories, to writing stories: "I used to make up stories for my sisters and cousins because I learned very early that I got the same pleasure from telling stories as I felt when I was a listener. Later, in fifth grade, I learned that when it was not possible to be soothed by hearing a story or by telling a story aloud, I could evoke that same feeling of well-being by writing down a story I made up myself" (160–61).

Once writing enters into storytelling, however, there is always the "danger" that, just as little writing storytellers are separated from home, their new words will be separated from the things and places to which they refer: "Fifth grade was when my sisters and I had to commute to Albuquerque to school, and I was very unhappy. Mrs. Cooper, the fifth-grade teacher, asked us to make up a story that used the words in our spelling list at least once. The spelling list had the word *poplar*, and I remember I had a character sliding down the smooth bark of the poplar tree. Of course I had no idea what a poplar tree looked like" (161). This seemingly innocent account of the young Leslie's first encounter with nonreferential writing, with writing about things that one has not experienced, precedes and implicitly provides an interpretive frame for the story of the quarrel between Grandma A'mooh and Aunt Susie over a book whose author intentionally used words alienated from their referents in order to encourage Pueblo readers to alienate themselves from their traditional ways: "A book was the cause of the only big quarrel my great-grandmother ever had with her daughter-in-law Aunt Susie. The old-time Pueblo people abhorred confrontations, especially with family members. So I was almost grown and Grandma A'mooh had passed on before my mother ever discussed the incident. The quarrel had occurred years before, and few people knew about it; but Grandma A'mooh was very fond of my mother and told her the story" (161). The book was *Stiya: A Carlisle Indian Girl at Home*, which was copyrighted in 1891 by Marion Burgess, whose initials are phonetically represented as "EMBE" on the title page. The book is dedicated to "Tonké, Who Shared the Pleasures and Sorrows of a Trip Among the Pueblos." It is illustrated with photographs, the first of a young Indian woman, wearing a long-sleeved dress buttoned up to her chin, standing next to what appears to be a fainting couch. She is identified in the caption as "Stiya, Carlisle Indian Girl." Who this young woman was is not disclosed, but her photographic image lends verisimilitude to the fictive Stiya, who narrates her story in the first person. Interspersed in the chapters of the book are photographs of miserable-looking, barefooted Pueblo children, a very stiff-looking Pueblo woman balancing a water jar on her head, miserable-looking Pueblo women washing clothes in a creek, three burros covered with enormous loads of wood, a "Sun-Dance at Catholic Mission," Taos, and the neat campus of Carlisle Indian School.

Silko lambastes this book, which, according to her, was written to be sent to all graduates of Carlisle as part of a campaign to keep them from returning to their old ways:

> As soon as the parcels from Carlisle began to arrive at the post office, there must have been a stir of excitement among the Carlisle graduates. Those who had graduated some years before were quite curious about the book. Aunt Susie would have been one of the first to finish reading *Stiya* because she loved to read. Grandma A'mooh began reading the book but, as she read, she became increasingly incensed at the libelous portrayal of Pueblo life and people. There was a particularly mendacious passage concerning the Pueblo practice of drying meat in the sun. The meat was described as bloody and covered with flies. Grandma A'mooh was outraged. (163–64)

The passage in question is probably the following:

> My mother, after making the fire, took down a piece of meat from a line. It was mutton, and had been cut very thin and

hung up on the line to dry, as people in civilized countries hang their clothes on lines to dry.

The line was stretched across the room from side to side, and was full of meat.

Flies?

If I should say that a million flies flew from the meat when my mother shook the line you would think that I was not telling the truth, but there were certainly thousands upon thousands of them. (*Stiya* 13–14)

It is not difficult to understand that Maria Anaya Marmon, member of the progressive faction at Laguna and alumna of Carlisle, would have been outraged at such a depiction of a Pueblo home. Furthermore, it is easy to understand why a devout Presbyterian and devoted spouse of a former governor of Laguna, who with his brother had coauthored the first Laguna constitution, and who had endured the bitter contention of the split between the conservatives and the progressives during the 1870s,[16] would want to burn a book in which "the brutal governor . . . was arrested and lodged in jail" (*Stiya*, unnumbered introductory page).

Enter Aunt Susie and the quarrel begins. In this quarrel Aunt Susie and Grandma A'mooh figure two ways to deal with the power of written words and photographic images to masquerade as the truth. *Stiya* is a first-person narrative mask that Marion Burgess dons in order to tell a sentimental version of the dominant narrative of acculturation. It is a cleverly mendacious interweaving of fact and fancy, of words and photographic images, of real persons and ethnocentric stereotypes that has as much claim to historical veracity as other books of the period like *Ben-Hur* or Adolf Bandelier's *The Delight Makers*. According to Silko's account of the quarrel, on the one side Aunt Susie advocated using the written lies of Western writers to rewrite the history of the West. On the other side, Grandma A'mooh advocated treating this writing as witchery and burning it:

Aunt Susie was a scholar and a storyteller; she believed the *Stiya* book was important evidence of the lies and the

racism and bad faith of the U.S. government with the Pueblo
people. Grandma A'mooh didn't care about preserving historical evidence of racist, anti-Indian propaganda; a book's
lies should be burned just as witchcraft paraphernalia is
destroyed. Arguments and face-to-face confrontations
between mother-in-law and daughter-in-law were avoided if
possible, but that day they argued over a book. (164)

In this quarrel and near book-burning, there are figured aspects of
the two attitudes toward writing between which Silko vacillates in
her fiction, her literary criticism, and her essays: One is a literalist
desire to reclaim orality, which is associated with truth and goodness,
and to reject writing as a deplorable swerve from truth and life.
The other is a writerly wisdom in which orality and writing are
interwoven in a syncretic and maternal vision of both Laguna and
Western culture. Grandma A'mooh represents the former. For the
devout Presbyterian wife of Robert G. Marmon, *Stiya* was a perfect
example of the letter that "kills" with an evil only Satan could be
behind. By likening *Stiya* to the paraphernalia of witchery, which
the Protestant great-grandmother would burn, Silko prefigures the
impossibility of dealing with the conflict between orality and writing
without entering into the equivalent of a philosophical debate on
the problem of evil. Just as Christianity has no definitive solution
to this philosophical problem, and must resort to conceiving evil
as a potential absence of being brought about by a deflection of the
will, or of personifying evil in a figure like Satan who reigns in a
domain of flames, so Grandma A'mooh literally would resort to
casting evil writing into the flames. She would simply imitate the
Spaniards' inquisitorial gesture, which according to Silko destroyed
the great libraries of the Americas, while reconstruing their Euro-
centric ideology of exclusion in a Pueblo mode.

In the debate Aunt Susie embodies an acceptance of writing as
part of the irrevocable syncretism brought about by European education; she embodies the need to defer reading and writing literally,
and ultimately to Pueblocize them meaningfully. At the point in

the debate where her mother-in-law's literalist, Protestant position would *traditionally* prevail, Aunt Susie cleverly uses part of the oral tradition, that is, the unwritten rules of Pueblo etiquette, in order to subvert the bibliophobic tendency in orality, to save the book with the intention of deflecting its power and using it against the culture in which it was written. Aunt Susie, the writing historian, envisages turning the poisonous *Stiya* into exegetical medicine. In doing this she removes the book from the library on Silko's side of the family and defers to future generations the rewriting of the entire history of a people.

> Aunt Susie could not persuade my great-grandmother that the book should be spared for future Pueblo historians. So finally Aunt Susie said, "Well, if you are going to burn the book, then give it to me." According to Pueblo etiquette, it would have been unthinkable for my great-grandmother to refuse her daughter-in-law's request for the book, especially since my great-grandmother was about to destroy it. So Grandma A'mooh gave Aunt Susie her copy of the *Stiya* book, and our side of the family didn't have a copy of the notorious book. Years passed before I ever saw a copy of the book, in the rare book room of the University of New Mexico Library in Albuquerque. (164–65)

No matter the outcome of this quarrel, the libelous tale of Stiya is destined, like *Ben-Hur: A Tale of the Christ,* to be absent from the library on Silko's side of the family. This absence marks a quarrel, a conflict, a split, a hidden *wound* in the family story that is passed on to Silko by her mother, the maternal storyteller missing from *Storyteller.* Thus, Silko must defer reading the notorious but little known book until she has already started rewriting it, until she has been properly formed as a postmodern Laguna medicine woman who writes to cure quarrels at home and at Laguna. As writing medicine woman she writes a special kind of text in which orality and writing are used to rewrite both the books burned by the Spaniards and the books written by Anglo-European invaders to deprecate

Pueblo culture. One tendency in Silko finds these books worthy of the fire, but another tendency, that of the writing storyteller and of Aunt Susie, would rewrite these books in their absence. For Silko such a rewriting is what the contemporary florescence of Indian writers is all about:

> Books like *Stiya*, purportedly written by Indians about Indian life, still outnumber books actually written by Indians. It is because of books like *Stiya* that Native American communities concern themselves with the origins and authorship of so-called Indian novels and Indian poetry. Books have been the focus of the struggle for the control of the Americas from the start. The great libraries of the Americas were destroyed in 1540 because the Spaniards feared the political and spiritual power of books authored by the indigenous people. As Vine Deloria has pointed out, non-Indians are still more comfortable with Indian books written by non-Indians than they are with books by Indian authors.
>
> Now, fewer than five hundred years after the great libraries of the Americas were burned, a great blossoming of the Native American writers is under way. (165)

Storyteller, Ceremony, Almanac of the Dead, and *Gardens in the Dunes* are part of the restoration of the "great libraries of the Americas."

CHAPTER 1

BEARS

Writing and Madness

"This is my helper," he told Tayo. "They call him Shush.
That means bear."
—SILKO,
Ceremony

Wovon man nicht sprechen kann, darüber muss man schwei-
gen. (Whereof one cannot speak, thereof one must be silent.)
—WITTGENSTEIN,
Tractatus Logico-Philosophicus

Bears are identified with Pueblo shamans in particular: "Of
all the curing societies, Keresan, Zuni, or Tewan, Bear is the
particular patron. The doctors or shamans are called bears;
by drawing on the bear paws which lie on the altar the shamans
impersonate bears; the paw is the equivalent of the mask. It is
believed that shamans have power literally to turn into bears, just
as bears may divest themselves of their skins and become people"
(Parsons, *Pueblo Indian Religion* 189). In an early novella, of which
only an excerpt has been published, Silko depicts a young Pueblo
man, Humaweepi, being taken by his uncle into the mountains on
a journey that culminates with a vision of a boulder that is also a
giant bear.[1] This journey can be construed as a coming-of-age rite
during which Humaweepi, an orphan who has been raised outside

of the pueblo by his uncle, realizes that he is a shaman. Humaweepi's seeing this bear is reminiscent of Silko's own vision of a giant bear about which she writes in *Storyteller.* This chapter comprises a comparative reading of these two narratives, as well as of a passage from the curing scene in *Ceremony* and of "Storyteller," in which bears figure. I shall focus on the interrelation of writing and orality and madness in this reading.

As Humaweepi is led up a mountain by his uncle, he takes off his moccasins to walk barefoot and sleeps where deer have nested. By moving away from the pueblo and shedding items of clothing and human practices, Humaweepi is symbolically and literally positioning himself on the threshold between culture and nature. The vision of the bear takes place after he and his uncle have come upon an unnamed lake that Humaweepi does not seem to know. Its sudden appearance stirs in him the desire to ask a question, which, however, is neither spoken in direct discourse nor reported in indirect discourse: "Humaweepi had never seen the lake before. It appeared suddenly as they reached the top of a hill covered with aspen trees. Humaweepi looked at his uncle and *was going to ask* him about the lake, but the old man was singing and feeding corn pollen from his leather pouch to the mountain winds" (165; my emphasis). It is as if the uncle's offerings and singing shush the question, silently suspending it in a timeless realm where Humaweepi no longer perceives words just as words but also as natural things:

> Humaweepi stared at the lake and listened to the songs. The songs were snowstorms with sounds as soft and cold as snowflakes; the songs were spring rain and wild ducks returning. Humaweepi could hear this; he could hear his uncle's voice become the night wind—high-pitched and whining in the trees. Time was lost and there was only the space, the depth, the distance of the lake surrounded by the mountain peaks. (165)

Perhaps Humaweepi "was going to ask" where the lake came from and what its name was.[2] However this may be, Humaweepi appears to have been led by his uncle into a special spiritual realm where the boundaries between words and things, between myth and reality, between past and present, between time and space, between question and answer, between representation and knowledge have been relaxed if not erased.[3]

From a distance Humaweepi sees a boulder on the edge of the lake. Up closer, however, when his uncle silently indicates it with a gesture, this boulder is a giant bear: "Finally the old man motioned for Humaweepi to come to him. He pointed at the gray boulder that lay half in the lake and half on the shore. It was then that Humaweepi saw what it was. The bear. Magic creature of the mountains, powerful ally to men" (165). The use of the definite article and the epithet "magic" in these lines of indirect discourse, as well as the coincidence of boulder and bear, suggest that this is a spirit bear. Humaweepi's response is to make an offering and to intone a song, asking it for its power:

Humaweepi unrolled his buckskin bundle and picked up the tiny beads—sky-blue turquoise and coral that was dark red. He sang the bear song and stepped into the icy, clear water to lay the beads on *the bear's head, gray granite rock,* resting above the lake, facing west. [my emphasis]

"Bear
   resting in the mountains
   sleeping by the lake
Bear
   I come to you, a man,
   to ask you:
Stand beside us in our battles
   walk with us in peace.
Bear
   I ask you for your power
   I am the warrior priest
   I ask you for your power
   I am the warrior priest."

(165–66)

Humaweepi's singing these words is said to effect in him an understanding of what the bear song means. He shares this understanding with his uncle in an exchange of silent gestures: "It wasn't until he had finished singing the song that Humaweepi realized what the words said. He turned his head toward the old man. He smiled at Humaweepi and nodded his head. Humaweepi nodded back" (166). It is possible to read this avuncular smile and shared nod as the silent acknowledgment that what Humaweepi realizes, in singing this song that ends with the words, "I am the warrior priest," is that he is bear, he is shaman. This he realizes in the songs and stories that have been passed on to him by his uncle and in his vision of the bear in the granite boulder. To a certain extent the power for which he asks the bear is already part of Humaweepi's store of songs and stories.

If this reading is incorrect, then, "what the words said" would remain silent, unspoken in direct discourse and unreported in indirect discourse. The meaning that Humaweepi realized would be left silently figured in the smile and shared nods and in the song. If this reading is correct, then the third-person narrator has made it possible for the reader to understand Humaweepi's realization that he is a shaman in an act of translation. Given Humaweepi's traditional oral upbringing by his uncle, it is plausible to assume that the narrator is providing a translation of the words of the bear song from a Pueblo language into English. Humaweepi's pueblo is left unnamed. From a realistic and historical perspective, the oral language he and his uncle speak could be either Keresan, or Tiwa, or Tewa or Towa. In not naming a specific pueblo, Silko is leaving this text open to a reading in which Humaweepi could be from different pueblos. It is also possible to construe this anonymity as a sign that Humaweepi and his uncle are from an imagined or fictional pueblo. Thus they could also be speaking a fictional or an imagined language. Quite literally such a language would not be an oral language, as it has never been spoken; nor would it be a written language. It is a silent imaginary language, neither oral nor written, that is translated into English in writing. [4]

One can read this episode of Humaweepi's vision of the spirit bear and boulder as emblematic of the special kind of writing that recurs not only in Silko's bear stories, but also in her novels and essays. Humaweepi's vision can be construed as his exercising a power of spiritual interpretation owing to which he reads the boulder not as inanimate matter but as a living glyph that encodes and embodies the meaning of his journey up the mountain. Seen from this perspective, Humaweepi's initiation as a shaman consists partly in his learning how to read the story of his own life in natural glyphic writing. As he sees the lake, the boulder, the giant sleeping bear, and as he sings, Humaweepi is spatially and temporally experiencing a realm where language has ontological efficacy. In this realm speaking words is inseparable from creating the things to which the words refer. It is a realm where questions grounded in distinctions between myth and reality have been passed over in silence.

That Humaweepi sees the "magic creature of the mountains" as both "the bear" and a boulder at the same time does not appear to strike him or his uncle as in the least unusual. Nor does the narrator show signs of finding this sleeping bear/boulder odd. There is no ironic gap between the third-person narrator's point of view and that of Humaweepi and his uncle. The narrative point of view in the passages quoted here can be likened to that of so-called magic realism.[5] Such a narrative point of view can also be compared to Victor Turner's ethnological description of the "total perspective" of the initiand experiencing liminality: "Liminality is thus a period of structural impoverishment and symbolic enrichment. It is essentially a period of returning to first principles and taking stock of the cultural inventory. To be outside of a particularized social position, to cease to have a *specific perspective,* is in a sense to become (at least potentially) aware of all positions and arrangements and to have a *total perspective*" (576–77; my emphasis). In *Humaweepi, the Warrior Priest,* the total perspective of Humaweepi and his uncle is bear empowered. The narrator can only share this perspective with them in silence, in writing. In this story the bear-boulder is a metaphor for the third-person narrative perspective or vision.

The short first-person narrative of Silko's first deer hunt in *Storyteller* (77–79) can also be read as a coming-of-age story. Indeed, young Leslie Marmon, somewhat like Humaweepi, does not appear at first to be aware that silently awaiting her during her journey to Mount Taylor, where she joins her uncles, cousins, and father in her first deer hunt, is a special vision of "a giant brown bear" (77). No ritual gestures are said to be performed before, during, or after this vision. Uncle Polly is not depicted chanting or spreading pollen into the wind like Humaweepi's uncle. Yet, in this short narrative there are signs that young Leslie Marmon is experiencing a liminal and total perspective as she quietly undergoes a private initiation as more than a hunter. There are several signs of liminality in the story: At thirteen Leslie is on the threshold between childhood and adult womanhood. Neither the old .30-30, which she says was *borrowed,* nor the status of grown-up hunter—connoted by carrying this high-powered rifle—appears to have been completely conferred on her yet. For this reason, she relates that she was cautious at the time to pass over in silence any possible sign that she might not yet be ready to make the transition into the adult world of her uncles and cousins who have brought her up the mountain, not yet ready to wield a power that, judging from the report of the borrowed rifle, could be construed as even higher than that carried by her father: "When I was thirteen I carried an old .30-30 we borrowed from George Pearl. It was heavy and hurt my shoulder when I fired it and it seemed even louder than my father's larger caliber rifle, but *I didn't say anything* because I was so happy to be hunting for the first time" (77; my emphasis). It turns out that during this hunt young Leslie experiences a power that may be greater than that of her father and of the other hunters, who appear all to be male. This higher power makes it possible for her to return from Mount Taylor not with a dead deer, but with a story that is alive with silent ursine meaning: "I didn't get a deer that year but one afternoon hunting alone on the round volcanic hill we called Chato, I saw a giant brown bear lying in the sun below the hilltop" (77).

This story of the giant brown bear, however, like the signs that the loud and heavy .30-30 may still be too much for her to handle, will be silenced. Silenced because seeing this bear seems also to be a sign of something that young Leslie knows better than to speak about: "I never told anyone what I had seen because I knew they don't let people who see such things carry .30-30's or hunt deer with them" (78). Why? For what reason would "they" (presumably members of the Marmon family) not let Leslie hunt deer with a high-powered rifle if she told of having seen the bear? It is tempting to reason that from the perspective presumably of her family, "people who see such things" might be perceived as mad, or, less negatively, as being in a betwixt and between where madness and bear power cannot be told apart.

Silko's personal story of seeing the giant brown bear on Mount Taylor resembles in some aspects her story of Humaweepi's initiation as a shaman. In both stories the giant bears and boulders are situated in a betwixt and between. Humaweepi's bear, which lies half in the lake, half on the shore, straddles two elements, water and earth. Young Leslie's giant brown bear lies sleeping between fall and winter, around that transitional time of year when bears go into hibernation and hunters make preparations for winter. Neither bear is said to be awake; thus both occupy a state that can be construed as on a threshold between life and death.

Nevertheless, there are important differences in the characters and in their experiences. Obviously Humaweepi is male and Leslie is female. The male appears to be a full-blood who has not been to grammar school, but who has been taught orally by his uncle. The female is a mixed-blood who has gone to school, where she has learned, among other things, to read and write. Humaweepi sees from a distance a boulder, then from up close a bear. Leslie sees from a distance a bear, but then, in this version of her story, does not go up close to look at it. (There is another version told in "An Essay on Rocks" that I will take up shortly.) Humaweepi's bear is silently pointed out to him by his elderly uncle. Young Leslie has been separated from her uncle and cousins in the course of the hunt and sees the bear on her own. Humaweepi, who is unarmed, is not in the least afraid of the bear and puts beads on its granite head. Young Leslie, armed with the borrowed .30-30, appears to fear getting close to the bear.

The two most important differences between Humaweepi's vision and young Leslie's, however, lie in the area of intentions and verbal responses to the bear. First, on the male side, Humaweepi's uncle apparently intentionally takes his nephew up the mountain as part of a coming-of-age ceremony that includes a vision of the spirit bear and his initiation as a shaman. On the female side, young Leslie is taken to Mount Taylor in order for her to bag a deer in the flesh and return as a full-fledged hunter. There is no suggestion whatsoever that young Leslie's uncles are aware of the bear before, during, or after the hunt. Second, Humaweepi sings the bear song, requesting power and protection from the bear, whereas young Leslie silently asks herself the question: "Dead or just sleeping, I couldn't tell" (77). Thus, the nonliterate full-blood male evokes and celebrates his vision of bear power, and his being initiated as a warrior priest, with a traditional song, whereas the literate mixed-blood female poses a silent question. It is my hypothesis that the meaning of Silko's bear story lies silenced in the untellable difference between sleep and death to which this silent question refers. Writing, I shall argue, is inseparable from this question and from the act that decides this question in a conflation of creation and interpretation.

In "An Essay on Rocks" (*Yellow Woman* 187–91), the bear story included in *Storyteller* is retold differently in an even shorter version: "Once while I was deer hunting I saw a giant bear sleeping on a rock in the sun; when I got closer there was only the great basalt boulder amid the patches of melting snow" (191). This very short rewritten version of the bear story differs both from Humaweepi's story, in that the young warrior priest sees a boulder from a distance and a sleeping bear from up close, and from the story in *Storyteller*, where young Leslie sees a bear from afar but does not approach for a look from up close. In this succinct rewriting of the story, Silko does not tell or question whether what she saw was a bear or a boulder, nor does she ask the question from *Storyteller*: "Dead or just sleeping"?

The point of "An Essay on Rocks" is to demonstrate that rocks are living glyphs, in which, owing to photography and special power, Silko can record and read invisible glyphic narratives. The logic and imagery of this essay overlap the imagery and logic of Silko's bear story. For Silko, her family's practice of photography, like writing, is silent storytelling. Photographs, Silko argues, can be put together into a narrative to show what cannot be seen with the normal naked eye. In this sense they resemble writing, which can show things, suggest to one's readers meanings that cannot be told with clarity and simplicity, except at the risk of one's hearers taking this clarity to be a sign of something awesome and ineffable.

"An Essay on Rocks" resonates with Silko's personal interest in stones. In this odd and entertaining essay Silko relates her vision of the giant bear almost as an afterthought to the story of how in the vicinity of her house (near Tucson) she had perceived a rock in a distant arroyo to be, first a horse head, then a blackened carcass, then a half-buried safe. Accompanying the essay are black and white photographs of the rock in the arroyo, seen first from a distance, then from closer and closer. In this tale of rocks in transition, Silko subtly leaves undecided whether "the angle of the sun or the shift in shadows on the snow next to the rock" (191) combined with her imagination are responsible for her differing perceptions, or whether some innate power residing in the rocks themselves is responsible for this vision.

In a companion essay, entitled "On Photography," Silko speculates that an electromagnetic power residing in objects themselves works together with a similar power innate in some photographers to produce and represent photographically differing perception: "My father, Lee H. Marmon, learned photography in the army. *But to me it is still magic.* The more I read about the behavior of subatomic particles of light, the more confident I am that photographs are capable of registering subtle electromagnetic changes in both the subject and the photographer" (*Yellow Woman* 180; my emphasis). In this passage the phrase, "But to me it is still magic," is odd. The logic of the contrastive conjunction, "but," seems to be grounded in a context that is not explicitly evoked. In other words, Silko seems to be saying that even though her father learned photography in the least magic of places (U.S. Army military occupational school), this art nevertheless entails a magic that her father could have passed on to her, just as "medicine" would be passed on by an older person to a younger person who is to become a shaman. Here Silko is speculating that what is "magic" in a photograph is that it comprises not just traces on paper of the chemical reaction that occurs when a photographer uses an objective lens and a shutter to expose a portion of film to visible light reflecting off her or his photographic subject in order to produce a visually realistic image, but that it also comprises traces of a transition of "invisible" subatomic energy between this subject and the photographer that produce a magically realistic image. In other words, photographic realism is magic realism. In this transition of subatomic energies the conceptual boundary between subject and object, which is posited as a given in classic Western epistemology and physics, as well as the physical boundary between visible and invisible electromagnetic radiation, which is posited as a given by modern physics and physiology, would be questioned as they are in postmodern epistemology and in contemporary physics and chaos theory. The photographer's "gift" of invisible electromagnetic power takes on aspects of the problematic givens of modern science. Just as writing can be understood as silent traces of the effable and the *in*effable, so photography (i.e., etymologically light + writing) can be envisaged as silent traces of the visible and the *in*visible. Writing, like photography, can be effected from a total perspective, yielding a narrative of magic realism, especially when its subject-object is the "magic creature of the mountains."

Just as Humaweepi can see the sleeping bear in the boulder, owing to the visionary power that awakens in him through his uncle's spiritual guidance, so Konomi Ara, having spent three years reading and translating *Ceremony* into written Japanese characters, can "see" and record Japaneseness radiating in Silko's face:

> Professor Konomi Ara, my Japanese translator, photographed me outside my house in Tucson. Months later, when I saw

the photograph in a Japanese publication, I was amazed and delighted to see how Japanese I appeared. *How does this happen?* Perhaps the way the photographer feels about her subject affects the outcome. Professor Ara had spent three years translating my novel *Ceremony* into Japanese; thus, in a few seconds, she was able to translate my face into Japanese. (*Yellow Woman* 181; my emphasis)

It would appear that Silko believes that the answer to her question— "How does this happen?"—lies in a still unexpounded scientific hypothesis that would identify the electromagnetic genealogical affinities, which Silko and her translator share, with the spiritual power that enables Tayo to see his Uncle Josiah's face "translated" into the face of the Japanese prisoner he is ordered to kill (*Ceremony* 7–8). In a sense, the vision that brings Tayo to the verge of madness is a photo-mytho-graphic total perspective. He sees what old Betonie tells. According to the mixed-blood medicine man, Tayo's seeing old Josiah's face in the Japanese prisoner "isn't surprising" (124). He is only seeing the state of affairs as it was thirty thousand years ago. He is seeing that the Pueblo and the Japanese share the same distant ancestors. These ancestors, according to the Japanese, are descended from the Goddess of the Sun. Tayo is seeing from a total perspective what Professor Ara's photograph shows silently radiating from Silko's face: the Rising Sun.

Silko continues in the essay entitled "On Photography" to liken the photographs of rocks and other debris in arroyos around her home outside of Tucson to "glyphs," in which she can read "photo narratives":

Obsessively, I photographed the dry wash below my ranch house. Stone formations with Hohokam cisterns carved in them appeared as sacred cenotes, and flattop boulders looked as if they were sacrificial altars. Then, after the summer storms, I began to photograph certain natural configurations of stones and driftwood left by the floodwater. The photographic images of the stones and wood reminded me of *glyphs*. I could imagine there were messages in these delicate arrangements left in the wake of a flash flood. As I began to look at the prints, I realized each roll of film formed a complete *photo narrative,* although that had not been my intention as I pressed the shutter release. *Most of the narratives were constructed from the image of the "glyphs" I "saw" in the debris in the bottom of the arroyo.* (181; my emphasis)

By disavowing that these glyphic narratives were part of her conscious intention when she "pressed the shutter release," Silko leaves open the possibility that her photography traces silent stories told by someone else of pre-Columbian times in the Southwest. Here the electromagnetic visionary power of the imagination to influence the photographic image becomes the power to read and to transcribe glyphic narrative. Although, in this essay, she does employ the term "magic" to describe her experience of photography (180), she also explicitly speculates that future scientific inquiry will allow us to understand these photoelectric phenomena: "Perhaps photographs register ambient bursts of energy in the form of heat or X rays as well as light. Thus photographs reveal more than a mere image of a subject, although it is still too early for us to understand or interpret all the information a photograph may contain" (181). Here the total perspective includes both the traditional Pueblo perspective and the contemporary or future worldwide scientific perspective. As it is with glyphic photo narratives, so is it with novels: invisible photoelectric radiation is to the photographic process what the spirits are to the writing process. Some texts, like *Storyteller,* where the text is sown with photographs taken mostly by her grandfather and father, and *Sacred Water,* where Silko's photographs are interspersed with writing, combine the two.

But even if it is still "too early for us to understand and interpret all the information" in these glyphs recorded by Japanese and Laguna photographers, it is nevertheless time for us to return to *Storyteller* and attempt to explicate at least some of the untellable and of the invisible silently sleeping in Silko's bear story. This will include articulating two questions that the writing storyteller has rhetorically passed over in silence when constructing this text.

In the passage that follows the question, "Dead or just sleeping, I couldn't tell" (*Storyteller* 77), without the speculation about the magic realism of photography and total perspective generated in my reading of Silko's essays on rocks and on photography, a skeptical reader might, in the spirit of so-called scientific objectivity or of common sense, ask whether the giant bear Silko saw was *real or just imaginary*. Without literally writing this question, Silko acknowledges that it is apposite at this point in the narrative by mentioning the possibility of visual problems that could have been caused by physical strain on the eyes and by expectation and desire on the imagination: "I was cautious because I already knew what hours of searching for motion, for the outline of a deer, for the color of a deer's hide can do to the *imagination*. I already knew how easily the weathered branches of a dead juniper could resemble antlers because I had walked with my father on hunts since I was eight" (77; my emphasis). In a cleverly veiled rhetorical gesture Silko puts forward the knowledge gained from five years of prehunting experience with her father in order to preemptively shush the reader who might ask whether the bear was *real or just imaginary*. In order to keep this question and the conceptual dichotomy that informs it quiet in her text and in her reader, Silko first implies that if imagination and eyestrain were responsible for a visual misperception, it would be a deer that she would see, not a giant bear.[6] Second, she tells how in order to assure herself of her power of perception, she calmed herself, becoming almost as still as the giant bear in the distance, moving only her eyes in a silent quest for an older uncle or cousin to witness her vision: "So I stood motionless for a long time until my breathing was more calm and my heart wasn't beating so hard. I even shifted my eyes away for a moment hoping to see my uncle Polly or my cousin Richard who was hunting the ridges nearby" (77–78). But the only possible avuncular figure in Silko's first-person narration of this scene is the reader, who, in a gesture that paradoxically reduces and maintains the distance between perceived and perceiver, between nurtured and nurturer, can smile and nod at the first-person female narrator as they share what is silenced, as they magically understand that this is a glyphic bear

who is medicine. This glyphic medicine both poisons and heals . . .
but I am getting ahead of myself.

The second question the reader could ask about the bear is
whether it is *supernatural or just natural.* This question and the dichotomy that informs it are also rhetorically preempted in the narrative. Before the young hunter shifts her eyes back to the giant bear,
she consults her memory of bears and reasons that this bear is
quite unusual; in size alone it surpasses all regional bears and maybe
even all bears: "I knew that there were no bears that large on Mr.
Taylor; I was pretty sure *there were no bears that large anywhere.* But
when I looked back at the slope above me, the giant brown bear
was still lying on the sunny slope of the hill above patches of melting
snow and tall yellow grass" (78; my emphasis). In having the young
hunter reference in her memory the physiological dimensions of
known bears, either from oral hunting stories—where bears do have
a tendency to grow larger as the story is retold—or from written
zoological accounts that are supposed to be factually informed by
the perspective of scientific objectivity, or even from children's books
like the "worn-out little book that had lost its cover" in which
Grandma A'mooh used to read "again and again" to Leslie and
her sisters the story of Brownie the Bear "with such animation and
expression . . . the way a storyteller would have told it" (*Storyteller*
93), the writing storyteller cautiously avoids awaking the questions
about the bear's ontological status, or explicitly saying that the bear
is magic.

Lying rhetorically silenced in the text are the two questions about
whether this bear, which seems to be the biggest bear in the world,
is a figment of young Leslie's imagination or a supernatural creature that appears to bestow special power on the young writing
storyteller. Just as the old uncle's singing and offering corn pollen
to the mountain winds turns words into natural things, thereby
shushing Humaweepi's question about the lake, so the nascent
writing storyteller will erase the boundaries between the imaginary
and the real, the supernatural and the natural, generating the total
perspective of magic realism that silences the dicey questions, which

could be posed from a scientifically objective perspective, and nurturing the untellable.

Having passed over in silence both questions that from the perspective of scientific objectivity the skeptical reader would probably feel obliged to voice, the first-person writing storyteller leaves her young self as motionless as the bear, as motionless as a printed word on a page, suspended in space and in mind, to wonder how she might "tell" the only explicitly but silently posed question: "Dead or just sleeping" (77). She will let this question hibernate within her, carefully nurturing it, acting as if the boundary between death and sleep depended on one's perspective and one's patience. At the same time she shows wise respect for the animal who in size is greater than any known bear and whose power is much higher than that which has been temporarily loaned to her for the hunt: "I watched it for a long time, for any sign of motion, for its breathing, but I wasn't close enough to tell for sure. If it was dead I wanted to be able to examine it up close. It occurred to me that I could fire my rifle over its head but I knew better than to wake a bear with only a .30-30" (78).

The old borrowed .30-30, which the young hunter knows is not powerful enough to stop this giant bear dead in its tracks, were it real and natural—much less supernatural—and just sleeping, could, however, annihilate the vision of the bear. One can see this by envisaging the following scenario from an objective perspective: The young hunter fires the .30-30 over the bear's head. The bear still does not move. The young hunter approaches to examine the bear up close and discovers either that it is dead or that there is nothing there, or, as in the abbreviated rewriting in "An Essay on Rocks," that "there was only the great basalt boulder amid the patches of melting snow" (191).[7]

Rather than letting the young hunter risk a confrontation with a sleeping real bear, be it natural or supernatural, or with a dead bear, or with *no* bear at all, the first-person writing storyteller in *Storyteller* walks her newly realized self away from the bear. In doing this she paradoxically defers or silences the realization of what the vision means. She leaves the feeling that something uncanny and highly powerful is blowing in the wind behind her at Chato, this ancient site of volcanic eruptions from the depths of the earth:

> I had only moved my eyes, and my arms were getting numb from holding the rifle in the same position for so long. As quietly and as carefully as I probably will ever move, I turned and walked away from the giant bear, still down wind from it. But the big dark bear remained there, on the south slope of Chato, with its head facing southeast, the eyes closed, motionless. I hurried the rest of the way down the ridge, listening closely to the wind at my back for sounds, glancing over my shoulder now and then. (78)

Here the young writing storyteller could be glancing back with thoughts left by other stories from bear country, such as the one in *Ceremony* (128–30), which is included in *Storyteller* (207–9). In this "verse" narrative, a child, who has wandered away from his human family and joined a bear family, must be called back by a medicine man. This calling back, which involves making "mother bear sounds" (209), must be accomplished according to prescribed ceremonial steps in order to keep the child from being left suspended in the betwixt and between. Even when these steps are followed, it seems, the child cannot return the same:

> They couldn't just grab the child
> They couldn't simply take him back
> because he would be in-between forever
> and probably he would die.
>
> They had to call him.
> Step by step the medicine man
> brought the child back.
>
> So, long time ago
> they got him back again
> but he wasn't quite the same
> after that

not like the other children.
(Storyteller 209)

Silko, however, does not have a medicine *man* to call her back. The
writing storyteller who is awakening within her prescribes the
medicine necessary for the return: Writing will be her bear paw.
Like the child in this verse story from bear country, like Shush,
who uses the bear paw to help old Betonie lead Tayo through the
Navajo Red Antway in *Ceremony,* like Humaweepi when he comes
back from the mountain, the young hunter will not be the same
when she leads herself back to kith and kin from her transitional
experience on Mount Taylor. She will have silently and carefully
taken the first steps toward becoming a medicine woman who
writes to nurture and ceremonially resurrect in herself her ancestors
in states and languages that are ontologically and epistemologically figured in bear stories. Not being "quite the same" after having
been called back from the bears can be understood as having brought
back some of the "in-between" where the child risked remaining
and dying. The space into which she silently rebirths herself and
her ancestors remains a liminal and a mixed space, a textual space
where orality and literacy are interwoven in a perspective that
yearns to be total. This space is traversed with stories and questions
that Silko still must silence as she continues to write today from
her home outside of Tucson.

Thus, rather than force an end to the undecidability, the young
hunter reasons according to the liminal logic of the writing storyteller: Unlike Humaweepi, who lays beads from his medicine bundle
on the "gray granite rock" that *is* the sleeping bear's head, Leslie
defers an examination of the giant bear up close, thereby deferring
telling. She leaves lying not only the bear and the sleeping questions about this giant bear's status, but also the question about
the reasoning of a young hunter who passes over such a story in
silence: "I never told anyone what I had seen because I knew
they don't let people who see such things carry .30-30's or hunt
deer with them" (78).

These words can be read to imply that Silko rejects her vision of
the bear, and in so doing rejects becoming a shaman, a medicine
woman. These words can also be read to imply that her telling of
this vision would be read by her family to mean that she was men-
tally unstable, and thus not safe to hunt with a high-powered rifle.
Silko leaves the interpretation of these words up to the reader. My
reading, which I support with the comparison with Humaweepi,
is that Silko does not reject the vision of the bear or the realization
that she is to become a medicine woman. But unlike Humaweepi,
who is a male, full-blood, nonliterate, and traditional member of a
fictional pueblo, Silko is a female, mixed-blood, and literate member
of a very real pueblo tradition in which writing and orality are inseparably interwoven. She will accept the vision in a mode that is
informed by both orality and literacy. What the young hunter cannot
tell, in either sense of this word, will be silenced and nurtured in
writing. She will defer telling about her vision of the bear until she
is accepted as a writing storyteller whose narrative perspective is
that of the postmodern medicine woman. Silko will not come of age
until she writes and publishes *Ceremony*, for which she is known
throughout the entire world.

On the following page Silko continues the silently deferred story
of differing perception, writing in verse[8] of herself as a somewhat
older young hunter:

Two years later, on the north side of Chato, my Uncle
Polly was rewarded for his patience by the "old man
of the mountain" as my uncle had called him—the mule
deer whose antlers were as wide as a gun rack. As soon
as the big buck had gone down, Uncle Polly signaled
so those of us close by could go help.

(79)

As she moves around the volcanic hill in response to her uncle's
signal that "the old man of the mountain" has rewarded hunterly
patience, Leslie finds herself again in the liminal setting of two
years earlier. Her patient waiting for an answer without telling is

rewarded as she "deliberately" moves up close to the place where
she had seen the giant brown bear:

> As I cut across the south slope to reach my Uncle
> I realized it was middle afternoon almost the same
> time of day as before, except this year no snow
> had fallen yet.
> I walked past the place *deliberately.*
> *I found no bones,* but when a wind moved through the
> light yellow grass that afternoon I hurried around the
> hill to find my uncle.
> Sleeping, not dead, I decided.
>
> (79; my emphasis)

Finding "no bones" there, or in other words, seeing *nothing* there,
if read in the spirit of Western scientific objectivity, could be taken
to indicate either that the bear was sleeping or that there was *no
bear* there two years earlier. Such a reading would not put an end
to the undecidability of the story. For the writing storyteller, however, finding no bones there is silently "telling." She sees *nothing,*
but feels in the wind *something* that causes her to hurry around the
hill to find her Uncle Polly.[9] Rather than reading "no bones" to indicate undecidability about whether there was or was not a bear
there two years before, she effects a spiritual reading in which finding
"no bones" annihilates death and quickens the bear sleeping in
her visionary story, which she still, apparently, does not tell, but
will eventually write. The spiritual and writerly narrative point of
view of the emerging writing storyteller and young hunter—what
Victor Turner refers to as the "total perspective" characteristic of
liminality—not only refuses to let the giant bear die, it also refuses
to annihilate it according to the logic of the letter, to give it and the
figurative imagination up to nothing. Seen from a Western Judeo-
Christian perspective, this would amount to simulating an ex nihilo
creation of one's ursine self. Seen from a modern so-called objective scientific perspective, this would amount to Silko's writing about
nothing. Seen from the writing storyteller's syncretic perspective,

this would amount to a writerly, spiritual, and dialectical gesture that conflates creation and interpretation and informs the conceptual space not just of *Storyteller* but of all of Silko's texts.

This writing generates a syncretic space in which Laguna and Western concepts meet in what Krupat has called Silko's dialectal dialogic. This is neither a Hegelian nor a Bakhtinian space. It is not a deconstructionist space, in which the writer and reader would turn tediously in hermeneutic whirligigs of undecidability, but it is a space in which the antinomies of Western metaphysics, which scientists, philosophers, and critics like Jacques Derrida, Paul de Man, and J. Hillis Miller have labored to deconstruct, are called transitions, or harmonies or balances. Above all, it is not a logo-centric and orthodox Pauline space in which the carnal letter kills, the spirit quickens, and writers like Silko are anathematized as idolaters or witches. It is a space of secondary orality, or textuality, in which the fertile letter of carnal spirituality rebirths and nurtures.[10] It is the space of the bibliophilic Marmon home in which the young hunter and her "father used to read at the table at lunchtime," or in which she used to "go find *Lolita* or *Lady Chatterley's Lover* half hidden under [her] dad's side of the bed" (158–59). It is the space of the *written* Navajo Red Antway ceremony in *Ceremony*. It is the space of *Almanac of the Dead* where a pre-Columbian Mayan manuscript prophetically informs the rewriting of the history of the Americas. It is the space of *Gardens in the Dunes* where the Messiah, his children, and his Mother join the ghost dancers and where Indigo, on the Grand Tour with Hattie and Edward, reads stones as glyphs of pagan European spirituality. It is the space of heresy in which Hattie has placed herself by writing a protofeminist thesis on an allegedly apocryphal gospel that she argues was written by Mary Magdalene, the Messiah's favorite prostitute. It is a space where the vehemently anti-Christian Silko can fondly recall her staunchly Presbyterian Grandma A'mooh reading to her grandchildren not only from *Brownie the Bear* but also from the Bible. It is a space where Presbyterian Laguna progressives can reside with their syncretic Catholic and non-Christian Laguna kith and kin. It is in this space that Silko lives and writes and publishes today. Silko, the writing medicine woman who no longer lives at Laguna, yet who adamantly refuses to give up the Laguna oral tradition, Silko, the internationally published American Indian writer, can best exercise the power she has as writing storyteller to rewrite Laguna spirituality by passing over the story of her glyphic bear power in silence as she "tells" this story to readers who, like the young hunter on Chato, hear with their eyes. Like the giant bear lying in the sun, the Laguna tradition is hibernating on the printed page of *Story-teller.*[11] Keeping in mind what has been said thus far about this mixed space, madness, glyphic bear power, nurturing, and writing, I would like to turn to the bear stories in *Ceremony,* the text that embodies Silko's coming-of-age.

In an interview with Dexter Fisher, which was published shortly after the appearance of *Ceremony* in 1977, Silko explicitly describes writing this novel as a cure for what appears to be not just Tayo's but her own tussle with madness. When asked "Why did you entitle the novel *Ceremony,*" Silko answered: "That's what it is. *Writing the novel was a ceremony for me to stay sane.* My character in the beginning of the novel is very sick. . . . And as Tayo got better, I felt better" ("Stories and Their Tellers" 20; my emphasis). In this passage Silko identifies her own psychological and physiological state during her stay in Alaska with that of her fictional character, Tayo, and with the alienation that some Lagunas, but not her father and uncle, experienced during and after World War II.[12] Thus, in writing of Tayo's return to health and harmony, she was literally writing her own way back from a dicey encounter between two perspectives that risked leaving her insane.

Such a description of the genesis of *Ceremony* recalls Silko's remark about having learned in the fifth grade that she could evoke the "same feeling of well-being [that she got from hearing a story told or telling a story aloud to herself] by writing down a story I made up myself" (*Yellow Woman* 161). In other words, in writing *Ceremony* while she was in Alaska, Silko was doing on a larger scale what she had learned to do in the fifth grade when she was away from storytelling grandmothers and aunts at Laguna. She was acting as her own medicine woman; writing was the medicine she ceremonially administered to herself. As I will argue in a reading of "Lullaby" in chapter 2 (and of the Mayan almanac in *Almanac of the Dead* in ch. 6), Silko has a tendency to view this scribal potion not only like a remedy but also like a poison.[13] Recurring in Silko's texts is an ambivalent attitude toward writing. Like glyphic bear power, writing can be perceived as both debilitating madness and as empowering medicine. Writing can be conceived both as the dead letter that kills and as spiritual carnality that quickens and nurtures by silencing the likes of patristic Christian exegesis and vacation Bible school.[14]

Tayo's "madness," it turns out, is visionary. His seeing Josiah's face in the Japanese prisoner affirms the interconnectedness of all life that is part of the Pueblo, the Navajo, and the Japanese worldviews. His reaction to the brutality of war in the Pacific is only madness when understood from the point of view of destructive Western thought. Western thought, like witchery, tends to deny the sacred interconnectedness of all life. The alleged crowning achievement of twentieth-century Western science is the harnessing of atomic energy, the use of which some white Americans judged appropriate to end the imperialistic dreams of the Land of the Rising Sun. As Silko sees it, the entire story of the atomic bomb, from the Manhattan Project to mining uranium ore at the Jackpile Mine on Laguna land, from testing the first bomb in New Mexico to bombing Hiroshima and Nagasaki, confirms the death-dealing insanity of the Western worldview based on conceptual dichotomies that objectify the earth and nature. Tayo's cure is effected by his learning how to see and to read the world in terms of transitions and patterns, not dichotomies and death: "He cried the relief he felt at finally seeing the pattern, the way all the stories fit together—the old stories, the war stories, their stories—to become the story that was still being told. He was not crazy; he had never been crazy. He had only seen and heard the world as it always was: no boundaries, only transitions through all distances and time" (246).

Bears and writing are involved in Tayo's cure. Having met and begun to tell old Betonie about his experiences before, during, and after World War II, but still feeling somewhat undecided about this unorthodox, mixed-blood medicine man, Tayo sees for the first time Betonie's odd helper:

> Behind the dog a boy about fifteen or sixteen came with an armload of firewood. He knelt by the fire with the kindling; Betonie spoke to him in Navajo and indicated Tayo with a nod of his head.
>
> "This is my helper," he told Tayo. *"They call him Shush. That means bear."* It was dark, but in the light from the fire Tayo could see there was something strange about the boy, something remote in his eyes, *as if he were on a distant mountaintop alone* and the fire and hogan and the lights of the town below them did not exist. (128; my emphasis)

Not only does the name of this extremely taciturn boy mean bear in Navajo, "shush" is also an interjection used in English to request silence.[15] Immediately following the description of the remote mountaintop look in Shush's eyes, there is the verse narrative (mentioned above) telling of a small child who wandered away from his kin and had to be called back from the bears. This narrative, whose exact narrative status in the text is passed over in silence, is center-justified on the page and typeset as if it were a poem. It is one of the twenty-eight embedded texts that Robert M. Nelson has likened to the narrative backbone of *Ceremony.* This bear story, which is the second of two stories from bear country included in *Storyteller* (207–9), might be one of the two embedded texts that Robert M. Nelson finds not to be "appropriated, sometimes verbatim, from preexisting ethnographic print texts rather than immediately from remembered oral performance." It is not clear whether this embedded bear narrative is one of the clan stories whose telling in *Ceremony* has upset Silko's cousin, Paula Gunn Allen,[16] but both the manner in which it is told and its content make it plausible that this could be a story told by Aunt Susie or Aunt Alice to young

Leslie and her sisters in order to warn them about the consequences
of straying from the grownups when away from the pueblo.

Owing to a lack of speaker attributions in the text, in other words,
owing to the writing storyteller's having silenced the origin and
status of this narrative, it is unclear whether old Betonie is supposed to tell this bear story at this point in order to inform Tayo
about Shush, or whether the passage is embedded here in order to
allow the reader access to a story that Tayo or Betonie, or both
Betonie and Tayo, have heard told, or could have read for that
matter. Whatever the case, the bear story can be read to bestow
reality—the reality of magic realism of the oral and the written
Laguna tradition—on the existence of bear people. The remote look
in Shush's eyes, which suggests he is alone on a distant mountaintop removed from any manifestation of contemporary culture, as
well as Tayo's apparent recognition that Shush, like the anonymous
child in the embedded narrative, is a bear person, causes Tayo to
feel uneasy: "Tayo stood up and moved around the fire uneasily;
the boy took some ribs and disappeared again behind the hogan"
(130). Betonie perceives Tayo's uneasiness and reassures him:

> The old man put some wood on the fire. "You don't have to
> be afraid of him. Some people act like witchery is responsible
> for everything that happens, when actually witchery only
> manipulates a small portion." He pointed in the direction the
> boy had gone. "Accidents happen, and there's little we can
> do. But don't be so quick to call something good or bad.
> There are balances and harmonies always shifting, always
> necessary to maintain. It is very peaceful with the bears; the
> people say that's the reason human beings seldom return. It
> is a matter of transitions, you see; the changing, the becom-
> ing must be cared for closely. You would do as much for the
> seedlings as they become plants in the field." (130)

About such an accident one can pose questions informed by Western
conceptual dichotomies such as human/beast, insane/sane, and
evil/good. Old Betonie obviously does not launch into a sociological

discourse on the benefits of cultural relativism or the ethnocentric perils of understanding the world through a grid of traditional Western logical dichotomies. He does, however, shush the questions about Shush that appear to worry Tayo here. He gently chides Tayo and subtly suggests that the boundaries drawn between the conceptual dichotomies that inform the judgment that Shush is a witch—or a psychopath—are not nearly so fixed as persons like Tayo's teachers and alleged buddies would have him believe. Old Betonie's discourse obviously is not explicitly about deconstructing conceptual dichotomies, but about maintaining shifting balances and harmonies, about transitions and nurturing. Here he speaks not only of Shush, whose appearance and behavior suggest he may indeed be caught up in a transition betwixt humans and bears, but also of Tayo. Tayo is caught between Anglo-European culture and Indian culture, between the belief that he is insane and the understanding of his predicament through what Robert M. Nelson has termed a "constellation" of three modes of reality: Tayo's subjective experience, the Story of the People, and the Landscape ("Place and Vision" 282–84). Shush, Betonie, and the old bear people will soon help Tayo take the first steps toward this constellation in the Red Antway, which Silko has most likely accessed through writing.[17] Writing, the medicine that she administers to bring herself and Tayo back from a metaphorical and ceremonial encounter with the bears, informs Silko's project to cure herself of mixed-blood anxiety.

At this point in the text there is a note introduced with a center-justified title:

NOTE ON BEAR PEOPLE AND WITCHES

Don't confuse those who go to the bears with the witch people. Human beings who live with the bears do not wear bear skins. They are naked and not conscious of being different from their bear relatives. Witches crawl into skins of dead animals, but they can do nothing but play around with objects and bodies. Living animals are terrified of witches. They smell death. That's why witches can't get close to them. That's why

people keep dogs around their hogans. Dogs howl with fear
when witch animals come around. (131)[18]

How is one to situate and understand such a note within the text?
How does the status of this note differ from that of the embedded
narratives? Perhaps this is one of the notes from the "brown spiral
notebook with a torn cover" that old Betonie thumbed through as
he was "diagnosing" Tayo:

> Betonie dug down into the cardboard boxes until dust flew
> up around his face. Finally he pulled out a brown spiral note-
> book with a torn cover; he thumbed through the pages slowly,
> moving his lips slightly. He sat down again, across from Tayo,
> with the notebook in his lap.
> "I'm beginning to see something," he said with his eyes
> closed, "yes something very important." (125)

Perhaps this note has a status in the text similar to that of the
"Note on the Deer Dance" that Silko includes in a letter to James
Wright, apparently in order to provide him with cultural knowledge
necessary for evaluating one of the poems she has sent him (*Delicacy and Strength of Lace* 9–10). Whereas the identity of the narrator
of the embedded bear story, owing to a lack of speaker attribution
and to its being typeset in center-justified verse style, is undecidable,
the narrative status of this note can be construed as self-reflexively
textual and deconstructive of the Western categorization of different
kinds of discourse. Like a footnote in a poem by T. S. Eliot, or in a
short story by Borges, this note not only provides information about
the cultural context to the reader, but in so doing it also tends to
erase the boundary between writing as fiction and writing as scholarly discourse. It also silences the boundary between the written
and the oral.

Like many modernist and postmodernist texts, *Ceremony* eludes
attempts of the critic to theoretically articulate and define the boundaries by which writing can be classified and confined as a type of
discourse (such as anthropological or philosophical or theological
or oral or written) or as a literary genre, such as the novel, the epic,

the short story, the drama, or the poem. This so-called novel is written and narrated betwixt and between the discourse boundaries used to construct a theory of traditional or modern genres. It is a liminal text in which the writing storyteller's understanding of ceremony, that is, of discourse, is in transition.[19]

Robert M. Nelson has argued that Silko has reappropriated into living Laguna tradition the museumified ethnographic expropriations transcribed and translated in *Keresan Texts* by Franz Boas and Elsie Clews Parsons.[20] He compares Boas and Parsons's book to one of the "boxes and boxes of human bones and 'artifacts' in a museum warehouse somewhere, waiting to be sorted and displayed in the museum—or, if they get lucky, repatriated back to Indian Country" ("Rewriting Ethnography" par. 14). His reading of the center-justified embedded narratives as resembling vertebrae and serving as vertebrae for the narrative of *Ceremony* is clever and rhetorically apposite. His suggestion that Silko has graphically translated the conventional oral phrase of closure, "that long is my aunt's backbone," into textual graphics is insightful:

> Continuing to exercise the conventional Keresan backbone trope, working to assemble story in the way that Badger Old Man works for healing in the old stories, Silko then lays out the embedded texts in her novel so that formally these "bits and pieces" of Laguna traditional story, far from being positioned peripherally with respect to the prose narrative of Tayo's adventures, rather represent the very backbone—the spinal column—of the novel, the skeleton of story that Tayo's story, the prose narrative, takes shape upon and fleshes out. (par. 9)

In other words, Silko, the writing storyteller, silences this oral Keresan trope that indicates narrative closure and turns it into a glyph. In this glyph can be read not only the old oral stories but also a pattern of thought characteristic of Silko in which, through what could be described as writerly back-formation, the oral tradition turns out to have been written all along. This writerly back-formation is metaphorically figured in old Betonie's reference to the "brown spiral notebook with a torn cover" (125). What Betonie reads in this notebook allows him to begin "to see something." It is almost as if Betonie's reading, not out loud but while "moving his lips slightly," is a self-reflexive textual metaphor that mirrors *Ceremony* as a text in which medicinal writing informs the oral tradition that informs the rewritten ceremony. In such a circular figure, what Betonie is reading includes the story in which he and Tayo figure. The role of this "brown spiral notebook" presages the role of the old Mayan book and notebooks that form the vertebrae of *Almanac of the Dead*. As I argued in the introduction and continue to argue throughout this book, Silko rewrites Laguna culture in such a way that the oral tradition is written out by ancestors at Cliff House in a perfect and ontologically privileged language.

Shush himself joins the writing ancestors as he helps Betonie prepare the sand painting for the Red Antway ceremony: "The helper worked in the shadows beyond the dark mountain range; he worked with the black sand, making bear prints side by side" (*Ceremony* 142). As he leaves these black sand prints, it is as if Shush is using his "bear paw," that is, medicine, to "write" his own name. This writing is part of the ceremony intended to cure Tayo of his doubts about his sanity. In other words, Shush is writing his own ursinity—which could be perceived as madness from a Western perspective—to cure Tayo of this Western perspective, which has poisoned him physically and spiritually. Like Derrida's writing as pharmakon, Shush's bear paw as writing is both medicine and poison. To write, in this scene, is to shush Tayo's fears about madness and Silko's fears about being mad because she is both medicine woman and writer.

If Betonie is to be believed, those ancestors from thirty thousand years back are, according to the myths of their country, descendants of the Goddess of the Sun. I have already likened Tayo's seeing Josiah's face in the Japanese prisoner to Silko's appearing Japanese in the photograph that the Japanese translator took of her and included in the Japanese edition of *Ceremony*. Silko's use of white space on the pages with embedded words and narratives can be likened to a practice in Japanese scroll painting:

> The essence of Japanese balance is found in the term *yohaku*—literally "white space." Coined long ago, it referred to the background or untouched areas in ink painting. The elegance-in-proportion of the empty space in a given framework was admired as much as the brush strokes themselves. In scroll painting, minimal suggestion was preferred to literal representation, thus allowing the viewer to participate in his mind's eye and complete the interpretation. (Blakemore 200)

The similarity of the white space on the pages of *Ceremony* to *yohaku*, especially in the opening pages where the word "Sunrise" is set alone, center-justified at the top of an otherwise blank page that is followed by a page of which at least four-fifths is blank (4–5), and in the closing page, where only the words "Sunrise, / accept this offering, / Sunrise" (262) are slightly asymmetrically centered, must be heightened in the Japanese translation where, rather than English words, written Japanese characters appear. Silko's elegant use of this *yohaku*-like blank space on important pages of *Ceremony* can be read as a postmodern and cross-cultural trope of balance in deferral, of shushed bear stories in which what is passed over in silence is admired as much or more than what is literally brushed in.[21] This Japanese aesthetic, which is implicit in *Ceremony,* comes of age in the translation into Japanese. This is a remarkable demonstration of how writing and translation are anything but static and impoverishing of the old Pueblo stories. Indeed, they are nurtured and enriched in a logic and aesthetic of inclusion that make themselves explicit as Silko's writing career develops.

On the final page, the written characters and the white space form an ending that is open and that points spatially and temporally, back and ahead, toward the Land of the Rising Sun, as well as toward a shorter text, "Storyteller." This long short story, which is set in Alaska and which Silko wrote at the same time she was working on *Ceremony,* begins not with sunrise but with the apparent frozen arrest of the sun in the white arctic sky during the solstice. "Story-teller" is informed not only by this story of the sun, but also by the story of a giant polar bear and a hunter.

Published in *Puerto del Sol* in 1975—the year in which Silko returned from her stay in Alaska—"Storyteller" can be read not only as "an allegory on the essentialist position, an allegory that will be tested and contested in the remaining stories in *Storyteller*" (Jaskoski 22), but also, like *Ceremony*, as a healing writing in which the writing storyteller passes over in silence a madness with apocalyptic overtones. This healing writing indicts the narrative of Anglo-American law, which Silko had studied for three semesters and then abandoned in order to pursue graduate study in literature and writing, because she finally realized that "injustice is built into the Anglo-American legal system" (*Yellow Woman* 19).

This allegory also derides the notion of Western scientific objectivity, the belief in technology, and the Christian missionary morality according to which man is supposed to be master of nature and of woman. In "Storyteller" and in the personal stories linked to this unsettlingly ambiguous story, it is the carnal letter that quickens and the spirit of patristic Christian exegesis that kills. This quickening is partly effected by knowledge, both carnal and cultural, which is conceptually present in the sexual metaphors used to describe storytelling.

The two principal Yupik[22] characters in "Storyteller" are the "old man" and the "girl." Both are storytellers. Neither is named. Central to the story that the old man is said to tell endlessly are a giant polar bear and a hunter, which thematically echo Silko's story of seeing a giant bear while hunting. The old man and the girl are depicted in such a way that characters, both Yupik and non-Yupik, may detect signs of marginality and even madness in their storytelling as well as their behavior. When the story opens, the girl, who has been placed in jail awaiting trial for allegedly being responsible for the death of the local storekeeper, excitedly yells and randomly utters swear words in English in order to get the jailer's attention. When the jailer gets to where she is, it appears that she informs him in

Yupik that the sun is frozen in the sky. Such talk could easily be construed as typical of what goes on in a mental institution. Whether the jailer, an assimilated Yupik who refuses to speak his mother tongue, thinks she is mad or not is passed over in silence, the same silence that constitutes his response to her apocalyptic enunciation to him: "He came and stared at her. She didn't know if he understood what she was telling him until he glanced behind her at the small high window. He looked at the sun, and turned and walked away. She could hear the buckles on his heavy snowmobile boots jingle as he walked to the front of the building" (18). It is no more possible to tell, however, whether the girl is correct in interpreting the jailer's looking at the sun through the small window as his having understood what she is talking about, than it is to know the meaning of the jingling buckles on his snowmobile boots. For, if the girl understands the motionless sun and the dissolution of boundaries between the sky, the earth, and the water to be signs of the arrival of the final winter about which the old man has talked and allegorized in his story of the hunter and the giant polar bear, the assimilated Yupik jailer could just as easily understand these signs as nothing more than the usual meteorological and astronomical phenomena that occur during the summer solstice in the arctic.[23]

There are similarities between the white dissolution of natural boundaries in the description of the solstitial landscape that the Yupik girl is reading apocalyptically and Tayo's perception of himself as a disembodied cloud of white smoke that has merged with the white walls of the Los Angeles psychiatric ward: "For a long time he had been white smoke. He did not realize that until he left the hospital, because white smoke had no consciousness of itself. It faded into the white world of their bed sheets and walls; it was sucked away by the words of doctors who tried to talk to the invisible scattered smoke" (14). At one point in the story, after the girl has returned to her village from her one school year in Bethel and learned that her grandmother has died during her absence, her perception of her own body is described in a manner that somatically recalls Tayo's alienated disembodiment: "She sat beside the old man at his place on the river bank. She poked the smoky fire for him, and felt herself growing wide and thin in the sun as if she had been split from belly to throat and strung on the willow pole in preparation for the winter to come. The old man did not speak anymore" (26). There is a lot going on in the unbrushed white space of this story. For one thing, as Kenneth Lincoln has pointed out, the repetition of the recurrent motif of a splash of red in the whiteness brings to mind images of wine and blood on snow, of the girl's first menstrual blood, of her sex with the redheaded white man, of her first being seduced by the old man, who may or may not be her grandfather, but who appears to be taken for her grandfather by the people in the village, of revenge in which "blood will out" (Lincoln 229–31). There is also an echo in Silko's story of a tale found in Yupik oral tradition in which "the sun is a transformed woman who fled to the skyland followed by her brother, who became the moon and who continues to pursue her" (Fienup-Riordan 263). The reason for the flight and the pursuit are found in the brother's incestuous desire for his sister:

> Variations of this tale are told all across the Arctic. Nelson Island oral tradition attributes the origin of the sun and the moon to the lust of one of five brothers for their younger sister. Although at first unaware of the identity of her lover, one night the sister marks him with soot from his lamp. The next day she confronts her brothers in the *qasgiq* [the men's house], identifying the culprit by the mark of soot. Thereupon she flees from the *qasgiq* and up into the sky, followed by her brother, who comes dragging his pants and carrying his empty bowl. There she transforms into the sun and her brother becomes the moon. (263)

Despite evidence provided by witnesses that the storekeeper's death was an accident, the girl insists that she intended to kill him to avenge her parents' death, and that she did this by patiently devising a scheme whereby she could use his lust to lure him into chasing her out onto the treacherous ice-covered river. It is for this reason that she is in jail. The court-appointed lawyer, having failed to persuade her to change her story of revenge, resigns himself to telling a narrative of her mental confusion in order to defend her: "The attorney exhaled loudly; his eyes looked tired. 'Tell her that she could not have killed him that way. He was a white man. He ran after her without a parka or mittens. She could not have planned that.' He paused and turned toward the cell door. 'Tell her I will do all I can for her. *I will explain to the judge that her mind is confused'"* (31; my emphasis). The irony here, traversing the gap between the legal and medical point of view of the attorney and the Yupik point of view of the defendant, is apparent. The attorney simultaneously does all he can to legally defend his client, which equals doing all he can to fail to understand her and all he can to condemn her Yupik perspective. Where she sees transitions and balances, where she reads the vast white expanses from a total perspective, he narrowly reads her reading as a sign of mental confusion.

This sign of mental confusion or madness she shares with the old man, the principal storyteller in the story. From the time when the old man starts to tell his story of a giant bear and a hunter, his demeanor and his words could be construed not only as confused and confusing, but also as the result of senile dementia:

> His breathing was wheezy and fast; his hands gestured at the sky. "It is approaching. As it comes, ice will push across the sky." His eyes were open wide and he stared at the low ceiling rafters for hours without blinking. She remembered all this clearly because he began the story that day, the story he told from that time on. It began with a giant bear which he described muscle by muscle, from the curve of the ivory claws to the whorls of hair at the top of the massive skull. And for eight days he did not sleep, but talked continuously of the giant bear whose color was pale blue glacier ice. (22)

Endlessly, day and night, while awake and asleep, he tells this story in such a way that he almost appears to embody storytelling gone berserk: "Inside, he dozed and talked to himself. He had talked all winter, softly and incessantly, about the giant polar bear stalking a lone hunter across Bering Sea ice" (26). As he grows physically weaker he shows what could be construed as symptoms of the kind of behavior associated with Alzheimer's:

> He did not recognize her anymore, and when he spoke to her, he called her by her grandmother's name and talked about people and events from long ago, before he went back to telling the story. The giant bear was creeping across the new snow on its belly, close enough now that the man could hear the rasp of its breathing. On and on in a soft singing voice, *the old man caressed the story, repeating the words again and again like gentle strokes.* (27; my emphasis)

In this description of the old man's voice caressing the story, storytelling and having sex are metaphorically united in a way that might indeed be appropriate for a world in which the origin of the sun is found in a story of incestuous lust and pursuit.

When a state trooper comes to question the girl about what happened to the storeman, the old man again behaves in a way that is hard not to take as a symptom of dementia: he "suddenly sat up in his bed and began to talk excitedly, looking at all of them—the trooper in his dark glasses and the housekeeper in her corduroy parka. He kept saying, 'The story! The story! Eh-ya! The great bear! The hunter!'" (31). Whether the trooper and the housekeeper think the old man is crazy is passed over in silence. Here Silko uses what can be called an inverted *style indirect libre* (discussed in ch. 5). In the classic *style indirect libre,* the third-person narrator passes from a so-called objective and perspicuous point of view, shared with the interpretive community, down into the subjective point of view of the character. This produces a cold and condescending narrative irony. The writing storyteller, however, empathizes with the storytelling old man in a self-referential trope that doubles irony back on itself. With this trope the writing storyteller, rather than condescending to the point of view of the storytelling old man, equalizes him with herself, making it possible for the community of discerning readers to see that the incessantly told story of the bear and the hunter is the story of what the girl has done to the storeman.

To diagnose the old man and the girl as mad is only one possible interpretation. And as interpretation, with the exception of the lawyer's decision to tell the judge that the girl's "mind is confused," it is passed over in silence. The interpretation, in which the girl's mind would not be confused and the old man would not be senile, is specified only as "the story."

As Jaskoski has pointed out, this story of the bear and the hunter is not literally told in the text. According to Jaskoski, if this story is to remain "true," it cannot be told in the text, it must remain absent, owing to the "essential mendacity" of language, which, Jaskoski contends, Silko is interrogating in "Storyteller." Owing to its absence, the story cannot be construed as lying, as it would be were it written out in English. Jaskoski maintains that the absence of the story is consonant with Silko's criticism and disparagement of translations of informants' stories by ethnologists. This leads her to reason tautologically about essentialist thought in a way that echoes Silko's not telling her bear story, but contradicts Silko's shushing this story in writing:

> The old man's story can never be truly told in "Storyteller," because the pages of a book are the pages of a book and not the presence of the old man, his voice, his language, and his performance. Hence, it is the absence of the man's story that is the story "without any lies," and it is this absence, this centripetal inertia, that continually draws the story back into silence, that preserves the integrity of the old man's storytelling and makes it a figure for the protagonist's unflinching resolution to maintain her own integrity no matter the cost. (17)

This cost, it turns out, according to Jaskoski, is an essentialist point of view that freezes the world in dark apocalyptic silence, a gesture that symbolizes the refusal to acknowledge even the slightest possibility of multiculturalism, cultural relativism, and translation across cultures.

Jaskoski's reasoning skims around a paradox similar to the one Derrida treats in his article on Benjamin's essay on translation ("Des Tours de Babel"). What the translator cannot reach, the equivalent of a perfect pre-Babelian language, Silko imagines as the perfect but doomed being of the Yupik story. Ontologically the status of the old man's story is similar to that of Humaweepi's understanding of his uncle's ritual singing, the lake, and the bear-boulder. Thus, in order to avoid a doubly debilitating displacement, owing first to Silko's having to relate the story in English (she does not know Yupik) and second to her relying on writing to depict orality, Silko allows silence, or absence, to represent the ineffable and untranslatable story.[24] This is a strategy made possible by secondary orality, or textuality, to which Silko will resort in different ways. It is the same non-Yupik technology, writing and print, which has brought about the alienation of Yupik culture from itself, that enables Silko to tell this story.

Silko's own commentary on her story suggests not only that the unfamiliar northern landscape was at least partly responsible for the alienation she experienced in Alaska, but also that she undertook to overcome this alienation by writing about the interior landscapes of her characters. With these interior landscapes she could identify, and in identifying, she could relate to the exterior landscape, thereby assimilating it:

> My favorite story is one that isn't set in the Southwest, but I love my characters in it. It's called "Storyteller," and it's set in the tundra of Bethel, Alaska. It's a long short story, and it sets out what the relationship of the storyteller to people is. The story is interesting to me and I like it, perhaps because the landscape is different, because I find a common point where I can relate to the land, regardless of whether it's land I'm from or not. That's a big step for me, to go to a completely alien landscape. I managed. What I did in that story finally was to get the *interior landscapes of the characters,* and yet they are still related to the tundra and the river because that's how she does the guy in. I love that story just because I

like the characters and how she does the guy in. ("Stories
and Their Tellers" 22–23; my emphasis)

Getting to "the interior landscapes of the characters" produces a
disorienting and ambiguous depiction of an apocalyptic white otherness from which Silko returns not by telling stories to herself, like
the old man, but by writing these stories for herself and for the
Gussuck readers who, like Silko, cannot understand Yupik. In this
allegory, were she only an oral storyteller like her two anonymous
Yupik storytellers, she would remain forever in the betwixt and
between, stopped like the sun at the solstice, frozen in the absolute
essence of Yupik meaning. Rather than using white space on pages,
as she does in *Ceremony* and in *Storyteller* in a manner that recalls
the Japanese concept of *yohaku,* to balance what is inked in, she
would leave everything blank on the page.

But since Silko is not Yupik and because she is a writing storyteller, the signs of alienation—of madness—in the story of the giant
polar bear and the hunter, which the old man endlessly tells to himself and to the "girl," and which Silko must literally pass over in
silence here because it is told only in Yupik, become part of the
same landscape where Silko had gone hunting and seen the giant
brown bear, over which she passed in silence in order to return.
According to the logic of the writing storyteller, this landscape is
textually spiritual. It dialectically lifts itself above the logic behind
the spirit of Western scientific, legal, and exegetical inquiry. The
oral storyteller relies on the writing storyteller in order to avoid
the final winter, just as young Leslie in the fifth grade relied on
writing to undo the feeling of alienation away from home. Likewise,
Silko writes "Storyteller" and *Ceremony* to bring herself back from
arctic alienation, from the blank page where she may have felt like
that girl-sun trapped in a solstice that might just end in totally mad
whiteness. Like the Yupik girl's lawyer, John Silko, the supervising
lawyer for Alaska Legal Services, did not seem able to bring Leslie
Silko back from this whiteness. Passed over in silence in the interview with Dexter Fisher, John Silko, from whom Leslie Silko later

severed herself in an apparently unpleasant divorce, may have told a story to the judge about his storytelling spouse during that divorce to which Leslie refers elliptically in her letters to James Wright.

Although the Yupik girl is not a writer, she does introduce a sign into the natural landscape and meteorological condition that she "uses" in order to do in the storeman. She saves herself from being lost in the frozen white-out condition that resembles an ultimate winter by referring to the red color of the tin that she had earlier nailed to her house:

> She moved slowly, kicking the ice ahead with the heel of her boot, feeling for sinews of ice to hold her. She looked ahead and all around herself; in the twilight, the dense white sky had merged into the flat snow-covered tundra. In the frantic running she had lost her place on the river. She stood still. The east bank of the river was lost in the sky; the boundaries had been swallowed by the freezing white. But then, in the distance, she saw something red, and suddenly it was as she had remembered it all those years. (30)

In a parallel with Silko's writing, the Yupik girl has nailed up the red tin not consciously as part of a plan, nor in order to provide insulation for her house as have the Yupik villagers, but for aesthetic reasons alone: "The village people were using the strips of tin to mend walls and roofs for winter. But she nailed it on the log walls for its color" (28). The white-out—a dissolution of boundaries—can be construed as a metaphor for madness. Nailing up the red tin metaphorically figures Silko's writing her way back from an encounter with madness. The red tin also recalls explicitly the motif of revenge in that the girl remembers something red on the ground near her parents' dead bodies.[25]

There are, however, in the text, signs that one can be attracted to this madness, signs of a desire to remain among the bears, to go berserk, so to speak. These are signs of a yearning to be overcome with an interior vision of wintry ursine beauty like the anonymous character in "Story from Bear Country" in *Storyteller:*

Their [i.e., the bears'] beauty will overcome your memory
like winter sun
melting ice shadows from snow
And you will remain with them
locked forever inside yourself
> your eyes will see you
> dark shaggy and thick.

(205)

In the essay "Interior and Exterior Landscapes," the tone of which is angry and political, Silko's commentary on "Storyteller" literally amounts to an interpretive rewriting of her story that is absent from the written text:

> *A sudden storm develops. The hunter finds himself on an ice floe offshore. Visibility is zero, and the scream of the wind blots out all sound. Quickly the hunter realizes he is being stalked, hunted by all the forces, by all the elements of the sky and earth around him. When at last the hunter's own muscles spasm and cause the jade knife to fall and shatter the ice, the hunter's death in the embrace of the giant, ice blue bear is the foretelling of the world's end.* (Yellow Woman 46–47)

A comparison of the above passage with the passage from "Storyteller" reveals the former to give a more explicitly apocalyptic closure to the story of the great bear and the hunter:

> The hunter had been on the ice for many hours. The freezing winds on the ice knoll had numbed his hands in the mittens, and the cold had exhausted him. He felt a single muscle tremor in his hand that he could not stop, and the jade knife fell; it shattered on the ice, and the blue glacier bear turned slowly to face him. (32)

In her commentary on "Storyteller" from "Interior and Exterior Landscapes," Silko foregrounds the conflict between the insane belief of Western technology and science that the forces of nature can be objectified and mastered and the Yupik spiritual and intuitive relation in which nature and culture, the land and man, are not thought to be opposed in a conceptual dichotomy:

> Although the white trader possessed every possible gar-
> ment, insulation, heating fuel, and gadget ever devised to
> protect him from the frozen tundra environment, he still
> dies, drowning under the freezing river ice, because the
> white man had not reckoned with the true power of that
> landscape, especially not the power that the Yupik woman
> understood instinctively and that she used so swiftly and
> efficiently. The white man had reckoned with the young
> woman and determined he could overpower her. But the
> white man failed to account for the conjunction of the land-
> scape with the woman. The Yupik woman had never seen
> herself as anything but a part of that sky, that frozen river,
> that tundra. The river's ice and the blinding white are her
> accomplices, and yet the Yupik woman never for a
> moment misunderstands her own relationship with that
> landscape. (45–46)

In paraphrasing and identifying strongly with her anonymous Yupik character's revenge for the murder of her parents, Silko is passing over in silence the coming-of-age aspect of the Yupik story. Red on white can figure the first menstrual blood, as well as her own writerly struggle to overcome the otherness she experienced in the Alaskan landscape. In this essay Silko's vehement bashing of Western culture and her growing tendency to speak out about its mad tech-nological arrogance effect in her a swing away from the writing storyteller's understanding of her own dialogic and dialectical link to writing. This particular reading of her own story is an example of one of the attitudes toward writing between which Silko vacillates in her fiction and essays. Here a literalist desire to reclaim orality and to reject writing as a deplorable Anglo-European swerve from truth and life is dominant. It is a swing toward the position occupied by the Bible-reading Presbyterian Grandma A'mooh, who would burn *Stiya*, and away from the position of Aunt Susie, the writing scholar, historian, and storyteller, who uses the etiquette of Laguna oral tradition to appropriate the mendacious book, leaving behind, almost passed over in silence, since it is told by Leslie's mother, the story of why the book is absent from Leslie's family household.[26] In this angry swing Silko reads Yupik culture in terms of a literalist apocalyptic narrative: "For the Yupik people, souls deserving punishment spend varying lengths of time in a place of freezing. The Yupik see the world's end coming with ice, not fire" (45).

Not only can one discern possible echoes of Robert Frost in this vision of punishment in an afterlife that Silko attributes here to the Yupik, but one can detect traces of a rhetoric of hell-ice and damnation such as might have informed sermons preached at the end of the nineteenth century by Moravian missionaries like John Kilbuck.[27] Such an apocalyptic rhetoric would permanently close the passages between worlds through which the cyclical movement of souls among animals and humans is assured in traditional Yupik narrative and ritual, at least according to the ethnological studies of Ann Fienup-Riordan (45–47). In "Storyteller," however, the writing storyteller is less ideologically angry than Silko in her commentary. The attitude of writerly wisdom, as embodied by Aunt Susie, in which orality and writing are interwoven in a syncretic vision of both American Indian and Western culture, can be discerned, as well as the literalist and essentialist desire to reclaim orality. The problem with the literalist reclamation of orality in this story—as Jaskoski suggests but does not explicitly state—is that rather than opening a passage either to the precontact worlds and traditions of the Yupik, or to a new postcolonial world of political independence, bilingualism, and celebration of tradition, such as the one that, according to Ann Fienup-Riordan, the Yupik are now attempting to create, it effects closure for all, white and Yupik. Couched in a language that has overtones of both science and religion, Silko's vision of the postapocalyptic world, in which the white man, like the storeman, will ultimately get what he deserves, is not unlike a Manichaean version of the ultimate triumph of evil: "When humans have blasted and burned the last bit of life from the earth, an immeasurable freezing will descend with a darkness that obliterates the sun" (*Yellow Woman* 47). There are problems with this vision of justice, as can be ascertained in *Almanac of the Dead,* where Lecha's memories of a stay she had in Alaska can be read as a rewriting of the story in "Storyteller," in which the indigenous person who is one with the land and climate triumphs over the hubristic Westerner who thinks his or her technology assures superiority.

CHAPTER 2

BACK TO THE TEXT

"Lullaby"

The land grant documents alerted the Pueblo people to the value of the written word; the old books of international law favored the holders of royal land grants. So, very early, the Pueblo people realized the power of written words and books to secure legitimate title to tribal land. No wonder the older folks used to tell us kids to study: learn to read and to write for your own protection.

—SILKO,
*"Books: Notes on Mixtec and Maya Screenfolds,
Picture Books of Preconquest Mexico"*

To write is often still suspect in our tribal communities, and understandably so. It is through writing in the colonizers' languages that our lands have been stolen, children taken away. We have often been betrayed by those who first learned to write and to speak the language of the occupier of our lands. Yet to speak well in our communities in whatever form is still respected. This is a dichotomy we will always deal with as long as our cultures are predominately expressed in oral literatures.

—JOY HARJO,
Reinventing the Enemy's Language

"Lullaby" opens with the image of Ayah, an aging Navajo woman, reaching out childlike toward the luminescent snow that is beginning to cover her:

> The sun had gone down but the snow in the wind gave off its own light. It came in thick tufts like new wool—washed before the weaver spins it. Ayah reached out for it like her own babies had, and she smiled when she remembered how she had laughed at them. She was an old woman now, and her life had become memories. She sat down with her back against the wide cottonwood tree, feeling the rough bark on her back bones; she faced east and listened to the wind and snow sing a high-pitched Yeibechei song. (*Storyteller* 43)

Ayah's reaching out toward the falling snow, which is likened to freshly sheared and washed wool and associated with light and purity, can be construed as an emblem of the paradoxes around which this story is woven: The cold snow, which will soon blanket Ayah and her spouse, brings memories of a warm, luminous, and happy past. Natural elements, the snow and the wind, rather than being presented as life-threatening, are construed metaphorically as life-cherishing cultural artifacts, blanket and song. Ayah's is a figurative gesture toward a natural mother in which she metaphorically becomes a baby again, in which her smile reflects her joyous maternal laughter at the same gesture made by her infant children toward the snow. These images that paradoxically unite opposites, old age and youth, nature and culture, cold and warmth, life and death, function like the metaphorical backbone of Silko's written storytelling. Just as Ayah gestures toward the family activity of weaving, uniting her dark and abject present with her luminous and joyous past, so Silko's writing gestures toward the world that Ayah has lost owing to writing. Just as it is paradoxical that the present cold snow evokes in Ayah memories of warmth and childhood, so it is paradoxical that writing is called on to restore an oral world that it is shown to have deeply wounded if not destroyed. "Lullaby" is metaphorically and thematically informed by the ambivalent attitude that Silko recurrently demonstrates toward writing and literate culture. Silko's text is to the preliterate past what the wind and the snow are to Ayah: a warm blanket to wrap oneself in and a song lulling one to sleep, not death.

That past, toward which Silko's text reaches out, is evoked as an idyllic maternal scene in which three generations of Navajo women are woven together as they weave, contrasting with the present of the narrative where Ayah sits alone, coldly wrapped in an unraveling olive drab blanket. This blanket is a gift from the first male to be mentioned in the story. Its origin is the U.S. Army, an institution with which there are few pleasant or maternal associations in Silko's writing. This mention of the male is shushed by Ayah's memory of weaving almost as soon as it is made:

> Ayah pulled the old Army blanket over her head like a shawl. Jimmie's blanket—the one he had sent to her. That was a long time ago and the green wool was faded, and it was unraveling on the edges. She did not want to think about Jimmie. So she thought about the weaving and the way her mother had done it. On the tall wooden loom set into the sand under a tamarack tree for shade. She could see it clearly. She had been only a little girl when grandma gave her the wooden combs to pull the twigs and burrs from the raw, freshly washed wool, her grandma sat beside her, spinning a silvery strand of yarn around the smooth cedar spindle. Her mother worked at the loom with yarns dyed bright yellow and red and gold. (43)

The faded unraveling army blanket obviously contrasts aesthetically and functionally with the colorful and home-woven blankets of the past: "The blankets her mother made were soft and woven so tight that *rain rolled off them like birds' feathers.* Ayah remembered sleeping warm on cold windy nights, wrapped in her mother's blankets on the hogan's sandy floor" (44; my emphasis). To liken these Navajo blankets to "birds' feathers" is to imply that they are so artfully woven that they are natural. This natural artfulness in the blankets is associated with protective warmth, life, autonomy, brightness, the maternal, and the indigenous. It is contrasted with the male, the cold, the faded, the foreign, the absent, death, and writing.

Writing first explicitly enters the narrative and is woven into this paradoxical emblem of the story as Ayah recalls how she and Chato learned that their elder son would not return from the army:

> It wasn't like Jimmie died. He just never came back, and one day a dark blue sedan *with white writing* on its doors pulled up in front of the box-car shack where the rancher let the Indians live. A man in a khaki uniform trimmed in gold gave them a *yellow piece of paper* and told them that Jimmie was dead. He said the Army would try to get the body back and then it would be shipped to them; but it wasn't likely because the helicopter had burned after it crashed. All of this was told to Chato because he could understand English. She stood inside the doorway holding the baby while Chato listened. Chato spoke English like a white man and he spoke Spanish too. (44; my emphasis)

Instead of Jimmie or his dead body, which Chato tells the white government official they do not want back, Ayah and Chato receive a yellow piece of paper.[1] No doubt this piece of yellow paper has writing on it, since in all likelihood it is a telegram notifying them of Jimmie's death in combat, certifying that Ayah's and Chato's first-born son has been sacrificed by Uncle Sam to the warlike god of Western expansion. It is as if the writing, delivered by a white man in a car with white writing on its doors, becomes another link in a chainlike textual metaphor, prefigured by Jimmie's sending the army blanket, which also has taken his place as well as the place of the Navajo blankets. Sitting wrapped in the unraveling Army blanket, Ayah is figuratively wrapped in the story of the death of herself and her people as the U.S. government has written it.[2]

Chato, who is multilingual and literate, translates into Navajo what the white man has told him in English, which is probably also what is written on the yellow piece of paper. "Then Chato looked at her and shook his head, and then he told her, 'Jimmie isn't coming home anymore,' and when he spoke, he used the words to speak of the dead" (45). Here Chato is said to use a different vocabulary, or a different morphological form—the narrator does not provide a detailed linguistic description but only translates into English Ayah's Navajo thought about her own maternal language—to distinguish a referent that is dead from one that is living. Chato's translation of the meaning of the writing on the yellow piece of paper into the distinctive Navajo form used to speak of the dead potentially sets up for Ayah an association between these "words to speak of the dead" and writing. For Ayah, it is as if writing, like the special usage in Navajo, must refer to the dead. From this point on Ayah can easily associate writing with loss and death and see in it something threatening that she cannot understand, just as she cannot understand English. Since Navajos customarily do not speak the name of a deceased person for a period of one year following that person's death,[3] writing could also be associated by Ayah with not uttering the name of her son, who in Navajo was named "for the summer morning" (44). Thus, writing could easily be perceived by Ayah as something dead that has silenced her, coldly severing her from the summer morning embodied in Jimmie's Navajo name, replacing the spoken name with incomprehensible marks on a piece of paper, leaving her out in the cold.

This silence seems to carry over into Ayah's apparent failure to follow Navajo tradition by grieving openly during the customary four-day period. Ayah is not said to have participated in any mourning ceremony or purification. The loss of Jimmie causes her to turn her anger and grief inward, extending the traditional four days of ceremonial mourning, which should provide closure, to a lifetime of repetitive and inefficacious grief. Silent grieving for Jimmie is her repeated response to other suffering and losses, which come from Chato having made himself dependent on the white rancher, from his having bound himself to the white man's writing culture with its contracts, laws, wages paid in printed paper money, and government agencies and institutions that allegedly provide health care and welfare:

She didn't cry then, but she hurt inside with anger. And she mourned him as the years passed, when a horse fell with Chato and broke his leg, and the white rancher told them he wouldn't pay Chato until he could work again. She mourned Jimmie because he would have worked for his father then; he would have saddled the big bay horse and ridden the fence lines each day, with wire cutters and heavy gloves, fixing the breaks in the barbed wire and putting the stray cattle back inside again.

She mourned him after the white doctors came to take Danny and Ella away. She was at the shack alone that day they came. It was back in the days before they hired Navajo women to go with them as interpreters. She recognized one of the doctors. She had seen him at the children's clinic at Cañoncito about a month ago. They were wearing khaki uniforms and they waved papers at her and a black ball-point pen, trying to make her understand their English words. (45)

Obviously, Ayah does not understand either the spoken or the written English words. She does, however, understand from the look in the white doctors' eyes that they intend to take Danny and Ella. Thus, she could easily reason that the writing on the papers they are waving will replace her children, just as the yellow piece of paper replaced Jimmie. Not understanding what is written on the papers, but nevertheless apparently implicitly understanding the link between writing and power, she attempts to take the story of her children into her own writing hand. She proudly and blindly mimics the whites, writing her own name on the paper. Thereby she becomes not the author of, but a character in, the story of death and alienation that the whites have written:

She was frightened by the way they looked at the children, like the lizard watches the fly. . . . Ayah could see they wanted her to sign the papers, and Chato had taught her to sign her name. It was something she was proud of. She only wanted them to go, and to take their eyes away from her children.

> She took the pen from the man *without looking* at his face
> and she signed the papers in three different places he pointed
> to. She stared at the ground by their feet and waited for them
> to leave. But they stood there and began to point and gesture
> at the children. (45; my emphasis)

Seeing the gesture toward the children repeated by the whites, which
is to say, seeing that her attempt to write her own story has failed,
that she has reduced herself and her children to powerless signs in
the white text, she grabs the referents and flees into the surrounding
hills. The doctors leave and come back the next day when Chato is
there. Thus, they have a polyglot translator-interpreter who attempts
to explicate to Ayah that the disease (apparently tuberculosis) that
her grandmother had passed on to the children is the reason the
children must become characters in the white man's written story:
"The doctors came back the next day and they brought a BIA
policeman with them. They told Chato they had her signature and
that was all they needed. Except for the kids. She listened to Chato
sullenly; she hated him when he told her it was the old woman
who died in the winter, spitting blood; it was her old grandma who
had given the children this disease" (46). Seen from Chato's literate
point of view, the doctors are using writing and the law not to signify the children's death, but to keep them from dying, to cure them
of tuberculosis. This cure will also entail the two children's assimilation into literate Anglo culture. The Navajo tradition, at this point,
becomes entangled with the disease that the Navajo grandmother
has allegedly passed on orally to the younger generation. Writing
will make possible not only the cure of tuberculosis, it will also
cure the children of being Navajo. Ayah figuratively knows this, as
she associates writing and those who use it with mendacity and
loss: "'They don't spit blood,' she said coldly. 'The whites lie.' She
held Ella and Danny close to her, ready to run to the hills again. 'I
want a medicine man first,' she said to Chato, not looking at him.
He shook his head. 'It's too late now. The policeman is with them.
You signed the paper.' His voice was gentle" (46). Seen from a

cross-cultural point of view, Ayah's saying that she wants a medicine man amounts to her saying that she wants the Navajo ceremonial equivalent of writing, which has been used to procure a Western cure for the children.[4] The Navajo cure would consist of live song and colorful sand painting, performed in Ayah's presence. The white man's cure, represented by black ink on the white paper that Ayah has signed, forces Ayah to accept silently the absence of her children, of the persons doing the curing, and even the absence of herself to herself. In putting her name on the paper, on which her children's names also figure, and which she does not even get in place of the children, she has sundered herself from what constituted her reason for being: her oral maternal presence and her Navajo identity. Chato, who taught her the incomplete rudiments of literacy, thereby making it possible for her to mimic the white writer and afflict herself with self-alienation, tries to comfort her by gently voicing his understanding of the workings of writing culture. Like the unraveling army blanket, Chato's words about legal writing are coldly and inadequately comforting. This Navajo polyglot figuratively imitates the white critic and translator and writes himself into the white story of the West as a powerless and contemptible character: he will soon be a pathetic literary stereotype, a drunken Indian, a marginal character in a story he himself has neither authored nor adequately understood.

The children's institutional treatment for tuberculosis will also amount to their being "cured" of the oral culture and the Navajo language, as Ayah can painfully foretell in Danny's speech during the last time the children are brought back to see her. During this visit, Danny poignantly reenacts his older brother's having been replaced with a sheet of paper. When he tried to answer Ayah, "he could not seem to remember and he spoke English words with the Navajo. But he gave her a scrap of paper that he had found somewhere and carried in his pocket; it was folded in half, and he shyly looked up at her and said it was a bird" (49).

Helen Jaskoski has offered an excellent close reading of this story. She provides a great deal of ethnological information about Navajo

culture and relies on contemporary Western psychology and genre
theory to view the story less as a narrative text than as a poetic
reflection on loss, death, grief, and mourning. Jaskoski emphasizes
the contrast between Ayah's inner life, where Navajo culture "lives"
in all its spiritual richness and beauty, and the squalid outer life of
poverty, suffering, indignity, physical debility, and alcoholism that
afflict the couple. She goes to some length to explain how the story
can be construed as a healing ritual when certain exterior elements
in it are interpreted according to a Navajo worldview:

> At the opening of the story, Ayah hears the wind sing a Yeibi-
> chei [sic] song. The term *Yeibichei* is often translated as
> "Holy People," and Yeibichei, or Yei People, are comparable
> to spirits; they are powerful beings who inhabit sacred
> mountains, springs, and other holy sites, and they also
> represent certain natural forces. Their connection to sacred
> places is more than merely residential, however; in English
> they are sometimes designated as the "inner form" of a par-
> ticular place, suggesting something more like a soul. . . .
> Navajo philosophy and worldview regard the universe as
> essentially animate, or as theologians might say, ensouled.
> Yei People are powerful creators and healers, and so they
> are called upon in ceremonies, especially rituals for healing
> the sick or injured. A Yeibichei song is a sacred song in a
> religious ritual, and the song that Ayah hears in the wind
> suggests that her story may be understood as a healing ritual.
> (26–27)

If Ayah's story is understood as a healing ritual, then Silko is standing
in for the Navajo medicine man whom Ayah asked for and did not
get. Jaskoski goes on to point out that the song at the end of the story,
the lullaby that Ayah sings to Chato as they lie freezing, probably
to death, resembles in form and content the English translations of
many Navajo sacred songs. She contends that the imagery in this
song—father sky, mother earth, brother winds, sister rainbow—
allows one to construe it as Ayah's equivalent of a chantway healing
ceremony.

Jaskoski suggests, however, that Ayah's ceremony remains interior. Thus, she implies, the ceremony is in need of a reader to interpret it, to see into that sacred inner place that is the meaning of her story:

> The ideal [Navajo] life is conceived as a journey along the correct, fruitful, beautiful road (the pollen path or rainbow path) which will take the individual back to the original— that is, the perfect—harmonious balance with the universe. Though Ayah's brief journey to the bar and along the road home appears outwardly to be rambling and dreary, inwardly it is leading her to a "sacred place" where she will experience healing. Following the implications of this reading, we may consider that the story offers its own healing ritual, hinting of the great traditional ceremonies that restore the individual and community to harmonious balance. (29)

Jaskoski's interpretation, though astute, becomes a figure for literary interpretation that is informed by Western literary concepts:

> The *tragedy* and *pathos* as well as the beauty of Ayah's journey are precisely that it is made as a purely interior voyage; she has neither the extraordinary attention and care that a chant-way ceremonial involves nor the possibility of communicating her healing with surrounding family and neighbors. She and Chato have only each other and the past. (29; my emphasis)

Tragedy and pathos are concepts that entered Anglo-European literary theory through the translation and collation of surviving copies of Aristotle's *Poetics* during the Renaissance. Ayah's "tragedy and pathos" could be said to emerge from her being an oral character whose hubris leads her to attempt to assume the role of author in a written text, but who misses the mark (cf. *hamartia*, Aristotle's tragic flaw), inscribing her name in the story of the Indian as tragic victim. Like Medea or Antigone or Clytemnestra, Ayah is heroic as long as she has vanished into the text. No one really wants to live next door to a tragic heroine.

The critical language Jaskoski employs in her detailed reading of the Navajo symbolism around which, she convincingly argues,

Silko has constructed her story, is informed by literary concepts that belong to the very culture Ayah hates. This, however understandable it may be, is not all. Jaskoski appears to be portraying Silko as having had recourse to discourse categories and concepts of Western genre theory: "'Lullaby' is cast in the mode of pastoral elegy" (22). In categorizing this story as a "pastoral elegy," Jaskoski is casting Silko in the role of a modern humanist who has melded together into one form, or one mode of discourse, two Greco-Roman forms that were revived during the European Renaissance. Both are traditionally written forms. One, the pastoral, an escapist form, uses written lyric, drama, or narrative to depict shepherds, shepherdesses, and other nonliterate rural characters enjoying a sunlit life of song and love in the country. The other, the elegy, an introspective form, uses written lyric to lead the reader through meditation on death and the transience of the world, usually to philosophical or religious consolation. The very notions of elegiac individual introspection and interiority evolve in a culture that has interiorized writing. In other words, Ayah's "purely interior voyage" is brought about by a literary form not found in oral cultures.[5]

Jaskoski emphasizes the damage white man's literate culture and English have done to Ayah and Navajo culture, but she falls into a slight but telling equivocation when she attributes to Ayah the thought that her "literacy" was responsible for her greatest loss:

Ayah's world has been contaminated and damaged by these alien elements, which have entered her life by way of a language she has learned to hate. She has lost everyone close to her, and she sees the English language, speakers of English, and even *her own literacy* in English as the means of that loss. Proud of knowing how to sign her name, she had *unwittingly* signed the papers that allowed her children to be taken from her, and *seeing the damage her literacy has accomplished*, she has blamed her husband all the years since then "because he had taught her to sign her name. Because it was like the old ones always told her about learning their language or any of their ways, it endangered you." (24; my emphasis)

Perhaps from the point of view of an absolutely pure oral culture, Ayah's having learned to write the letters in her name could be construed as literacy. As mentioned above, by writing her name on the paper she does not so much sunder herself from her children as sever them and herself from her own Navajo essence, from her own being, from her own self-identity, which is one with maternal orality. From the point of view of a writing culture, however, Ayah is not literate. She is illiterate, or at most, barely subliterate. Furthermore, from the point of view of a writing culture, Ayah's refusal to learn spoken and written English, except for her extremely rudimentary knowledge of writing her name, is responsible for her loss of Danny and Ella to the government doctors. Had she been truly literate, she never would have signed the paper. Ayah's illiteracy or subliteracy—not her literacy—is the means of her loss. To point out the paradox or the dilemma that arises from this double reading of Ayah caught up in a pathetic and tragic liminal area between pure monolingual orality and multilingual literacy, however, is to risk incurring the censor of certain critics of American Indian literature and American Indian writers who insist on the irrelevance of Western theory when writing about Indian literature. To exclude Western literary theory, which, however much we may dislike it, is inseparably interwoven with literary writing in Anglo-European languages, is to make a hubristic gesture similar to that of Ayah when she signs her name to the documents.

Jaskoski seems to vacillate between expressing her open awareness of the dilemma in which Native American literature and criticism find themselves, which arises not only from the overlap of oral and written points of view but also from the dialectical relationship between literary text and criticism, and a somewhat guilty willed blindness to it. This has already been pointed out above in her use of terms like "pastoral elegy," "tragedy," and "pathos." This willed critical blindness can be detected in the conclusion to her reading of "Lullaby," in which she elaborates on the "pathos" (31) of the story by gently equating the critical aspect of Silko's text with two photographs of great-grandmother Marmon printed in

Storyteller. She reads the two photographs as glossing Ayah's story. I agree that these two photographs silently "gloss Ayah's story" (31), just as Silko's written story silently glosses the silence and mourning in Ayah's shushed story by providing the literacy she did not acquire. I am not quite so certain, however, that Silko's great-grandmother "regards the reader with patience and serenity" (31), as Jaskoski maintains for the photograph on page 211. It is not difficult to see in the great-grandmother's gaze surprise, severity, suspicion, and impatience at being interrupted.[6] The "pathos," not just of "Lullaby" but of all of Native American literature, is that Silko's written story, even without the two photographs, gently but forcefully makes the argument that the only way Ayah could have preserved her warm, bright, colorful Navajo past is by learning how to read and write English, and that by doing this, she opens herself up to cross-cultural interpretation that might steal or assimilate her Navajo identity. By including in *Storyteller* the two photographs of Grandma A'mooh, one showing her reading aloud as Marmon family tradition, the other depicting crocheting, Silko reinforces the argument that the only way the indigenous past can be maintained or rebirthed is through adapting Western technology to Indian culture. This is dicey, as all texts, like photographs, are open to interpretation. Grandma A'mooh is not only looking at the reader as she pauses from her crocheting (also a non–Native American craft), she is looking at her mixed-blood grandson, Lee Marmon, who is using a non–Native American mimetic technology that he learned in the U.S. Army to capture the image of her for posterity. Her mixed-blood great-granddaughter will include this image as gloss in a book that tells the story of how literacy and orality were irreversibly interwoven in Laguna storytelling.

What does it mean to say that these photographs gloss Ayah's story? The term *gloss* in Latin, French, and English is fraught with a story of paradoxical translations. First, *glossa* in Latin designates an obscure or foreign word that needs explanation or translation. Then, over time, *glossa* comes to designate the words of explanation or translation. At the end of the Middle Ages near the beginning of the Renaissance, in Latin, French, and in English this word comes to designate explanatory verbiage that obfuscates. In contemporary English, *gloss* maintains these two antithetical meanings among multiple usages that all involve writing. In defining *gloss,* the entry in the *American Heritage Dictionary of the English Language* (4th ed.) implies that the development of the term and the concept belongs to a writing culture. Ong probably would affirm this. In very briefly tracing the term to its etymological root, the entry leaves open the possibility that the history of the term parallels the history of writing being accused of corrupting the lost orality that lies hidden in the Greek word for tongue from which Latin *glossa* and English *gloss* is derived.

Ayah's reaction, however, when Chato glosses the piece of paper she has signed, is maternal fury. She severs herself from him, seemingly blaming the male, the heteroglossic, the written patristic. Ayah does not want gloss. She wants neither photographs nor olive drab army blankets nor yellow pieces of paper. She wants the maternal presence, generational continuity, and pure luminous clarity associated with her own oral culture and brightly colored blankets.

In the conclusion to her reading of "Lullaby," Jaskoski suggests the lightly veiled existence in Silko's text of a kind of writing that is associated with luminous presence and life, rather than absence and obscure death. Unlike the writing in printed government documents and in laws that made it possible to take Indian children away from their parents, allegedly for their own good, this luminous kind of writing is put into practice by Silko and her bibliophilic family. Unlike the ethnological writing that desiccates oral stories and makes them resemble dusty old artifacts in a museum or in some box stored in the basement of the Smithsonian by ethnologists like Franz Boas and Elsie Clews Parsons, this writing quickens the old stories and images, restoring them to a present that banishes the very concept of a historical past.[7] This writing is artfully natural. Its naturalness has its source in indigenous figures and images (Spider Woman, ceremonial sand painting, Navajo weaving, Yeibechei songs, etc.) that are explicitly or implicitly construed as metaphors

for writing by literate Indians and critics of American Indian literature. Neither weaving nor crocheting is indigenous in origin, but
owing to metaphor or to photography, each art can be endowed with
living, indigenous, natural presence and associated with continuity
and life, rather than with absence and death.

Silko's text clearly suggests a cross-cultural misunderstanding
between the white culture that erects tombs in which to inter bodies
and the Navajo culture that does not erect tombs. Nevertheless,
Chato and Ayah get a figurative tomb for Jimmie, whether they
like it or not, in the yellow piece of paper given them by the U.S.
government. Jaskoski suggests that the hogan in which Ayah was
born, and back into which Ayah and Chato moved after the rancher
had evicted them from the boxcar shack, takes on the appearance
of a tomb (30).

Ayah supposes that had Jimmie been present, his knowledge of
writing would have kept her from being tricked into severing her
maternal ties with Danny and Ella: "If Jimmie had been there he
could have read those papers and explained to her what they said.
Ayah would have known then, never to sign them" (46). But Jimmie
had been sundered from her by the army, for which he had probably
signed up, without foreseeing that his signature would put him in
the helicopter that would carry him away to the vanishing point in
the story of his noble patriotic sacrifice for Uncle Sam. Thus, once
Ayah has unwittingly signed on as a character in the white narrative
of conquest, expropriation, and assimilation, she sunders another
family tie by refusing to sleep with Chato, because he taught her
the rudiments of writing: "She hated Chato, not because he let the
policeman and doctors put the screaming children in the government car, but because he had taught her to sign her name. Because
it was like the old ones always told her about learning their language
or any of their ways: it endangered you" (47). It is only when the
weak and aging Chato's economic ties with the white world have
been callously severed by the unnamed rancher in whose boxcar
shack they have been living that Ayah resumes with him ties that
now appear as much maternal as conjugal:

She slept alone on the hill until the middle of November when the first snows came. Then she made a bed for herself where the children had slept. She did not lie down beside Chato again until many years later, when he was sick and shivering and only her body could keep him warm. The illness came after the white rancher told Chato he was too old to work for him anymore, and Chato and his old woman should be out of the shack by the next afternoon because the rancher had hired new people to work there. (47)

This white rancher comes close to being a stereotypical villain in a melodramatic portrayal of greed destroying spirituality in a belea-guered environment. Although Ayah and Chato return to live in a hogan, raise sheep, and plant a garden, five years of drought leave them caught in the bureaucratic web of U.S. government handouts just as they are wrapped in the frayed olive drab army blanket in the final scene.

Danielson reasons that Ayah is in control of her own story, because she is associated with Spider Woman: "The husband, Chato, is evi-dently drinking himself into discouraged oblivion. But the struc-tural context of the spider web, combined with the story's imagery, associates Ayah with Spider Woman, and thus with control over the making of her life" (335). Danielson, in an interpretation of the key passage in which the contact zone is explicitly portrayed in a scene inside the bar, contends that the men in the bar fear Ayah's mythic power: "'In past years,' Silko writes, 'they would have told her to get out. But her hair was white now and her face was wrinkled. They looked at her like she was a spider crawling slowly across the room.' . . . This is not a lowly or contemptible spider. What the bar customers fear is mythic power" (336).

Jaskoski, elaborating on Danielson's interpretation, labels this passage from *Storyteller* "overdetermined" (25), by which she appears to mean open to conflicting interpretations according to at least two cultural codes. To a certain extent Jaskoski glosses the text in a manner that acts out Krupat's description of *Storyteller* as a text that is dialectically dialogical. She attributes misperception to the men in the bar, whose cultural point of view is probably Chicano. Implicitly opposed to the Chicano misperception is correct perception, which she attributes to the informed reader who can see from two points of view at the same time. This can be seen in her assertion that this passage "is a moment of critical truth" for the reader of the story: "the informed reader will understand how it is that she knows the men ought to fear her, whereas those who remain outside Ayah's frame of reference, like the men in the bar, will think they see only a delusional old woman" (25–26). The problem could be summed up: Ayah, the writing storyteller who is narrating in third-person free indirect discourse, and the informed reader know the men fear her, even though the men do not know this. In reading this as a moment of "critical truth" rather than as an example of irony, or of dialogic paradox, or of indeterminacy that suspends valid interpretation between two codes, Jaskoski is saying that the normative voice of this text is pan-Indian and written. The irony, however, is that the moment of dialectical quasi-sublation, the moment of the invalidation of the voice or the point of view of the men in the bar, is also the moment that the writing storyteller becomes the ontological and epistemological ground for the truth. This is the moment when the narrative perspective is nearly total. This can be seen as ironic in the larger context of Navajo culture being portrayed as owing its survival to the literacy that has unraveled it.

It is also possible to read Ayah as having transcended the world of human language, as having returned to that universal language— the Weibechei song of the wind and the snow—that is not a language but perfect harmony and unmediated being. This is not just something that happens in Ayah's interior space; it is a hierophany that combines interior and exterior space, past and present. Like other female characters in Silko's text, Grandmother A'mooh, Aunt Susie, old Yoeme (in *Almanac*), Mama, and Grandma Fleet (in *Gardens*), Ayah has been translated into a realm outside of linear time and communication into a mythical and sacred language that is ontologically privileged.

Jaskoski makes writing and photography necessary to the continuation of Ayah's culture when she states that in Silko's text the two photographs of literate Grandma A'mooh "gloss Ayah's story not only in their contrast with the ravages of loss and decline Ayah has endured but also in their silence" (31). The Western art and crafts Grandma A'mooh is practicing, reading aloud and crocheting, as well as photography, which Lee Marmon practiced as he took this picture of his grandmother, are part of the Marmon tradition. When Jaskoski states that by "relating Ayah's thoughts and memories to the reader, 'Lullaby' breaks Ayah's silence and reveals her ceremony" (31), when she ends her gloss by stating that "in a sense, then, the text of the story contains some of the wisdom Ayah should have been able to transmit to the younger generations of her family, and the reader of the story has the opportunity to stand in the place of those grandchildren" (31–32), she is making the continuation of Ayah's culture depend also on the reader of *Storyteller*. She is making Ayah's wisdom comprise the lesson Silko's great-grandmother and great-aunts taught her: "learn to read and to write for your own protection" (*Yellow Woman* 160). She is saying that Silko's text, like the Navajo blankets that Ayah remembers weaving and sleeping in, is artfully woven to the point that its literariness can be taken for orality. Just as the army blanket and then the yellow sheet of paper took the place of Jimmie, so Silko's text takes the place of the U.S. government document. In other words, Silko wraps Ayah in a blanket of textuality, or secondary orality, in such a naturally artful way that we cannot tell it from a Navajo blanket. Woven by the writing storyteller and a critic like Jaskoski, "Lullaby" becomes the *maternal blanket* in which the vitality of Navajo ceremony is warmly wrapped. Like the giant bear Silko saw but did not look at up close on her first deer hunt, this Navajo vitality is "[s]leeping, not dead" (*Storyteller* 79).

Thus, it is the writing storyteller and the literary critics who spin a new web in which Ayah's story can grow. Ayah can only imagine herself to be Spider Woman in the contact zone. Her minimal literacy disqualifies her from spinning and weaving in this cross-cultural zone. In order to spin and weave again as she, her mother, and grandmother had in the past, in order to assume the mythic and narrative power of Spider Woman, Ayah either needs to learn to read and write, or she needs the writing storyteller. She needs literate women like Grandma A'mooh, Aunt Susie, or Leslie Marmon Silko. She needs the very writing that wounded her to heal her. She needs readers and critics. Without the writing storyteller's use of metaphor, allusion, symbolism, gloss, and silence, Ayah's nurturing song, "Lullaby," is only a song to die by.

CHAPTER 3

"THE BATTLE OF PIE TOWN," OR LITTLECOCK'S LAST STAND

On June 10, [1885] one of Pradt's scouting parties took up the trail of a raiding party of four fleeing north. The trail was lost in the northern Datils, but non-militia Indians picked up the trail. Three of the raiding party turned south and disappeared. The remaining raider, a renegade Laguna named Huisia, was tracked down and killed. On June 21, Major Pradt directed recall of all patrols and the assembly of all his troops for return to Laguna. He also sent a courier to notify colonel Marmon of the withdrawal in accordance with the governor's message.

—AUSTIN N. LEIBY

All I know of my great-grandpa Marmon
are the stories my family told
and the old photographs which show him
a tall thin old white man
with a white beard
wearing a black suit coat
and derby hat.
He stands with his darker sons
and behind the wire-rim glasses he wore
I see in his eyes
he had come to understand this world
differently.

—SILKO,
Storyteller

L eslie Marmon Silko's "A Geronimo Story" is set in the 1880s. It was a time when newspapers in Arizona and New Mexico often ran sensational stories about the attempts of the U.S. Army, under the command of General George C. Crook, to protect white settlers from raiding Apaches led by the legendary Geronimo. It was also a time when Walter G. Marmon, George H. Pradt, Robert G. Marmon (Leslie Marmon Silko's paternal great-grandfather), and John M. Gunn served as officers in the Third Battalion, New Mexico Volunteer Militia. All of these men had married into Laguna families and taken Laguna clan vows. Company I of the Third Battalion was composed entirely of men of Laguna Indian ancestry. A brief account of the formation of this militia unit and its involvement both in regional and national drill competitions and in active duty campaigns against Apache raiders, thieves, and rustlers was written out by Robert G. Marmon on the back of a muster roll from the period. It appears that one of Robert G. Marmon's motives for writing this account was to ensure pensions for the old soldiers and to prepare for a ceremony celebrating the remaining Laguna Regulars. According to Austin N. Leiby, who researched and in 1973 published an article commemorating the Laguna Regulars, that ceremony took place on "a mild but sunny afternoon in late August of 1917" at which "a U.S. Department of Interior official solemnly handed certificates of service and pension to 'The Last of The Marmon Battalion'" (Leiby 211).[1] Leiby's research comprised talking with persons at Laguna, including members of the Gunn, Pradt, and Marmon families, and examining documents in their possession. Specifically mentioned among these family members is Mrs. Walter K. Marmon, who is better known to Silko's readers as Aunt Susie.[2]

Silko first published "A Geronimo Story" in 1974, the year following the publication of Leiby's article.[3] Thus, she could have been aware of Leiby's research and his contact with Aunt Susie and other members of the Laguna families in question. She possibly even could have read his article before completing "A Geronimo Story." However this may be, I shall read "A Geronimo Story" as the writing storyteller's quiet attempt to construct a text that views through the lenses of anti-assimilationist Indian ideology the story told in the "historical" documents that were written by Silko's great-grandfather and his brother and that served in part as the basis for Leiby's article. In this text there is an interweaving of the oral and the written from Marmon family stories, although there is no explicit mention of the "historical" documents. There is also a rhetoric of silence that posits an Indian cultural logic of inclusion and equality in contrast to the white logic of exclusion and hierarchy. In this meeting of the two logics, the unspoken and the unspeakable carry more weight than the spoken. This text has as its principal ideological goal to debunk and deflate the grand narrative of Manifest Destiny and of the taming of the Wild West by military conquest in the Indian Wars. In order to do this, the writing storyteller must shush certain voices at Laguna, for these voices might tell a different story in which the Laguna Regulars do not go deer hunting, but chase down and perhaps kill a Laguna renegade. There is the suggestion in this story that Silko's great-grandfather's identity might be as elusive as the Apache warrior who, according to old Yoeme in *Alamanac of the Dead* (224–32), the U.S. Army mistakenly called Geronimo and who was really never captured. One of the goals of "A Geronimo Story" is to lead the reader to see that neither the old bearded white man in the photograph of the "Remaining Members, Troop F, Company I, 1917" published by Leiby (212)—who may be the captain who wrote out the story of the Geronimo campaign of the summer of 1885 on the back of an old muster roll—nor Geronimo can be captured and understood in a historical narrative informed by the logic of exclusion and hierarchy.

Andy, the first-person narrator, tells about accompanying his uncle, Siteye, on one of the campaigns against Geronimo and other Apaches in which the Laguna Regulars participated. Despite the existence of many details about topography, including the names of towns and geographic formations, there is a vagueness in Andy's story. Neither the year of the campaign nor the year when the narrator is telling his story is mentioned. Even Geronimo may be absent from the geographical area in which the story is set. According both to Siteye and to Captain Pratt, who is the commanding officer of the Laguna Regulars, the legendary Apache warrior is still at White Mountain. This, it turns out, in an interesting logical twist, is the very reason that Siteye, Captain Pratt, and the rest of the Laguna scouts go to Pie Town:

> "Where are we going?" I asked him again, to make sure.
>
> "Pie Town, north of Datil. Captain says someone there saw Apaches or something."
>
> We rode for a while in silence.
>
> "But I don't think Geronimo is there. He's still at White Mountain."
>
> "Did you tell Captain?"
>
> "I told him, and he agrees with me. Geronimo isn't down there. So we're going down."
>
> "But if you already know that Geronimo isn't there," I said, "why do you go down there to look for him?" He just looked at me and smiled. (214)

In Siteye's smiling silent look lies a special understanding of storytelling. Siteye is teaching Andy that a good story is quickened not just by well-spoken and carefully chosen words, but also by what should give one pause in between those words: "It was beautiful to hear Siteye talk; his words were careful and thoughtful, but they followed each other smoothly to tell a good story. He would pause to let you get a feeling for the words; and even silence was alive in his stories" (215). Siteye is teaching Andy that the end of "A Geronimo Story" is not the mythical Apache warrior, nor is it the "truth" of the historical narrative of the Indian wars. Rather, it is their absence, their elusiveness. Storytelling here comprises a web in which the eloquence of silence makes it possible for Siteye, Andy, and the writing storyteller, relying on a logic of inclusion and equality, to paradoxically exclude the main proponent of a logic of exclusion and hierarchy.

That the destination of the Laguna Regulars is stated specifically to be Pie Town, and not just the Datil Mountains or the area around

Quemado, is a detail that Andy repeats several times. On the one hand, it is possible that by setting the story precisely in a real place with an Anglo rather than a Hispanic name, Silko is endowing with historical and geographical realism her critical focus on Major Little-cock, the Indian fighter with whom Siteye and the Laguna Regulars have an encounter. Pie Town is an actual settlement located just west of the continental divide at the intersection of U.S. 60 and New Mexico 603. In the summer of 1885 Major George Pradt and Captain Robert G. Marmon led New Mexico Volunteer Militia forces, including the Laguna Regulars, into this area, where Apaches, who at the time were reported to have broken away from the White Mountain Reservation, are depicted in historical accounts as having carried out some raids.[4] On the other hand, it appears that Silko's choice of Pie Town as the name of an actual white settlement in the 1880s as well as Andy's explanation for that somewhat whimsical name—"They would have good food. I knew that. This place was named for the good pies that one of the women could make" (219)—are anachronistic and inaccurate. According to accounts given by persons who lived in and around Pie Town in the 1920s, 1930s, and 1940s, the pies and the name first made their appearance several decades after Geronimo had given up raiding for good. "Pie Town was known simply as 'Norman's Place' at first" (Myers 67). Clyde Norman started making and selling pies in the 1920s, and only after he had put up a hand-stenciled sign that read "Pie Town" did the settlement become known by this name.[5] Thus, not only is Andy misremembering the name of the place where he, his uncle, and the rest of the Laguna Regulars stayed, but he also appears to be misinformed about the gender of the pie-maker. What is going on here? Is this Silko's or Andy's anachronism? Are we justified in attributing this apparent anachronism to Andy telling the story from the temporal point of view of the 1920s, after Pie Town had received its name? This would be the decade from which Silko dates the intriguing photograph of the Laguna Regulars that she includes in her text (*Storyteller*, photograph 22: "The Laguna Regulars in 1928, 43 years after they rode in the Apache Wars. *Photograph: Unknown*").

Thus the writing storyteller could be situating Andy's story chronologically with the photograph. If so, how reliable is Andy as a narrator? How reliable is the writing storyteller as a narrator? Likewise, how reliable are the inhabitants of Pie Town as narrators?

Siteye, in a wry allusion, compares the fate of the white settlers and the soldiers holed up at Pie Town to that of George Armstrong Custer and his cavalrymen at the Battle of the Little Bighorn: "'Looks like all the white people in this area moved up here from Quemado and Datil. In case Geronimo comes. All crowded together to make their last stand.' Siteye laughed at his own joke" (220). Siteye's joke also implicitly puts the Apaches in the place of the Sioux and the Cheyenne who defeated Custer. This opens the way to an implicit comparison and contrast of the Laguna Regulars with those Plains Indians whose much debated triumphant battle was followed by defeat and surrender. In Silko's text Siteye's joking as well as his use of cross-cultural sexual innuendo will prove to be more effective in defeating the white man than arrows and bullets. Siteye's joking is intertwined with the writing storyteller's own joke that provides the white officer in command at Pie Town with a name that suggests he is not well endowed. This lack of endowment holds both in the realm of understanding humans, as opposed to animals, and in the hierarchical realm in which a male allegedly acquires rank according to the size of his phallus: "'It was some Major Littlecock who sent out the Apache alert. . . . He says he found an Apache campsite near here. He wants us to lead him to Geronimo.' Siteye shook his head. 'We aren't hunting deer,' he said, 'we're hunting people. With deer I can say, "Well, I guess I'll go to Pie Town and hunt deer," and I can probably find some around here. But with people you must say, "I want to find these people—I wonder where they might be"'" (220).

By having her narrator tell of Siteye talking about the difference between going to Pie Town to hunt deer as opposed to hunting people, Silko links the thematic opposition between bestiality and humanity, around which the ethnic conflict in this story is structured, to the themes of natural endowment and the displaced telos. In the verbal conflict between the officious, mean-spirited, bigoted, and poorly endowed Littlecock and the wise Siteye, the largest of the Laguna Regulars, who mounts a huge horse named Rainbow, the white army officer characterizes a story that is dominantly linear, telic, and progressing toward lethal closure (i.e., the extermination of the American Indian), while the Laguna scout characterizes a story that is nonlinear, open, and quickening. In setting a manhunt that turns out to be a deer hunt in Pie Town, Silko may be wittingly setting her story on a rhetorical and linguistic rather than geographical and historic battleground. Indeed, the name Littlecock semantically foretells the outcome of the "battle of Pie Town," in which the major's racist slur equating the Lagunas with horses is deflected back onto him, resulting in his own sound rhetorical defeat.

The battle of Pie Town begins after Siteye has made his joke about the white people's last stand and has pointed out the difference between hunting deer and hunting people. The men have been smoking and talking after dinner. Mariano brings up the question of whether they will sleep in the kitchen where they have just eaten. Siteye makes a joke about their eating everything, which could be interpreted to imply that he thinks they probably should not sleep in the kitchen. Captain Pratt confirms that he thinks it might be "O.K. to sleep in the kitchen" (220). At this point Major Littlecock, who has eaten in the dining room where the Laguna Regulars, except for Captain Pratt, were not invited to eat, makes his entry: "Then Major Littlecock came in. We all stared, and none of us stood up for him; Laguna scouts never did that for anyone. Captain didn't stand up, because he wasn't really in the army either— only some kind of civilian volunteer that they hired because once he had been in their army" (220). The reaction of the Laguna Regulars and of Captain Pratt to this officer of superior rank is hardly in compliance with the following excerpt from the orders dated "February 12, 1883" and issued at Laguna by "Walter G. Marmon, Major 2nd Reg. N[ew]. M[exico].V[olunteer]. M[ilitia]. Commanding 1st Cav. Batt.":

8. It is the earnest desire of His Excellency the Governor, that the First Cavalry Battalion become thoroughly efficient in all that pertains to a well ordered and soldierly body of men. This end can only be attained by a determined and intelligent effort upon the part of both officers and men, and, in order to be effective, companies must be drilled, officers must fit them-selves for the proper discharge of their duties as such. All orders must be promptly obeyed. *Discipline and a spirit of sol-dierly pride and emulation must be encouraged.* (my emphasis)[6]

The failure of Captain Pratt and the rest of the Laguna Regulars to rise and stand at attention when Major Littlecock enters the kitchen verges on insubordination. Rather than deriving from the "spirit of soldierly pride and emulation" prescribed in Walter G. Marmon's orders and described by Robert G. Marmon in his account of the campaigns and the drill competitions in which the Laguna Regulars participated and won prizes,[7] Captain Pratt's and the Laguna Scouts' relaxed attitude toward military protocol, as described by Andy, sounds much more like it springs from the American antiwar spirit of the 1960s. Andy describes Littlecock as officious and arrogant. His military bearing and attitude inspire mockery and contempt rather than proud emulation. He is balding and fidgety. He pompously announces his plans for tracking Geronimo's raiders the next day and speaks of having "sophisticated communications" that enable him and his men to follow movements the Apaches have made unbe-knownst to the Lagunas. "Sophisticated communications," too, sounds more like 1960s language than part of the military terminology used in the 1880s to describe a network of mounted couriers and tele-graph lines. Nevertheless, these words are ironically apposite in the mouth of the man who is soon to be soundly defeated in the battle of Pie Town owing to a breakdown in cross-cultural communications.

Andy also describes Littlecock's bullying and condescending con-cern with the Laguna Regulars' failure to wear military uniforms:

He [Littlecock] smiled nervously, then with great effort he examined us. We were wearing our Indian clothes—white

cotton pants, calico shirts, and woven Hopi belts. Siteye
had his black wide-brim hat, and most of us were wearing
moccasins.

"Weren't you boys issued uniforms?" the Major asked.

Siteye answered him. "We wear them in the winter. It's
too hot for wool now." (220–21; my emphasis)

Either Major Littlecock or the writing storyteller needs to read more
carefully the policies and procedures set out by Walter G. Marmon to
be followed by the Laguna Regulars. It appears that no one among
the Laguna Regulars was "issued" uniforms. Walter G. Marmon's
orders of 1883 make it clear that officers "will at once procure for
themselves uniforms" and that commanders of companies "are
expected to use every effort in their power to have the enlisted men
of their companies uniformed as speedily as possible." Officers were
thus supposed to purchase their own uniforms and to help collect
contributions from civilians (ranchers, storemen, and others who
stood to benefit from the protection the militia would offer) to buy
uniforms for the enlisted men. The civilians' contributions were
expected, since "[t]he object of this organization is for the protection
of our people from Indian raids, thieves and rustlers, and [to]
strengthen the hands of the civil officers in the discharge of their
duties."

Robert G. Marmon depicts the Laguna Regulars as the only militia
group who fulfilled these orders; his mention of their uniforms can
be read to imply that they were worn during the campaign of 1885:
"In 1885 under telegraphic orders from Governor Lionel A. Sheldon
this Battalion under the Lieut Colonel and Major performed Active
Service in the field for more than a month during the Apache Campaign of that year. The command furnished their own horses etc.
Troop I was the only uniformed company having uniformed themselves at a cost of over $600—."[8] Troop I, it will be remembered,
was also the only company composed entirely of Lagunas. Leiby's
comment about uniforms, based on information he gathered from
persons at Laguna and from accounts written on the back of muster

rolls, depicts the Laguna Regulars as having "highly prized" their uniforms so much that "they were completely worn out in the campaigns of 1884 and 1885" (219–20). This depiction of the Laguna Regulars liking their uniforms conforms to Littlecock's preconceived ideas about Indian scouts in uniform:

> Littlecock looked at Captain. "Our Crow Indian boys preferred their uniforms," he said.
>
> There was silence. It wasn't hostile, but nobody felt like saying anything—I mean, what was there to say? Crow Indian scouts like army uniforms, and Laguna scouts wear them only if it gets cold. Finally Littlecock moved toward the door to leave. (221)

What is more telling here: the Laguna Regulars' silence, which, although Andy specifies its lack of hostility, certainly indicates a mounting tension in the kitchen, or Littlecock's unsophisticated refusal to recognize differences between what Crows and what Lagunas think about wearing uniforms? Or his racist, patronizing denial of manhood to the scouts from either tribe, which is signified by his designating them as "boys"?[9] Andy's use of the expression "I mean," and the tautological reasoning implicit in his insistence on there being nothing to say in answer to Littlecock's blatant racism and ignorance about cultural differences between tribes, echoes anti-establishment speech patterns of the youth of the 1960s.[10]

Littlecock apparently decides not to press the issue and moves for the door. It is at this point that Captain Pratt breaks the silence and *stands up*, not for Littlecock, but for the Laguna scouts whom he makes a point of calling "men," not "boys": "Captain stood up. 'I was thinking the *men* could sleep here in the kitchen, Major. It would be more comfortable for them'" (221; my emphasis). Symbolically and literally Pratt is subverting both military protocol and the major's condescending and racist verbal treatment of the Laguna scouts. He stands up when a subordinate would sit down, and he calls the scouts "men," not "boys." Andy describes the pallor in Littlecock's face as he reacts to Pratt's words and gesture. This pallor may signify that the poorly endowed major is experiencing some fear. However, it could also be Littlecock's exaggerated white character that Andy reads in his face. Andy uses this whiteness, which is inextricably entwined with racist arrogance and perhaps also with cowardice, to depict Littlecock as a caricature of the white man who paradoxically acknowledges the manhood of the Laguna "boys" by not speaking explicitly of it. Like Siteye, Littlecock uses silence and allusion, but he uses these rhetorical tools awkwardly, logically contradicting himself, while searching not to put into words the unspeakable threat that Laguna manhood poses to the white womanhood of Pie Town: "Littlecock's face was pale; he moved slowly. 'I regret, Captain, that isn't possible. Army regulations on using civilian quarters—the women,' he said, 'you know what I mean. Of course, Captain, you're welcome to sleep here'" (221). In this verbal clumsiness, which is perhaps a witting attempt to insult Pratt and hide behind military protocol, Littlecock implicitly sets up a three-tiered order that is symbolically telling. He allots Captain Pratt a marginal place associated with servants and women, the kitchen, which is still inside the confines of white humanity and "civilization." In a sense Littlecock is silently calling Pratt by a term that Andy will later say some white men used when speaking of him: "Squaw Man." The Laguna scouts, however, Littlecock places outside of humanity altogether.

Littlecock's smile, as he looks directly at the Laguna scouts and uses the English language to draw a boundary between them and humanity, can be interpreted as signifying a curious mixture of cowardice and self-satisfaction with his presumed linguistic and racial superiority. Perhaps he assumes that the Laguna "boys" will neither understand nor verbally contest what he is saying. Thus, he speaks to them as if they were really no different from the *dumb* beasts in the stable: "Littlecock smiled, he was looking at all of us: 'You boys won't mind sleeping with the horses, will you?'" (221). This time Siteye does not respond with silence or a smile. Obviously there is much to say about the relation between Lagunas, humanity, dumb beasts, and white men like Littlecock. Siteye returns the

major's direct look and utters a repartee that reverses the implications of the innuendo. Knowing that the major most likely cannot
understand the literal meaning of the words in Keresan, he verbally
puts the officious and racist officer in the place of a dumb beast:
"Siteye looked intently at the Major's face and spoke to him in
Laguna. 'You are the one who has a desire for horses at night,
Major, you sleep with them.' We all started laughing" (221). Of course
Littlecock, who gets mad, must assume the repartee, which Andy's narrative translates rather politely from the Keresan,[11] to be an insult.
Siteye, who certainly is not the first nor the last enlisted man to tell
an officer to occupy his time in such a fashion, is depicted as speaking English with no difficulty. In choosing to make his repartee in
Keresan, he linguistically includes Captain Pratt within the confines
of humanity and Laguna culture while rhetorically leaving Littlecock in the realm of bestiality in which the arrogant white racist
has placed himself by confronting the Lagunas and telling them
they are dumb beasts. Both literally and contextually Siteye's repartee
implies that it is the white officer, not the Lagunas, who sunders
himself from humanity with his bigoted allusion to Laguna bestiality and his militant confrontational attitude. Siteye has also placed
Littlecock in a position between cultures where he needs the help
of a fellow human being in order to understand and to act logically.
He needs a translator.

Littlecock makes one last attempt to pull Captain Pratt back
into the realm of his white racist worldview. The angry pale face
turns red as he issues a politely attenuated order to Captain Pratt
to act as interpreter: "Littlecock looked confused. 'What did he say,
Captain Pratt? Could you translate that for me, please?' His face
was red and he looked angry. Captain was calm. 'I'm sorry, Major,
but I don't speak the Laguna language very well. I didn't catch the
meaning of what Siteye said'" (221). Here Pratt opts to defuse a
volatile situation by using paradox, unspoken words, and modesty
verging on mendacity. He understates his knowledge of the Laguna
language. In saying he cannot translate, he both suggests that he is
not completely assimilated into Laguna culture and at the same

time paradoxically shows that he is, demonstrating his loyalty to his fellow scouts from that culture, thereby taking a stand with them without saying that he is doing so. Andy remarks on both Pratt's unusual command of the language and his quiet manner when narrating how the captain later joined them to sleep outside: "We built a big fire to sit around. Captain came down later and put his little teapot in the hot coals; for a white man he could talk the Laguna language pretty good, and he liked to listen to the jokes and stories, though he never talked much himself" (222). Captain Pratt, like Siteye, knows how to use silence meaningfully.

Indirection, humor, irony, the desire to avoid conflict, discretion with words, the apposite use of silence, valor, fairness, loyalty, and modesty are the values that Captain Pratt demonstrates and that Littlecock can only misunderstand as mendacity before he launches into a boisterous account of his own sophisticated but culturally irrelevant linguistic skills. During this tirade he addresses Captain Pratt as "Mr. Pratt," thereby linguistically demoting him and excluding him from the U.S. Army: "Littlecock knew he was lying. He faced Captain squarely and spoke in a cold voice. 'It is very useful to speak the Indian languages fluently, Mr. Pratt. I have mastered Crow and Arapaho, and I was fluent in Sioux dialects before I was transferred here.' He looked at Siteye, then he left the room" (221). Littlecock's learning these Indian languages is paradoxically part of his contribution to white culture's goal of stamping out indigenous languages in America either by extermination or by pacifying and forcing the tribes to abandon their own tongues and assimilate. Littlecock's reason to learn other tongues is grounded in a logic of exclusion and hierarchy. Pratt's reason to learn Laguna is grounded in a logic of inclusion and equality.

Thus ends the first half of the battle of Pie Town. Littlecock, despite the sound rhetorical horsewhipping he has taken, does not yet know he is defeated. Although he probably does not directly think it, anymore than he would explicitly say it, perhaps he indirectly hopes that Geronimo and his "boys" can still come to his rescue. After all, he would not be the first or the last great white commander in chief lucky enough to be assisted by his enemy in what he insists on viewing as the long war of civilized good against bestial evil.

It appears that after this little scene with Littlecock, Siteye would also like to see the Apaches ride into Pie Town. In the absence of Captain Pratt, he jokingly invents a future Geronimo story that resembles the story he told Andy about the time the Laguna Regulars refused to help the U.S. Army bury the putrescent corpses of white settlers who had been killed by Apaches:

> We walked down the arroyo, joking and laughing about sleeping out with the horses instead of inside where the white soldiers were sleeping.
>
> "Remind me not to come back to this place," Mariano said.
>
> "I only came because they pay me," George said, "and next time they won't even be able to pay me to come here."
>
> Siteye cleared his throat. *"I am only sorry that the Apaches aren't around here,"* he said. *"I can't think of a better place to wipe out. If we see them tomorrow we'll tell them to come here first."* (221; my emphasis)

Several questions silently lurk in the logic implicit in this enunciation: Is it possible that some Apaches may be in the vicinity, that Siteye has only assumed but does not know for certain that Geronimo is still at White Mountain? After all, Siteye himself has said that when one is "hunting people" one must ask, "I wonder where they may be" (220). According to Robert G. Marmon's account, the Laguna Regulars actually did engage some Apaches in the campaign of 1885. Is it possible that Siteye now more fully feels why Geronimo would already have broken away from White Mountain? After all, given the treatment the Laguna Regulars have just received from a major named Littlecock, what must the Apaches be getting from a white general named Crook. Is Siteye actually ready to throw in his lot with the Apaches? Leiby's story about the pursuit of raiding Indians during the campaign of 1885 ends with "one of Pradt's scouting parties" taking up the trail of a raiding

party and tracking down and killing the remaining raider, "a renegade Laguna name Huisia" (Leiby 225).[12] Could Siteye's verbal
encounter with Major Littlecock amount to him assuming the figure
of a renegade in Andy's account of this campaign?

Andy's narration, however, depicts Siteye as being opposed to
physical violence. By not speaking English, he becomes a rhetorical
renegade, winning this battle against Littlecock with speech acts:
"We were all laughing now, and we felt good, saying things like
this. 'Anybody can act violently—there is nothing to it; but not
every person is able to destroy his enemy with words.' That's what
Siteye always told me, and I respect him" (221–22).

Later that evening, after Captain Pratt has symbolically "rolled
himself up in his big gray Navajo blanket" and gone to sleep with
the men for whom he stood up, Siteye confides to Andy how he
thinks it is possible for the Lagunas to take a stand with Geronimo
while appearing to go on campaigns against the Apaches: "Before
I went to sleep I said to Siteye, 'You've been hunting Geronimo for
a long time, haven't you? And he always gets away.' 'Yes,' Siteye
said, staring up at the stars, 'but I always like to think that it's us
who get away'" (222). Here Siteye is a Laguna renegade whose
rhetorical tracks the reader can follow in the writing storyteller's
text, but, at least as long as he is riding with men like Captain Pratt
who refuse to play the role of *traduttore* (translator) and *traditore*
(traitor), he will not be killed.

Next day, bright and early, the rhetorical battle of Pie Town
continues:

> At dawn the next day Major Littlecock took us to his Apache
> campsite. It was about four miles due west of Pie Town, in
> the pine forest. The cavalry approached the area with their
> rifles cocked, and the Major was holding his revolver. We fol
> lowed them closely.
>
> "Here it is." Littlecock pointed to a corral woven with cedar
> branches. There was a small hearth with stones around it;
> that was all. (222)

Here Littlecock has interpreted the signs of this abandoned camp-site according to his lethal linear logic that makes Geronimo the end of the story. However, since he is not an experienced tracker in the Southwestern text, he must call on his rhetorical opponent to interpret the signs on which the fate of his logic and narrative depend. The reader, at the same time, is called on to read with great care the combination of silence and sparse words that make up Siteye's interpretation:

> Siteye and Sousea dismounted and walked around the place without stopping to examine the hearth and without once stopping to kneel down to look at the ground more closely. Siteye finally stopped outside the corral and rolled himself a cigarette; he made it slowly, tapping the wheat paper gently to get just the right distribution of tobacco. I don't think I ever saw him take so long to roll a cigarette. Littlecock had dismounted and was walking back and forth in front of his horse, waiting. Siteye lit the cigarette and took two puffs before he walked over to Captain. He shook his head.
>
> "Some Mexican built himself a sheep camp here, Captain, that's all." Siteye looked at the Major to make certain he would hear. "No Geronimo here, like we said."
>
> Pratt nodded his head. (222)

Andy has made it clear that Siteye, his mentor, is a master story-teller and a discerning reader of tracks. Now that we know that Siteye, the rhetorical renegade, may have changed his mind about whether Geronimo is still at White Mountain, how are we to inter-pret his interpretation of this campsite? How are we to understand Siteye's and Sousea's not even looking at the hearth and the ground closely? How are we to interpret the prolonged silence during which Siteye rolls himself a cigarette? Does this silence quicken his interpretation and the narrative, leaving them open to more than one meaning? How are we to interpret Littlecock's "walking back and forth in front of his horse"? On a symbolic level in which story-telling itself is the telos of this story, the white character's impatient vacillating movement before his mount embodies the extended pause during which the informing narrative balances between being lethal, linear, exclusionary, and closed and being quickening, nonlinear, inclusionary, and open. How are we to interpret Siteye's declaration of the obvious: "No Geronimo here, like we said"?

"No Geronimo here, like we said" is not a lie, no matter what the origin of the campsite. Geronimo is not there, for a sign is always the indication of an absence, not of a presence. Is Siteye repeating a variation on Pratt's move from the evening before, refusing to translate a Southwestern language Littlecock has not mastered in order to win the second half of the battle of Pie Town? May he not be indirectly declaring his adherence to Geronimo and his men while he defeats Littlecock by refusing to play the role of translator and traitor? In doing so he is also declaring his adherence to a humanity that includes the Apaches as well as the Lagunas. In such a scheme it is Littlecock whose own logic and narrative of Manifest Destiny make him a renegade to humanity.

However the reader may choose to answer these questions, according to Andy, Littlecock now knows he has not won the battle of Pie Town. He verbally restores Pratt to the rank of captain and continues his attempt to include this white man who sleeps with Indians within the confines of U.S. Army language and white reasoning: "Littlecock mounted; he had lost, and he knew it. 'Accept my apology for this inconvenience, Captain Pratt. I simply didn't want to take any chances'" (223). What Littlecock says, however, does not necessarily translate what he is thinking. Andy offers a reading of his face and of the silence that follows his implicit concession of defeat:

> He looked at all of us; his face had a troubled, dissatisfied look; *maybe* he was wishing for the Sioux country up north, where the land and the people were familiar to him.
>
> Siteye felt the same. If he hadn't killed them all, he could still be up there chasing Sioux; he might have been pretty good at it. (223; my emphasis)

Siteye confirms Andy's interpretation of Littlecock's silence and his "troubled, dissatisfied look." Offered here in a short switch into the *style indirect libre* in which the writing storyteller and Andy converge as narrator, Andy's and Siteye's reading is part of their rhetorical and logical victory over Littlecock's linear, lethal, and closed narrative. If Littlecock is wishing he were still up north, he could also be wishing he could kill Siteye and the rest of the Laguna Regulars who have inflicted a defeat on him without firing a shot. There are no two hands in Littlecock's logic; it is a mono-logic whose conclusion is death, exclusion, or extermination of the Other. In other words, legible on this white character's troubled and dissatisfied face is the realization that, should he follow his logic and insist that "the only good Indian is a dead Indian," he would be turning his rhetorical defeat at the battle of Pie Town into Littlecock's last stand.

Just as Geronimo, except as a name in the title, may be absent from the setting of "A Geronimo Story," so Robert G. Marmon appears to be absent both in person and in name from his great-granddaughter's story. Unless, as Jaskoski contends, he is figured in the fictional character, Captain Pratt. Jaskoski derives the so-called fictional character of Captain Pratt from the "historical" Robert G. Marmon by relying on the pejorative epithet, "squaw man," that Silko says was applied to her great-grandfather and that Andy learns, several years after his ride with the Laguna Regulars, was also applied to Captain Pratt:

> The allusion to the pejorative "squaw man" is one of the most specifically biographical references in Silko's novels and stories. The *fictional character* of Captain Pratt derives from Leslie Silko's great-grandfather Robert G. Marmon, who appears in three different photographs in *Storyteller.* The book opens with a picture of Marmon, his young wife—Leslie's beloved Grandma A'mooh—and their infant son, Leslie's grandfather Henry. Robert G. Marmon's image closes the text as well, in a later photograph showing him surrounded by sons, son-in-law, and two grandsons who are the author's father and uncle. A third photograph, placed immediately following "A Geronimo Story" shows "The Laguna Regulars in 1928, 43

years after they rode in the Apache Wars" (272). In the picture
Robert G. Marmon stands with a dozen other elderly men under a
great oak tree. The reader may feel invited to pick out an Andy,
a Siteye, a Mariano, or a George from the row of men calmly
gazing at the camera. (60; my emphasis)

This derivation of the "fictional character" from the historical
person stumbles over a historical fact: George H. Pradt (sometimes
spelled "Pratt") was an officer (lieutenant, captain, and then major)
in the Marmon battalion. As an adjutant major he was in command of Companies K and M during the 1885 campaign. Captain
Robert G. Marmon was in command of Companies I and L (Leiby
221).

According to Leiby, who, as mentioned above, is relying on
reports written on the back of old muster rolls, "Major Pradt was
ordered to assemble his combat group at San Rafael and to proceed
southeast and to the east of the Malpais (an area of an ancient volcanic flow) which lies south of Grants, and to cross the North Plains
on the east side while proceeding in the general direction of Quemado" (223). San Rafael lies to the west of Laguna and to the north-
west of Acoma. This itinerary is similar to the one followed by
Captain Pratt and the Laguna Regulars in Silko's story. Companies
K and M, however, were not made up of Lagunas, but of Spanish
Americans and a few Anglos who had married into local families
(219). "The other combat group," under the command of Captain
Robert G. Marmon, "would proceed south through Arroyo Colo-
rado and toward the gap between the Datil and Gallinas Mountains,
and then would swing west toward Quemado" (223). This combat
group comprised Company L, composed of Spanish Americans, and
Company I, composed entirely of Laguna Indians. According to
Leiby, Company I did depart from Laguna, like the Laguna Regulars
in Silko's story, but they followed an itinerary different from the
one Silko describes. Furthermore, it appears that the Laguna Regulars under the command of Captain Marmon did not even camp
near the present-day site of Pie Town:

The second group was the first to take up the line of march. Company I departed Laguna in the early afternoon of May 31. . . . The march was then taken up by the consolidated group after the noon break and reached the Alamocito district that day, having traveled a distance of about 30 miles. A base camp was set up, and the group remained in the district for four days. Patrols were sent out to the east and south, and they reconnoitered the entire area. Robert Marmon's report states that these patrols scouted "the adjacent country for a distance of 25 miles," which would indicate that the scouting parties operated as semi-autonomous units, perhaps remaining overnight in sub-camps. (223)

What is one to make of this tangle of similarities and differences between Silko's story and Leiby's historical account? It is certainly understandable, given the state of the documents on which Leiby had to rely as well as the age of his Laguna informants, that his narrative is somewhat entangled and contains "facts" that can be disputed. The date of the photograph of the Laguna Regulars, which Leiby gives as 1917 and Silko as 1928, is one obvious example. Should the reader even attempt to unravel the threads of fiction from the threads of history in Silko's text? Perhaps the photograph can help in sorting out what really happened. Is this photograph part of "A Geronimo Story," as Silko has stated on the opening page of *Storyteller* (1)? Can this story "be traced" (1) in this photograph? If one attempts to trace it in the photograph, one must remember the warning about the potential difficulty in figuring out the figure woven into the Indian basket containing photographs: "There is a tall Hopi basket with a *single figure* / woven into it which *might be a Grasshopper or / a Hummingbird Man*" (1; my emphasis). Jaskoski, in an attempt to interweave fictional and historical characters, points out Robert G. Marmon in the photograph on page 224 of *Storyteller* and then suggests that the reader might "feel invited" to fit the fictional characters of Silko's story to the photographic images of the real scouts. Silko, however, is silent about the identity of her great-grandfather and of the others in the photograph, except to name them all as "The Laguna Regulars in 1928, 43 years after they rode in the Apache Wars. *Photograph: Unknown"* (272).

Leiby has researched the identity not just of Robert G. Marmon, but of all the old soldiers in the photograph: "The 12 assembled warriors comprised the last remaining members of what had been Troop F, Company I, 3rd Battalion, 1st Regiment, New Mexico Volunteer Militia (Cavalry). They were: Fred Seracino, Topatata, Lowteya, Burns, Sinai, Tsitai, Goyetia, Levantonio, Angus Perry, George Pino, John M. Gunn, and Robert G. Marmon. They were better known as 'The Laguna Scouts'" (211). Sixth from the left is Tsitai! The reader may feel invited to phonetically equate the name of this large man, who is staring directly at the camera, with the Siteye of Silko's story. According to Leiby, the "members in the photograph were identified by Mrs. W. K. Marmon and by Mr. Wallace Gunn of Cubero, N.M., nephew of John Gunn. Identification was collated with names appearing in documents of the Governor's Papers, Edmund G. Ross, Militia, NMSRC" (228).

Jaskoski calls Silko's text "a deconstructionist parable in which the absence of Geronimo becomes the pretext for a deer hunt, and one of the subtexts is the permeability as well as the toughness of cultural and linguistic boundaries. The story celebrates hunting, storytelling, and the common human grounding of difference" (58). Jaskoski is on target. Silko's writing storyteller rhetorically embodies the defeat of Littlecock's lethal, linear, exclusionary, and telic logic that informs the narrative of Indian wars. According to this logic, the only good Indian is a dead Indian. The victory of Siteye's and Captain Pratt's nonlinear, quickening, open-ended storytelling, which is informed by an inclusionary logic, implies that the only good white man is a "Squaw Man." In this battle Littlecock is the butt of the irony, whereas Captain Pratt is the cross-cultural character who is shown traversing cultural and linguistic boundaries from a matronizing point of view that warmly equalizes him with the Laguna scouts he allegedly commands. In one sense, Silko's text shows how the demeaning racist epithet "Squaw Man," which Andy says white men sometimes used when referring to Captain

Pratt and which Silko mentions was applied to her great-grand-father (*Storyteller* 16), is apposite. According to the cultural code and protocol followed in Littlecock's quarters, Captain Pratt neither acts nor speaks like a "real" man. He does not refer to the Laguna scouts as "boys," as Major Littlecock does, and also as perhaps Robert G. Marmon did, at least according to Leiby (215). Rather he calls them "men" and puts himself on their level, opening the boundaries between white and Indian, sleeping with the Laguna men as well as with his Laguna spouse. He espouses his spouse's culture, without explicitly signaling himself as a renegade to white culture or to humanity.

In ironizing Littlecock's patronizing and condescending narra-tive and logic, Silko's text cannot but ironize the nostalgic narrative that informs Austin N. Leiby's "The Marmon Batallion and the Apache Campaign of 1885." This historical narrative of Indian wars and military conquest depicts the Laguna Regulars as "good old (Indian) boys" who silently received a written acknowledgment of their having helped win the wild Southwest, and who listened to taps before fading away in schmaltzy silence: "At the ceremony on the bluff in 1917, certificates were handed to each of the surviving warriors. A trumpet sounded taps from the opposite bank of the river. The assembled Indians and their families moved to the feast tables set under the broad limbs of the elms and oaks. The official of the Interior Department hurried off on his way back to Washington. The *silence of eternity* descended on the Marmon Battalion" (227; my emphasis). Silko's text uses Siteye's silence to subvert the nostalgia, sentimentality, and closure of Leiby's history. Staring silently, but not smiling, out of the photograph that follows "A Geronimo Story" in *Storyteller* are Tsitai and the remaining Laguna scouts, as well as two bearded "Squaw Men," Robert G. Marmon and John M. Gunn. In the silences that make up this Geronimo story, one can track the writing storyteller, the female narrator who speaks through Andy as if he were a mask, an Indian persona. Translating from the Keresan spoken by the Laguna Regulars, except when Littlecock and Captain Pratt speak in English, and when Siteye translates the tell-tale signs at the campsite (222), the writing storyteller is a figural "Squaw Man" who sleeps with Indians and within whom sleep white and Indian. The writing storyteller is a translator, who paradoxically confirms and subverts the Italian aphorism by being a "traitor" only to those, like Littlecock, who are renegades to humanity. Siteye, Captain Pratt, and the writing storyteller all use silence to renege on the logic of exclusion and hierarchy. All know how to quicken the lethal narrative of Manifest Destiny with silence. Just as the "language of love" that the ghost dancers speak in *Gardens in the Dunes* (32) is not "phonetically" transcribed, but is translated into English by the writing storyteller, so the meaningful silences of Siteye, Captain Pratt, and Andy are not betrayed when the writing story-teller quietly translates them into English. This silence figures an early language of love in Silko's writing, which Littlecock, despite his gift for Indian tongues, refuses to understand as it descends on him at the open ending of "A Geronimo Story."

CHAPTER 4

DIALOGIC WITCHERY IN "TONY'S STORY"

The date of August 10, 1680 is not celebrated today. Its historic importance is not observed. That is the date when the Pueblo tribal religious leaders united and expelled the Spaniards, who were trying to force their religion and economic slavery upon the people. What we can observe in retrospect is that, although Ruth Benedict, in her book Patterns of Culture, *classifies the Pueblos as predominantly peaceful in nature, the Pueblo people will defend themselves and have in the past.*

—JOE S. SANDO,
Pueblo Nations

If the Pueblos have conquered the dilemma of death, they do not know what to say about evil. Again, this is not unusual for nonuniversalistic religions. Witchcraft is the only general answer, and it is not a very good one.

—ALFONSO ORTIZ,
New Perspectives on the Pueblos

"Tony's Story," like other narratives in *Storyteller*, can be construed as a web of voices that speak from differing interpretive viewpoints. The voice of Leon, who has

been taught by Uncle Sam to talk like a good old Cold Warrior and
to see the world in terms of a conflict-friendly pursuit of "rights,"
and the initially conflict-phobic, traditional voice of Tony are the two
most visibly contrasted voices in this text. There is also the unset-
tling, high-pitched voice of the state policeman, which speaks for
or as Anglo–New Mexican law. There is the voice of the Interpreter
and the "old men" who interpret written Pueblo law to fault Leon
in his altercation with the violently abusive cop. And there is the
now-silent voice of old Teofilo, to which Tony harkens to form his
interpretive vision of the cop as a witch that he shoots and burns.

A. LaVonne Ruoff in her seminal reading of "Tony's Story" has
eloquently argued that Tony, in killing the state trooper who has
been harassing him and Leon, is performing a ritual exorcism, and
in so doing is implicitly appointing both himself and Leon to the
office of War Captain. As War Captains the two friends "represent
the twin heroes Ma'sewi and Uyuyewi who appear in many Keres
stories" (8). Thus, Ruoff suggests, in killing the cop-witch Tony is
exercising one of the rights of a War Captain, a right that is grounded
in the oral storytelling tradition. She supports this interpretation
with Elsie Clews Parsons's written ethnographic accounts of witchery: "Particularly relevant to 'Tony's Story' is Parsons's example of
the Laguna war captains' shooting a woman thought to be a witch.
Parsons concludes that at the time she was writing (about 1920), the
right of a war captain to perform such an act would not be questioned in most Keresan or Tewan pueblos or in Zuni" (5–6). Ruoff's
sympathetic interpretation of Tony's act implies that the crucial
issue here is whether a War Captain should still have the right to
shoot a witch today. Whether Tony has the right to decide that he
and Leon are War Captains is not, however, brought up. Indeed, it
seems likely, given their reliance on the "revised pueblo law-and-
order code" (125), that the "old men" in the story would question
Tony's implicit or explicit arrogation of this right. Thus at the heart
of Ruoff's interpretation lurks a question of rights, the pursuit of
which would entail interpreting the Laguna constitution, and the
talk of which Tony finds incomprehensible and indicative of Leon's

failure to understand what is being pursued: "I couldn't understand why Leon kept talking about 'rights' because it wasn't 'rights'
that he was after, but Leon didn't seem to understand; he couldn't
remember the stories that old Teofilo told" (127).

From Tony's point of view as the first-person narrator, Leon
fails to understand because, rather than harkening to the silent
inner voice of the deceased storyteller, he looks to writing and the
law. Where Tony turns inward to the *oral* tradition for protection
against the arm of the law, Leon pursues his conflict through written
appeals to higher legal authorities. While he awaits the deferred
justice he is seeking in the *written* law, Leon will trust in his .30-30:

> That afternoon Leon spoke with the Governor, and he pro-
> mised to send letters to the Bureau of Indian Affairs and to
> the State Police Chief. Leon seemed satisfied with that. I reached
> into my pocket for the arrowhead on the piece of string.
> "What's that for?"
> I held it out to him. "Here, wear it around your neck—like
> mine. See? Just in case," I said, "for protection."
> "You don't believe in *that*, do you?" He pointed to a .30-30
> leaning against the wall. "I'll take this with me whenever I'm
> in the pickup."
> "But you can't be sure that it will kill one of them."
> Leon looked at me and laughed. "What's the matter," he
> said, "have they brainwashed you into believing that a .30-30
> won't kill a white man?" He handed me back the arrowhead.
> "Here, you wear two of them." (127; my emphasis)

In pursuing in writing his conflict with the cop and pointing to the
.30-30, Leon is implicitly assuming that Pueblo law and his "arm"
can take on the long arm of New Mexico law on even ground. In
handling the arrowhead back with a sarcastic comment, Leon not
only belittles and rejects as superstition the beliefs Tony has received
from old Teofilo, he also symbolically refuses to accept the position
of War Captain. The War Captains, according to Parsons, "carry an
arrow point in a buckskin bag under their shirt" ("Notes on Ceremonialism" 121). Tony's understanding manifests itself as a special

vision, an interpretive insight, which he thinks enables him to see what remains unseen and unheard by Leon. Although this special vision comes from the oral tradition, Tony treats what he sees to be nearly "unspeakable" and refers to the cop as "it." The word "witch" occurs only once in the text when Tony mentions the "stories of witches" that ran with him in the dark (125). Indeed it seems that this vision induces in the seer a silence that recalls the silence of the voice of the deceased storyteller. This silence contrasts with Leon's loudness.

Leon's loudness and his acting like a drunken white man appear initially to constitute the problem central to this text:

> I saw him [Leon] standing by the Ferris wheel across from the people who came to sell melons and chili on San Lorenzo's day. He yelled at me. "Hey Tony—over here!" I was embarrassed to hear him yell so loud, but then I saw the wine bottle with the brown-paper sack crushed around it.
> "How's it going, buddy?"
> He grabbed my hand and held it tight like a white man. (123–24)

As Tony's story unfolds, however, something much more profoundly troubling than Leon's loud and drunken blustering appears: Patterns of silent signs that point to old conflicts between Western culture and Pueblo culture and also to conflicts within Pueblo culture itself begin to form. The figure of San Lorenzo, on whose feast day Silko has set the story, is one such sign: "I was happy, because I knew that Leon was once more a part of the pueblo. The sun was dusty and low in the west, and the procession passed by us, carrying San Lorenzo back to his niche in the church" (124). This procession is apparently carrying the saint's figure from its spruce-covered bower, where on feast days it presides over the dancers and receives offerings and prayers from the people, back to the oldest visible *construction* of Western culture in the pueblo. Thus this procession can be seen to figure the syncretism of the ceremony in a movement back and forth between Catholic Church and corn altar. Here San

Lorenzo is enshrined in cross-cultural irony. The dusty, dry return of the figure of this martyr to its niche in the church suggests the failure of the ceremony to bring an end to the drought and contrasts with the soon to be "martyred" Leon's "wet" return from the U.S. Army to his niche in the literally and legally "dry" pueblo. The recurrent motifs of desiccation and burning in the text, with which the silent signs are associated, are found both in Pueblo stories of Kaup'a'ta, the Gambler, and in European versions of this saint's life. According to Catholic hagiographic tradition—both oral and written—Lorenzo's martyrdom consisted in his being grilled over burning coals. It is perhaps more than a fortuitous coincidence that Leon is bloodily "martyred" on the scorched earth as the story opens and that the big cop, who is likened to Kaup'a'ta, is being burned at a shrinelike site as the story ends.

"Tony's Story," one of Silko's early texts,[1] is located at the confluence of a yellow-journalistic story and of oral storytelling: Silko reports that twenty-five years after the killing of Nash Garcia by Willie and Gabriel Felipe, stories about this incident were still being told at Acoma-Laguna High School (Evers 255). In this text Silko combines oral tradition with her education in literature at the University of New Mexico, and with her interest in law, in order to rewrite as a narrative of ethnic resurgence the journalistic and legal story that is a classic example of the narrative of assimilation (Bruner 139): For the journalists, the judge, and the jury, in the story written in the newspapers and told in court, Nash Garcia, the Mexican martyr for American law and order, played the role of the successfully assimilated New Mexican, whereas the Felipe brothers were cast as nonassimilated, pathetic drunken Indians, who ineptly pursued a conflict they were destined to lose by the author(ity) of the story of the West. In taking up her pen to rewrite this story, Silko was presciently acting according to what she would later conclude when she quit law school, namely, "that the only way to seek justice was through the power of the stories" (*Yellow Woman* 20). Tony too is seeking "justice" through the power of stories, but Tony does not see with the revised vision of the writing storyteller.

San Lorenzo enters the narrative through Silko's having changed the holiday from Good Friday (April 11, 1952), when Nash Garcia was killed, to San Lorenzo Day, August 10 (of an unspecified year). This change on the calendar opens the way to reading the yellow-journalistic story, which some Pueblos would probably like to forget, through the lens of a historical event that the seventeenth-century New Mexican ancestors of Nash Garcia undoubtedly would have preferred never to have experienced: It was on San Lorenzo Day in 1680 that the Pueblo Revolt began. Ironically, San Lorenzo's being in his niche in the church at the pueblo is a sign that the revolt of 1680, despite its initial success in purging the Pueblos of all things Spanish, ultimately failed, resulting in a continuation of the Pueblo-Catholic syncretism that had been an issue in a struggle between the Catholic friars and the Spanish colonial officials.[2]

Unlike Leon, who enters the story speaking loudly like a white man, the cop makes his first intrusion into the text under the sign of silence:

> He never said anything before he hit Leon in the face with his fist. . . . The tribal policemen knelt over Leon, and one of them looked up at the state cop and asked what was going on. The big cop didn't answer. He was staring at the little patterns of blood in the dust near Leon's mouth. The dust soaked up the blood almost before it dripped to the ground—it had been a very dry summer. (124)

Rather than replying orally to the tribal policeman, the cop stares darkly through his sunglasses at the "little patterns of blood" he has "authored." In these patterns can be read a silent answer to the question of "what is going on" in this text; this answer emerges as these little patterns form a larger pattern of blood in the writerly movement back and forth between Leon's being "martyred," the Pueblos being martyred by the Spaniards before and after the revolt of 1680, the Pueblos martyring the Spaniards during the revolt, San Lorenzo being martyred by the pagans, and the desiccated earth at the "end" of this story soaking up the blood of the cop, who plays the role of the New Mexican, Nash Garcia, martyr for American law and order: "He was on his back, and the sand between his legs and along his left side was soaking up the dark, heavy blood—it had not rained for a long time, and even the tumbleweeds were dying" (128–29). Tony's story, the story of the coming together of white and Pueblo, is written and rewritten in blood.

Like Popé's secret plan for the revolt of 1680, the date of which was allegedly communicated among participants by a form of pre-contact tribal "writing" similar to the Inca *quipu* (i.e., knotted cords, in which one knot was untied each day until the absence of knots indicated San Lorenzo Day) and "smoke signals" (!), which were allegedly used by participants to indicate their having understood the knotted cords (Silverberg 115), this answer is not spoken, but "read" by following the strands of different stories from knot to knot until smoke billows into the air from the burning patrol car. Like witchery, the unspeakable, the power of which in some cases arises from human blood mixed with substances like cornmeal, these patterns of blood mark points where the strand of Tony's story is tied to stories of dark powers, conflict, and madness.[3]

Tony's first inklings of his special vision are associated with medicine and darkness. Having returned from Albuquerque, where Leon waited for a long time before being "comforted" by the voice of Western medicine, Tony is silently stalked by the voice of Pueblo medicine: "Stillness breathed around me, and I wanted to run from the feeling behind me in the dark; and the stories about witches ran with me" (125). That night in a dream he sees the cop whose sunglasses appear as the stylized eyes on a kachina mask: "He didn't have a human face—only little, round, white-rimmed eyes on a black ceremonial mask" (125).

Relying on Parsons's written account, Ruoff contends that Tony's dream is "a form of clairvoyance, a technique used by many pueblo tribes for detecting witchcraft or witches" (6). What Tony sees, however, owing to this oneiric "clairvoyance," is not literally *clear*. The "little, round, white-rimmed eyes" are to the eyes behind the mask what the lenses of the sunglasses are to the cop's eyes, which

Tony never directly sees. In order for him to "see" that the cop is the unspeakable "it," he must interpret what he cannot see and what he sees in the dream according to what old Teofilo's silent voice says witches do with their *medicine:* "the big cop was pointing a long bone at me—they always use human bones" (125). What Tony sees in his dream is a silent sign pointing to other signs of power, all of which can be construed as long cylindrical instruments of power that can be abused: club, cane, and pen.

It is certainly not the voice of old Teofilo that Leon and Tony hear when the Pueblo elders respond to Leon's request for justice: "Leon even took it before the pueblo meeting. They discussed, it, and the old men decided that Leon shouldn't have been drinking. The interpreter read a passage out of the revised pueblo law-and-order code about possessing intoxicants on the reservation, so we got up and left" (125). Although this "law-and-order code" is Pueblo, both it and the office of the Interpreter have their origin in Western culture.[4] In insisting on his rights, Leon looks to this written Pueblo law, as well as to the U.S. Constitution, rather than to oral story-telling. What he gets is *dry* law read aloud to him by the Interpreter. Just as San Lorenzo is woven into the syncretic voice of Pueblo ceremonial tradition, so Leon's mentor in rights and arms, Uncle Sam, is inscribed in the Interpreter's voice, which points out to him that he has not yet properly returned to his niche in the *dry* pueblo. According to the old men's interpretation of the dry law, he should accept being bloodily martyred on the scorched earth by the fist of the law; he should conform to the ethnographic stereotype of the conflict-phobic Pueblo. Instead, Leon pursues conflict in writing: "That afternoon Leon spoke with the Governor, and he promised to send letters to the Bureau of Indian Affairs" (127). Silko no doubt views sarcastically such a paper chase after "rights."[5] Justice is pursued in her story by rewriting the paper chase of precedents and appeals as a "story of witches" told not according to the oral tradition, the voice of which is silent, but according to *written oral tradition,* textuality with its intertextual links.

Tony never sees behind the mirror lenses of the cop's sunglasses. These unseeable eyes of the law form a motif that can be
read to suggest that the big cop's ethnic origin is obscure, rather
than clearly Hispanic like that of Nash Garcia. This obscurity of
ethnic origin can be construed to link the cop to Kaup'a'ta, the
Gambler, a kachina surrounded by obscurity, whom Sun Man
blinds in the traditional Pueblo story that is transcribed and translated in Franz Boas's *Keresan Texts*.[6] Tony does, however, in a scene
in which he appears to associate the cop with the kachina of his
dream, see *himself* in these lenses:

> The cop studied Leon's driver's license. I avoided his
> face—I knew that I couldn't look at his eyes, so I stared at his
> black half-wellingtons, with the black uniform cuffs pulled
> over them; but my eyes kept moving, upward past the black
> gun belt. My legs were quivering, and I tried to keep my eyes
> away from his. But it was like the time when I was very little
> and my parents warned me not to look into the masked
> dancers' eyes because they would grab me, and my eyes
> would not stop.
> "What's your name?" His voice was high-pitched and it
> distracted me from the meaning of the words.
> I remember Leon said, "He doesn't understand English so
> good," and finally I said that I was Antonio Sousea, while
> my eyes strained to look beyond the silver frosted glasses
> that he wore; but only my distorted face and squinting eyes
> reflected back. (126)

Here Leon assumes the role of interpreter between Tony and the
voice of the law. From Tony's point of view there is irony in Leon's
interpretation of his silence: It is Leon who just does not understand
the cop's voice "so good." Tony's distraction can be read to indicate that he is referring to "stories of witches" to understand the
tonal meaning of the voice's high pitch rather than the meaning of
the words.[7] When Tony answers the cop's question, he voices his
"identity" while he looks at his own distorted image and eyes in
the cop's sunglasses. Figuratively reflected in the sunglasses are the

legal and religious alterations wrought on precontact Pueblo culture by the conquistadors and their friars. This scene can be construed as a specular *mise en abîme* of identity in which Tony is figuratively reading his legal identity, Antonio Sousea, which combines the name of a Catholic saint with an apparently Hispanicized Pueblo patronymic, in the distorted reflection he sees in the sunglasses. It is of a pre-Hispanic Pueblo land that Tony daydreams, before he decides for sure the cop is a witch, as he and Leon are trying to reach an isolated sheep camp: "The highway was empty, and I sat there beside Leon imagining what it had been like before there were highways or even horses" (128). This vision of the land, undistorted as Popé desired to see it again, is "invaded" in the narrative when Leon announces that he sees the big cop following them in the *rearview mirror.* Thus, as Tony looks back through his imagination at the land Popé allegedly envisaged as the goal of his revolt, Leon looks back literally and sees the ineluctable stalking New Mexican lawman, a black figure that keeps them from reaching their goal and even threatens to deprive Tony of his voice: "My body began to shake and I wasn't sure if I would be able to speak" (128). Tony, however, regains his live voice, apparently as he decides on the need of eliminating this figure, and soon begins to speak of the cop as "it," in contrast to Leon, who continues to refer to him as "he." Indeed, Leon assumes the cop is a white man, whereas from Tony's point of view the cop's ethnic origin is probably undecidable, like that of the witch that Silko portrays as winning a precontact witching contest by narrating the arrival of Europeans (*Storyteller* 130–37).[8] Tony portrays Leon as neither seeing nor understanding what he can read reflected in the cop's sunglasses as "it" races with them down a road leading deep into Pueblo land:

> "There's no place left to hide. It follows us everywhere."
> Leon looked at me like he didn't understand what I'd said. Then I looked past Leon and saw that the patrol car had pulled up beside us; the piñon branches were whipping and scraping the side of the truck as it tried to force us off the road. Leon

kept driving with the two right wheels in the rut—bumping and scraping the trees. Leon never looked over at it so he couldn't have known how the reflections kept moving across the mirror lenses of the dark glasses. We were in the narrow canyon with pale sandstone close on either side—the canyon that ended with a spring where willows and grass and tiny blue flowers grow. (128)

At the end of this wild chase is a place that appears almost untouched by dryness, the site of a spring like those associated with stories of the emergence. As they approach this shrinelike site, Leon continues to fail to understand:

> "We've got to kill *it*, Leon. We must burn the body to be sure."
> Leon didn't seem to be listening. I kept wishing that old Teofilo could have been there to chant the proper words while we did *it*. Leon stopped the truck and got out—he still didn't understand what *it* was. (128; my emphasis)

But old Teofilo's words are there only as the silent voice that needs the writing storyteller's medicine to enable the reader to see that "it," interpreted by old Teofilo, is witch, witchery, and exorcism, and also to enable the reader to see "it" as Leon sees "him," namely as a sick, violent bigot, who abuses his legal power, and who personifies blind (in)justice and the written dry law.[9]

Just as Tony sees that behind the appearance of the billy club is a witch's bone, so could the writing storyteller see that behind the appearance of this bone is the silver-tipped cane symbolic of the authority legally bestowed on the Pueblo governors by the U.S. federal government, or the pen of the authors of the "pueblo law-and-order code" and constitution. Both signify power that can be and has been interpreted to have been abused. Likewise, just as Tony, without seeing behind the cop's sunglasses, must interpret the eyes of the unspeakable, so could the writing storyteller understand that these invisible eyes, which follow Tony and Leon everywhere, reflect the eyes of a traditional Pueblo mythological figure,

Kaup'a'ta, the Gambler, who brings drought and death to the pueblo. Stories of the Gambler are knotted into this darkly enchanting weave of written Pueblo mythological tradition. Elsewhere in *Storyteller,* Sun Man, having been given "medicine" by Grandmother Spider, meets and "defeats" the Gambler, cutting out his eyes and throwing them into the southern sky before freeing his children, the rain clouds (169). Elsewhere in ethnographic accounts, the Gambler returns as a blind kachina, led in a dance by his old grandmother (Nelson, "He Said/She Said" 33). Reading these stories intertextually as interpretive lenses, one can see that Tony's actions recall those of Sun Man. Grandmother Spider, functioning as the writing storyteller, is leading the blind voice of the law in a dialogic dance in which the traditional "rights" of old age and youth are sublated in a new tradition in which her metaphoric medicine, like Plato's pharmakon, functions both as remedy and poison. From the writing storyteller's dialectical perspective, these eyes of the law, which, from the conquistadors' intrusion until today have blindly distorted the Pueblo, cannot be literally cut out and thrown into the sky. Popé tried it and failed. The Protestant progressives tried it and failed. But they can be made invisible behind the lenses of sunglasses, cut out, leaving the reader to interpret their invisibility as a figure of a vision that is not quite possible to visualize, yet.

Conceptually the cop-witch-kachina's problematic eyes are at a point in the text where insight meets blindness, being meets nothingness and writing meets the voice. It is at this point that the oral storyteller meets the writing storyteller. It is at a similar point in the grand narrative of the West that Saint Paul saw through a glass darkly. It is at a similar point in poststructuralist theoretical narrative that Paul de Man read the presence of absence in a figural whirligig of blindness and insight around which he believed literary texts to be constructed. It is at this point in the narrative of the intrusion of writing into oral culture that Jacques Derrida reads Plato's ambiguous pharmakon—mnemonic remedy and poison—and begins his deconstruction of logocentrism. It is at this point in the narrative history of the novel, a written genre in opposition to the traditionally oral monologic epic, that Bakhtin theorizes dialogism. But there is no need to bring additional saints or demons into our narrative at this point. The writing storyteller, Aunt Susie, San Lorenzo, and the cop will suffice, for in these syncretic figures oral Pueblo tradition meets written-oral Western tradition in a story of martyrdom and unsuccessful purgation. In the cop-witch, which conflates Anglo-American law and ceremonial kachina, which darkly reflects witchery and the abuse of the power of writing, the writing storyteller figures an image of the dark aspect of herself. As the unspeakable, the cop figures the letter, the law that dries up the oral source, the stalking power of writing that Tony attempts to exorcize in a gesture that repeats Popé's failed revolt. In Tony's failure the writing storyteller raises in sublation orality and literacy in a narrative vision of the Pueblo that at Laguna was underlined when Governor Marmon, in an attempt to attenuate the severity of the split between the "progressives" and "conservatives" ordered that the patron saint's image be returned to his niche in the church (Ellis, "Laguna Pueblo" 447).

As Tony is dragging the cop-witch's corpse across the hot sand, he looks for a last time into the sunglasses: "The dark glasses hadn't fallen off and they *blinded* me with their hot-sun reflections until I pushed the body into the front seat" (128; my emphasis). At this ultimate specular moment, Tony, in a Sun Man-like action—this is corroborated by the rain clouds' gathering on the horizon as the story ends—symbolically attempts to restore a precontact vision, a vision that he dreams will allow him to see himself and the land undistorted. He succeeds, however, only in momentarily blinding himself in the sunglasses where earlier he had read his distorted identity. In this specular moment these dark glasses show him a blinding vision of himself as Sun Man and as Kaup'a'ta. As blinder blinded, he sees the unseeable. Refracted in this oxymoronic blinding vision is the writing voice of Silko's own dialectical dialogic intention in *Storyteller:* to see herself and to allow the reader to see her through Aunt Susie's vision made whole; to knot herself and Aunt Susie's silent voice together as writing storyteller. To see the world of the living and the dead through Pueblo eyes that are both new and old.

Silko takes up the pen where not only Aunt Susie but also her great-grandfather Marmon put it down. Tony's having implicitly appointed himself and Leon to the office of War Captain constitutes a (re)vision of Pueblo law, which neither the old men nor Leon nor Leslie Marmon Silko appear prepared to accept. As the thick black smoke from the burning patrol car is rolling into the sky, Leon, in whom the Cold Warrior's drunken braggadocio has been sobered by the foreseeable consequences of burning the representative of New Mexico law, dialogues with Tony. From the western horizon, where they are gathering as rain clouds, the Pueblo ancestors look down on what Tony and Silko have wrought:

> "My God, Tony. What's wrong with you? That's a state cop you killed." Leon was pale and shaking.
>
> I wiped my hands on my Levi's. "Don't worry, everything is O.K. now, Leon. It's killed. They sometimes take on strange forms."
>
> The tumbleweeds around the car caught fire, and little heat waves shimmered up toward the sky; in the west, rain clouds were gathering. (129)

A. LaVonne Ruoff reads this ending as troublingly open: "The formation of rainclouds immediately after the murder seems to indicate that nature approves Tony's act, which has rid the pueblo of a menace. Nevertheless, Tony will be judged by neither Keres nor natural law but rather by non-Indian civil law. The conclusion of the story makes clear that the exorcism ritual is complete. What the conclusion leaves unclear are the consequences Tony will suffer for carrying out the ritual" (8). Tony may dream that as self-appointed War Captain he will not be tried, judged, and sentenced first to death and later to life in prison as were Willie and Gabriel Felipe, but Silko is under no such illusion. The point of her text, however, is not to judge, but to seek justice in written orality, to rely on "stories about witches" to rewrite the cop-killer narrative in such a way that the Felipes' conviction and Tony's likely failure to escape conviction point the bone at the blindness of relying on a .30-30 or of relying on the courts to eliminate the violent or nonviolent abuse of power. In figuratively arrogating the right to appoint himself War Captain, Tony not only implicitly assumes the right to interpret Pueblo law, but also the right of an inquisitor to "burn" the legal and literary narrative of assimilation along with the cop-witch-kachina. Here is where Tony represents only one tendency in Silko. This is where the writing storyteller sets herself apart from Tony. No matter how much Silko may dislike the law and the narrative of assimilation, no matter how much she may yearn for precontact orality, neither she nor her Aunt Susie burns books or witches.[10]

As the writing storyteller's revision of Pueblo tradition unfolds, patterns of blood—full-blood, mixed-blood, "white" blood—are written on the page. One such pattern, which is thematically linked to Tony looking into the big cop's sunglasses, can be traced from the knot in the textual web where writing and the Keresan voice are joined. In a gloss on the she-coyote story that was told in Keresan by Robert G. Marmon and transcribed and translated by Elsie Clews Parsons in Boas's *Keresan Texts*, Silko looks through the lenses of the old white lawgiver's glasses:

All I know of my great-grandpa Marmon
are the stories my family told
and the old photographs which show him
a tall thin old white man
with a white beard
wearing a black suit coat
and derby hat.
He stands with his darker sons
and behind the wire-rim glasses he wore
I see in his eyes
he had come to understand this world
differently.
Maybe he chose that particular coyote story
to tell to Parsons
because for him at Laguna
that was the one thing he had to remember:

> No matter what is said to you by anyone
> you must take care of those most dear to you.
>
>   (256; my emphasis)

It would appear that in her photographic vision Silko endows herself with a clairvoyance similar to the one Ruoff attributes to Tony in
his dream. Of course, Silko's vision is not unmediated. She neither
sees the eyes of her great-grandpa nor sees with his eyes. She sees
his eyes "figured" in a *photograph* and lets Marmon family stories
interpret them in such a way that she "imagines" how these eyes
saw. Her photographic clairvoyance, like Tony's oneiric clairvoyance,
testifies to her dream of a silent voice that is alive without writing.
Silko, like Tony, like Popé, also dreams of seeing the land through
precontact eyes. Silko, like Tony, like Popé, dreams of clairvoyance
to see witchery. But whereas Tony, in failing to see through the
lenses of the cop's sunglasses, opens the story onto the conflict
between the Gambler and Sun-Man, and darkly sees witchery's presence, Silko, in seeing through the lenses of her great-grandfather's
glasses, clearly sees *its* absence in the eyes of the ancestral lawgiver.
For Silko, Robert G. Marmon's eyes no longer saw like the eyes of
a white man: "he had come to understand this world differently."
And yet in those vague words about words, "no matter what is
said to you by anyone," can be read not only echoes of the racist
epithet "Squaw Man," which Anglos sometimes used when speaking
of the paternal founder of Silko's branch of the Marmon family (16),
not only the words of the racist hotel manager telling this paternal
figure to go through the kitchen when he was with his mixed-blood
sons (17), but also the whisper of Laguna voices saying that these
eyes of the white governor of Laguna, at the time of bitter contention between conservatives and progressives, were the eyes of a
witch and that his written Laguna law was witchery.[11] It is these
clairvoyant eyes that Silko, in her persistent daily attempt to balance
the Pueblo and the Western in her life, is attempting to fuse with
the failing full-blood Pueblo eyes of Aunt Susie. What Krupat calls
the dialectic dialogic of *Storyteller* is this fusion. In this written act

of visual orality, she exorcises the racist and nondialogic interpretation of her own green eyes in which both whites and full-bloods have read grounds to exclude her. These are the eyes that contributed to her being excised from the photograph of Indian schoolchildren taken by the obnoxious white tourist in an incident recounted in "Fences Against Freedom" (*Yellow Woman* 106). These are the eyes that have inspired her to see herself through the eyes of Kochininako: "I even imagined that Yellow Woman had yellow skin, brown hair, and green eyes like mine, although her name does not refer to her color, but rather to the ritual color of the east" (71). And Yellow Woman, as readers of "Estoy-eh-muut and the Kunideeyahs" know, is one of the strange forms "they" sometimes take on.[12] Writing is as much a part of Leslie Marmon Silko's vision of Pueblo culture as Yellow Woman and witchery.

CHAPTER 5

COYOTE LOOPS

Leslie Marmon Silko Holds a Full House in Her Hand

At Hopi he could get a fresh start; he could tell people about himself while they looked at the photos in the plastic pages of his wallet.

—SILKO,
Storyteller

It wasn't until I began this book
that I realized that the photographs in the Hopi basket
have a special relationship to the stories as I remember them.
The photographs are here because they are part of many of the
stories
and because many of the stories can be traced to the photographs.

—SILKO,
Storyteller

Leslie Marmon Silko's "Coyote Holds a Full House in His Hand" begins in medias res with a metaphorical twist on a common opening line of Coyote stories: "He wasn't getting any place with Mrs. Sekakaku, he could see that" (*Storyteller* 257).[1] Having perceived that he is *not* going there, but that he has been relegated to the static fringe of things by Mrs. Sekakaku's "warming

up leftover chili beans for lunch" (257) and by her talk of Aunt
Mamie's dizzy spells, the protagonist in this story begins by musing
about his situation in an extended passage that could be likened to
flashbacks in which, like Coyote, he loops around through similarly
ending beginnings in the past, to begin again.[2]

Digressing at some length through scenes from the protagonist's
youth, as well as through events from the recent past, and returning
to him sitting on the red plastic sofa in Mrs. Sekakaku's house, the
looping Coyote narrative introduces the protagonist as quite a
character. He is old enough to be graying, has avoided marriage
with the same nonchalance that he avoids work, and still lives in
his mother's house. He spends most of his time shuttling back and
forth between Laguna and Albuquerque, where he frequents "Indian
bars downtown," but has himself photographed in front of "fancy
bars in the Heights" that probably exclude Indians. Even though
he has dropped out of school after the seventh grade, he listens to
lawyers in the Federal Building and knows he could be a lawyer,
"because he was so good at making up stories to justify why things
happened the way they did" (259). He has depended on his mother
to cash her pension check to pay for enrollment in law school by
correspondence or COD mail-ordered items like the imitation leather
jacket he still wears. He likes to look at and imagine fondling plump
women such as the Mexican "postmaster"(257) and Mrs. Sekakaku.

There appears to be a gap between the point of view shared by
the protagonist's fellow Pueblos and the point of view of the character who begins the story seated, recalling and linking by free association events from his past experience. He perceives that others,
including his siblings and cousins, tell stories that cast him in a
less than favorable role. He, however, perceives their perceptions
to be misperceptions and is waiting for someone, like Mrs. Sekakaku, to understand:

Mrs. Sekakaku finally realized the kind of man he was. All
along that had been the trouble at Laguna, nobody understood just what kind of man he was. They thought he was

sort of good for nothing, he knew that, but for a long time
he kept telling himself to keep on trying and trying. But it
seemed like people would never forget the time the whole
village was called out to clean up for feast day and he sent his
mother to tell them he was sick with liver trouble. He was
still hurt because they didn't understand that with liver trouble you can walk around and sometimes even ride the bus
to Albuquerque. (258)

It is not difficult to read a suggestion of irony arising from the
gap between the protagonist's perception of himself and the other
characters' and the narrator's perception of him. Such an irony is
usually associated with the classic *style indirect libre* as exemplified
in novels such as Flaubert's *Madame Bovary*. In this narrative style
the author "alternates the supposed objective account of the third-
person narrator's voice with the subjective experience of a character
moving through the world. The former is presented as a given that
is in itself unproblematic for narrator and reader; the latter involves
an individual's perception and misperception. The gap between
the two gives rise to the familiar Flaubertian irony" (VanderWolk
276–77).

Silko's text, however, is written in a special version of the indirect free style discourse in which the third-person narrator gives
not only the protagonist's perceptions but also his interpretation of
the "supposed objective account" of his experience given by others.
This potentially puts into question the objectivity of all third-person
storytellers in the story, including the third-person narrator, and in
so doing gives rise to a gap in Silko's discourse in which there is,
indeed, irony. It is not, however, just the condescending irony that
arises from the gap between the supposed objective point of view
of a third-person narrator and a subjective character's misperceptions; rather, it is an ironizing of this irony, a spellbinding turning
of irony back onto itself that problematizes the objectivity that is
taken as a given in the classic *style indirect libre* and invites the
reader to experience a realm where subjectivity and objectivity are
suspended. In such a dizzying ironic discourse, realizing who the

character is means spinning together the warm and equalizing point of view of women like Mrs. Sekakaku with the cold and condescending point of view of the traditional Western narrative ironist.

There are several passages in the narrative where the reader is invited to experience the protagonist's experience of himself as enigmatically potent and irresistible. These passages are marked by a curious referential ambiguity of the pronoun *it*. Metaphoric language in these passages both contributes to the difficulty in determining a referent for the pronoun and suggests possible unnamed referents. The first such passage opens the Coyote loop: "He sat the magazine down on his lap and traced his finger over the horse head embossed on the plastic cushion. *It* was always like that. When he didn't expect *it, it* always came to him, but when he *wanted* something to happen, like with Mrs. Sekakaku, then *it shied away*" (257; my emphasis). The referent of *it* in the first occurrence in this passage could be the situation in which the protagonist currently finds himself, that is, "not getting anywhere with Mrs. Sekakaku" (257). However, with the second and third occurrence, *it* appears not to refer to the current situation with Mrs. Sekakaku but to a different and more desirable situation. In the fourth occurrence, the depiction of the behavior of the referent of *it* as shying away makes it possible to read this referent metaphorically as something *chevaline.* This *chevaline* shying is thematically anticipated by the protagonist "tracing" his finger over the embossed horse head, a gesture that opens the possibility that *it* in all four occurrences refers to something that is given to whims like a shy horse that has a will of its own.

A similar something like an outside will figures in the protagonist's self-flattering phallic interpretation of the *chevaline* metaphor he overhears spoken in Spanish by the matronly "postmaster":

The Mexican woman thought Pueblo men were great lovers—he knew this because he heard her say so to another Mexican woman one day while he was finishing his strawberry soda on the other side of the dry goods section. In the summer he

spent a good number of hours there watching her because
she wore sleeveless blouses that revealed her fat upper arms,
full and round, and the tender underarm creases curving to
her breasts. They had not noticed he was still there leaning
on the counter behind a pile of overalls; ". . . *the size of a
horse*" was all that he had heard, but he knew what she was
talking about. They were like that those Mexican women. (257;
my emphasis)

The referent of the Mexican postmaster's comparative metaphor is
itself left unspoken. The protagonist overhears, translates, and interprets only the words placed between quotation marks in the narrative. A supposedly objective and condescending reader could certainly
point out that, given the fragmentary status of the postmaster's
enunciation, it is not possible to rely on grammar either to validate
or invalidate the protagonist's interpretation of this metaphor as
referring to the phallic criterion used by the Mexican women to
measure Pueblo men as lovers. It is not even possible to know what
the topic of conversation was among the women, without assuming,
like the protagonist, that the only thing Mexican women talk about
is sex. Such a reader could read irony in this passage, seeing in the
protagonist's "subjective" reading of the metaphor a figure in which
his character is *embossed* like the horse head on the couch: he is so
self-centered, voyeuristic, ineffective, deluded, and inflated with his
own image of himself as a Laguna stud that he cannot possibly interpret "objectively" the pitiful figure he must cut when he hangs out
in the store drinking strawberry pop or when he brings the postmaster a heart-shaped box of candy. It is also possible, however, for
the reader to read the protagonist as an interpreter who consistently
relies on rhetoric rather than grammar to make sense of what he
experiences. Here, in interpreting the unspecified referent of the postmaster's *chevaline* metaphor to be a group of men including himself, he
selects the trope of phallic inflatability found in the treasure of Coyote
rhetoric.[3] In so doing he also traces one of the traits of his character.

Many of these figures involve olfactory perceptions and what
one could call olfactory reasoning. When the Mexican postmaster

silently ignores the heart-shaped box of candy, setting it aside unopened to gather dust, the protagonist understands this as a sign of her having *smelled* alcohol on his breath.

> —it was because she didn't approve of men who drank. That was the last thing he did before he left town; he did it because he had to, because liquor was illegal on the reservation. So the last thing he did was have a few drinks to carry home with him the same way other people stocked up on lamb nipples or extra matches. She must have smelled it on his breath when he handed her the candy because she didn't say anything and she left the box under the counter by the old newspapers and balls of string. (258)

In other words, from the point of view of the "objective" reader, the postmaster *smelled* that he is a drunken Indian. In so doing the postmaster and the "objective" reader would rely on a rhetoric of condescending, racist, anti-Indian stereotypes, rather than on the tropes of Coyote rhetoric. Interpreted according to the latter, the protagonist proves himself to be carefully bringing with him to the reservation what he cannot legally buy there. His logic is perfect. The "objective" reader can ground his/her objection to the protagonist's reasoning only in preconceived cultural figures of Indian debility, that is, in stereotypes. The racist "truth" of such stereotypes is validated by the law that prohibits alcohol on the reservation.

The protagonist motivates the postmaster's refusal to reciprocate his sweet love gift with an interpretation in which he relies on his nose for proof of her jealousy: "She didn't approve of perfumed letters and she used to pretend the letters weren't there even when he could smell them and see their pastel edges sticking out of the pile in the general delivery slot" (257), and "[t]he postmaster was jealous of the letters that were coming, but she was the one who had sent him into the arms of Mrs. Sekakaku" (258). The protagonist knows love and jealousy when he smells them. Grammatically or logically the "objective" reader cannot disprove the protagonist's olfactory reasoning.

The entry of a will into the protagonist, either from the outside or from the inside, is a metaphorically possible interpretation in a scene that occurs on the protagonist's way to Hopi. Once again the protagonist relies on his nose to reason. Once again this will is referred to in the text by the ambiguous use of the pronoun *it*. Like the protagonist, *it* is left virtually unnamed in the story,[4] but *its* supplementing the protagonist's will in the course of his interpreting events in the narrative is portrayed in tropes that readily link *it* to Coyote, the trickster-gambler named in the poker metaphor of the story's title. When *it* emerges as the protagonist is climbing Hopi mesa, *it* is linked to his breathlessness: "The last hundred feet up the wagon trail seemed the greatest distance to him and he felt an unaccustomed tightness in his lungs. He knew *it* wasn't old age— *it* was something else—something that wanted him to work for *it*" (260; my emphasis). Here in the first occurrence, *it* can be read as referring back to "an unaccustomed tightness in his lungs" or to the cause of this breathlessness. In the second occurrence, however, the referent of *it* is explicitly left undetermined, and in the third occurrence *it* is said to refer explicitly to "something" that has a will and appears not to be located anywhere in particular. While the language does not name what *it* is, it does make clear that in having a will of its own, *it* is separate from the protagonist's will, but seeks to become one with that will: *It* is "something that wanted him to work for *it*."

Coyote, who is often figured as coprophilic and coprophagous, and who is noted for being long-winded (both physically and verbally), would appear to be breathing in the protagonist as he recovers from his unexplained shortness of breath. This is suggested by his finding encouragement in an olfactory experience the reader might "objectively" take to be repulsively discouraging: "A short distance past the outside toilets at the edge of the mesa top he got his breath back and their thick odor reassured him" (260). Similar to his Clatsop Chinook cousin, who consults his own feces for advice, Coyote here seems to take counsel in the odor of the Hopi toilets.[5] In this olfactory reassurance can be detected not only the trope of

Coyote's practice of taking fecal counsel but also a vision of fecal equality among the Pueblos, a bit of olfactory reasoning understandable in the form of a silently voiced joke: The protagonist "smells" that Hopi turds stink just like those at any other pueblo.

As the exterior (or interior) will (or character) becomes more noticeable in the protagonist, the telling of the story itself begins to compete with the apparent end of the story. The protagonist's reason for going to Hopi appears at first to be copulation and possibly even marriage with Mrs. Sekakaku. The looping narrative and the dizzying irony formed by tropes from Coyote rhetoric impart to the story a self-referentiality that invites the reader to ask just who is telling this story and why. With coprophilic Coyote breathing in him, the protagonist now "senses" that the alleged Hopi superiority in matters of sex and magic is only apparent; it resides in the mistaken *belief* that the patronizing and condescending third-person narrators are actually objective. Spatially and temporally, the referents of *it*, the tropes of Coyote rhetoric, equalize all the Pueblos. In so doing, they attenuate the teleological structure of the narrative. They make it hard to determine what the end of the discourse is, hard to tell the difference between ending beginnings and beginning endings:

> He *saw* that one of the old toilets had tipped over and rolled down the side of the mesa to the piles of stove ashes, broken bottles and corn shucks on the slope below. He'd get along all right. Like a lot of people, at one time he *believed* Hopi magic could outdo all the other Pueblos but now he *saw* that *it was all the same from time to time and place to place.* When Hopi men got tired of telling stories about all-nighters in Winslow motels then probably the old men brought *it* around to magic and how they rigged the Navajo tribal elections one year just by hiding some little painted sticks over near Window Rock. Whatever *it* was he had come for, he was ready. (260; my emphasis)

What the unnamed protagonist thought he had come to Hopi for before Coyote entered or emerged in him—the end of "his" story in a telic sense, as he at first understands it, and the underlying meaning, the counsel that he took from the highly perfumed letters Mrs. Sekakaku had sent him—was an all-nighter, with him playing the role of the long-winded Laguna stud. What he finds on arriving, however, is another story in which condescending irony competes with the dizzying doubling irony of the Coyote story. Mrs. Seka- kaku takes him by surprise from behind right after he has "checked his reflection in the window glass of [her] front door" in order to verify that his image does coincide with the words "she had written after he sent her the photographs," that is, that "gray hair made him look dignified" (261). Here he is about to realize that she has assigned him a role in a story that she is telling. In this story she is another person and he, motivated by pride and vanity, is the lech- erous, gluttonous, and undignified butt of Hopi laughter: "The way the little dog was barking probably all the neighbors had seen him and were laughing" (261). As he conjectures that Mrs. Sekakaku's story is not about the mutually longed for tryst that he had read into her letters, he questions his own ability to interpret what is figured in a text: "At first he thought his understanding of the English language must be failing, that really she had only invited him over to Bean Dance, that he had misread her letters when she said that a big house like hers was lonely and that she did not like walking alone in the evenings from the water faucet outside the village" (261–62). On further reflection, he decides that Mrs. Seka- kaku's perfumed letters were bait in a trap, set to catch first his photographs, his gift, and then him in her story. At this point of interpretive hesitation and revision, he experiences a breathlessness similar to the one he felt before the fecal reassurance of Coyote rhetoric:

> She had lured his letters and snapshots and the big poinsettia plant to show off to her sisters and aunts, and now his visit so she could pretend he had come uninvited, overcome with desire for her. . . . The old auntie and the dizzy spells gave her the perfect excuse and a *story* to protect her respectability.

It was only 2:30 but already she was folding a flannel night-gown while she talked to her niece. And here he had been imagining the night together the whole bus ride from Laguna—fingering the creases and folds and the little rolls while she squeezed him with both hands. Their night together had suddenly lifted off and up like a butterfly moving away from him, and the *breathlessness he had felt coming up the mesa returned.* (262; my emphasis)

By this time the looping narrative has returned to the scene on which the story opened in medias res. Following this repeated breathlessness, *it* spontaneously reemerges in the protagonist as a storytelling character, the medicine man, whose story *it* invents as *it* goes along:

He was feeling bitter—if that's all it took then he'd find a way to get that old woman out of bed. He said *it without thinking—the words just found his mouth* and he said "excuse me ladies," straightening his belt buckle as he walked across the room, "but it sounds to me like your poor auntie is in bad shape." Mrs. Sekakaku's niece looked at him for the first time all afternoon. "Is he a medicine man?" she asked her aunt and *for an instant he could see Mrs. Sekakaku hesitate and he knew he had to say* "Yes, it's something I don't usually mention myself. Too many of those guys just talk about it to attract women. But this is a serious case." (262; my emphasis)

In other words—in Coyote words—the breath-voice-will-character in the protagonist speaks where Mrs. Sekakaku hesitates speechless, and in so doing, *it* assumes command as storyteller and interpreter. Rather than as gluttonous fool or lecherous clown, *it* now speaks the protagonist as medicine man. His self-effacing modesty about this heretofore untold power implicitly contrasts with the Hopi men's immodest storytelling about their fast hands and all-nighters in Winslow, while opening the way to his own handiwork inventing a "traditional" cure for Aunt Mamie.[6]

At this point the end of *its* story is unknown to the protagonist. Like the Hopi women, he is an auditor of as well as a character in the story that *it* is telling through him. In returning his focus to the end that initially brought him to Hopi, that is, sexual desire and the desire for a "fresh start" allowing him to escape his marginality at Laguna, the protagonist appears to risk losing his Coyote breath: "*It* was sounding so good that he was afraid he would start thinking about the space between the cheeks of the niece's ass and be unable to go on" (262; my emphasis). The spontaneous voice prevails, however, and *it* tells him as storytelling story and Coyote medicine man.

As mentioned above, neither the narrator nor the protagonist explicitly names *it*. Instead, *it* is referred to in vague terms, such as "momentum," which metaphorically combines the protagonist's storytelling impulse and the gambling metaphor of the story's title: "But the next thing he said was they had a cure they did at Laguna for dizzy spells like Aunt Mamie was having. He could feel a *momentum* somewhere inside himself—it wasn't hope, because he knew Mrs. Sekakaku had tricked him—but whatever *it* was *it* was *going for broke*" (262; my emphasis). This "momentum" would appear to be synonymous with the "Laguna luck" mentioned at the end of the story. It could perhaps be likened to the feeling gamblers speak of having when they are on a roll, when chance appears to be subject to the determinacy not of their own will but of some unexplained, benevolent will sometimes referred to exophorically as *it*.[7]

Following the logic of the gaming metaphor embodied in "going for broke," *its* end is the double-or-nothing stake in the game the protagonist is playing with the Hopi storytellers. The chips in this stake are words, which rather than being convertible into money are convertible into story, the coin of the realm that brings the secular and the sacred, the jocular and the serious, together in the special cure. It is a story in which pure chance seems paradoxically determined by the narrative *tradition* Coyote is *improvising*. It is a story in which the so-called real medicine men, "the medical doctors from Keams Canyon . . . and old man Ko'ite . . . from Oraibi" (257), who come from either somewhere in the Western world or in the Pueblo world, are trumped by the simulated medicine man who comes out of Coyote rhetoric. It is a story where, since the simulacrum precedes the "real," the distinction between the real and the simulated is set spinning in a dizzying irony. It is a story where luck and fate are character.

As was noted above, the emergence of *it* in the protagonist coincides with his regaining his breath. At the point where the protagonist definitively takes command of Mrs. Sekakaku's story, her sudden exhalation can be interpreted within a thematic of inspiration/expiration and inflation/deflation to signal that the Coyote voice not only has displaced her as storyteller but is also on its way to taking the wind out of the Hopi men's stories of superior sexual and medicinal potency. This depends on keeping the men marginalized in the kivas, which are the center of the sacred Bean Dance matters to which they are attending, away from the new center where Coyote is inventing a rhetorical cure for Aunt Mamie's dizziness:

> "Well, not so fast," he said even though his heart was racing. "It won't work unless everything is just so. All her clanswomen must come to her house but there can't be any men there, not even outside." He paused. He knew exactly what to say. "This is very important. Otherwise the cure won't work." *Mrs. Sekakaku let out her breath suddenly* and tightened her lips and he knew that any men or boys not in the kivas preparing for Bean Dance would be sent far away from Aunt Mamie's house. (263; my emphasis)

Once in command of the story, the protagonist becomes the center of the women's culinary attention, allowing him to satisfy his Coyote appetite, while he reflects on the willful capriciousness of *it*:

> He looked over at the big loaf of fresh oven bread the niece had brought when she came; they hadn't offered him any before, but now after she served him a big bowl of chili beans she cut him a thick slice. *It* was all coming back to him now about how good medicine men get treated and he wasn't surprised at himself anymore. Once he got started he knew just how *it* should go. *It* was getting *it* started that gave him trouble sometimes. (263; my emphasis)

Rubbing ashes onto the thighs of each woman of the Snow clan, one after the other, except Mrs. Sekakaku and Aunt Mamie, the protagonist steps outside of the linear temporality implicit in such a series of fondled female objects, experiencing what appears to be a timelessness in an ecstatic vision of soaring rhetorical uplift:

> The ashes were slippery and carried his hands up and around each curve each fold each roll of flesh on their thighs. He reached high but his fingers never strayed above the edge of the panty leg. They stepped in front of him one after the other and he worked painstakingly with each one—the silvery white ashes billowing up like clouds above skin dusted like early snow on brown hills, and *he lost all track of time*. He closed his eyes so he could feel them better—the folds of skin and flesh above the knee, little crevices and creases like a hawk feels canyons and arroyos while he is soaring. (264; my emphasis)

Having gripped some thighs "as if they were something wild and fleet like antelope and rabbits" (264), the protagonist gives special attention to Mrs. Sekakaku, whom he recognizes by the "dimple and pucker at the edge of the garter" (264). Then he comes down from this timeless vision to reenter a temporality that is distinctively linear. He sits breathless—deflated, so to speak—between the penultimate and ultimate objects of his medico-rhetorical attention: "*He was out of breath* and he knew he could not stand up to get to Aunt Mamie's bed so he bowed his head and pretended he was praying" (264; my emphasis).

At the beginning of this cure when all of the Snow Clan women have assembled, the protagonist glimpsed in their eyes a power that he then recognized to be greater than his: "The initiated girls and the women sat serious and quiet with the ceremonial presence the Hopis are famous for. Their eyes were full of the *power* the clanswomen shared whenever they gathered together. He saw *it* clearly and he never doubted *its* strength. Whatever he took, he'd have to run with *it*, but the women would prevail as they always

had" (263; my emphasis). The glimpse of this unnamed power
reinforces the protagonist's inability to know the end of the story
in which the feminine, the matronly, would prevail over the mascu-
line, the patronly. This unnamed power, which is linked with "ceremonial presence," is also referred to with the pronoun *it*. Thus,
when Aunt Mamie ultimately rises up on her own and goes over to
the fireplace for her turn, the end of *it* as the unnamed "power the
clanswomen shared whenever they gathered together" coincides
with the end of *it* as medico-rhetorical phallic Coyote power. *It*
would appear to have passed out of the now breathless protagonist
into Aunt Mamie, whose renewed ribald vitality accounts for the
efficacy of the special cure by Coyote rhetoric: "'I feel better already.
I'm not dizzy,' the old woman said, not letting anyone help her out
of bed or walk with her to the fireplace. He rubbed her thighs as
carefully as he had rubbed the others, and he could tell by the feel
she'd probably live a long time" (264). In this story it is ultimately
the women who wield the verbal phallic horse power, the equalizing
storytelling power in Silko's Coyote version of the *style indirect
libre*. The breathless protagonist knows this: "Whatever he took he'd
have to run with *it*, but the women would prevail as they always
had" (263; my emphasis). That power, linked with the Hopi ceremo-
niousness and with ribald vitality, ultimately deflates and debunks
both the stories told by Hopi men about their sexual superiority
and the verbal phallic Coyote breath—the Coyote trope of phallic
inflation—that has inflated the protagonist. In the Coyote loop *it*
deflates and debunks the "supposed objective account" of the narrator in the *style indirect libre*, but it cannot keep from also deflating
and debunking itself in the equalizing style of Coyote discourse.

Although, following the cure, Mrs. Sekakaku appears eager to
welcome the protagonist into her bed—she kicks aside the little
dog on which she had bestowed her affection earlier and symbolically blocks the opening of her oven to it—the protagonist senses
that the end of *it* as a story must remain ultimately rhetorical, oral,
and visual, rather than genital. The undetermined "whatever" (263)
the protagonist realized he would have to run with consists of pies

and piki bread, the photograph of himself with the women of the
Snow Clan in front of Aunt Mamie's fireplace, and the Coyote story
of Aunt Mamie's "cure" that is photographically and verbally
figured in his holding this "full house in his hand." Mrs. Sekakaku, whom the protagonist, on having received her written invita-
tion to come to Hopi, initially thought had "finally realized the kind
of man he was" (258) will no doubt experience some realization to
this effect when she or some of her clan sisters tell the story of
Aunt Mamie's cure. In order for the protagonist to avoid becoming
the subjective character in the condescending and patronizing free
style discourse that will erupt when the men emerge from the kiva,
his returning with culinary goodies and the story must remain the
beginning of a Coyote story. Otherwise this story could end as the
story of his being chased down the mesa, where he would wind
up breathless and battered or even dead, as Coyote sometimes is
in traditional Coyote stories. But this is not a traditional Coyote
story. The protagonist is not just Coyote, but a storyteller who
maintains his Coyote power by making his telling the story the
end and beginning of the story: "But he told her he had to get back
to Laguna right away because he had something important to tell
the old man" (265).

For Coyote the storyteller, roguish gambler, lecher, glutton, copro-
phile, wanderer, thief, cheat, spoiler, clown, pragmatist, bricoleur,
stud, and survivor, the story is always aleatory, never subject to
one's "own" will. The protagonist returns home, with a photographic
"vision" of the gaming pun—of himself as Coyote holding a full
house in his hand—which he will show and gloss as he continues
trying and trying with another gift for the Mexican woman: "He
set aside a fine-looking cherry pie to give to the postmaster. Now
that they were even again with the Hopi men *maybe* this Laguna
luck would hold out a little while longer" (265; my emphasis).
Thus, rather than coming to an end, the story "closes" as it opens,
with a narrative loop, perhaps even without the protagonist realizing
that in the "rhetoric" of *its* story *it* has poetically "pictured" him as
the character, Coyote.

Just as the unnamed will or story took over in the protagonist as he became Coyote–medicine man–storyteller, so the story appears to have wanted to take over in Silko as she was writing it. In a letter to James Wright, which she accompanied with a manuscript entitled "Coyote *Sits* With a Full House in His Hand," Silko wrote: "This is the story I told you I was working with in early August. *It* tried to become a novel during the second draft, but, after a week of fighting with *it*, I managed to determine that *it* should be a story" (90; my emphasis). Like her protagonist, Silko is fond of showing photographs to which stories can be traced. Holding *Storyteller* in his/her hand and having turned the last page of "Coyote Holds a Full House in His Hand," the reader can see a nearly entirely blank page and a photograph of Leslie Marmon Silko. Accompanied by three friendly dogs (one whose ratty coat makes it look a little like a coyote), dressed in what would appear to be men's western wear, she sits smiling out at us with a look of warm irony on her plump face. As we hold this photograph of the writing storyteller in our hand and trace in it the story we have just read, Leslie Marmon Coyote, like the oral storyteller dolls invented in the 1960s by Pueblo potters,[8] holds a full house in her/his hand. Should we let patronizing and condescending irony keep us from enjoying the matronizing and equalizing feel of Coyote rhetoric? *Ut pictura poesis.*

CHAPTER 6

ALMANAC OF THE DEAD

*The real reason I left Laguna and moved down here was that
I was going through a divorce and I had to leave. And I came
down here. I was called down here, actually, because of the
Almanac and the spirits. Besides being Laguna, I have Mexican Indian in me too. I have Cherokee, I have lots of tribes. I
have lots of callings, and lots of spirits.*

—LESLIE MARMON SILKO TO ELLEN ARNOLD

*The composition of vast books is a laborious and impoverish-
ing extravagance. To go on for five hundred pages developing
an idea whose perfect oral exposition is possible in a few minutes! A better course of procedure is to pretend that these
books exist, and then to offer a résumé, a commentary.*

—JORGE LUIS BORGES,
Ficciones

When *Almanac of the Dead* appeared in 1991, the reactions
of reviewers were mixed. Larry McMurtry and Richard
Erdoes were effusive in their praise, comparing Silko's
intellectual and literary accomplishment in this novel to that of
Marx and Tolstoy. Other reviewers criticized this long-awaited and

lengthy tome on grounds of its apparent homophobia, its obsession with the male member, its need of extensive editing, and its unbelievable plot.

Ever the rhetorical Coyote, Silko has employed a logic of inclusion to turn the negative reviews into testimony to her success. She interprets certain white male reviewers' emotional reactions to her massive book to indicate that some narrative force, similar to the unnamed Coyote-like referent in "Coyote Holds a Full House in His Hand," which she designates with the pronoun *it*, was at work in her while she was writing:

> Then these reviewers came along, certain white male academics—the one who had the hardest time was a political science professor at Yale who did the *USA Today*, but I noticed the *Newsweek* and *Time* reviewers, both white males, were very up-front about their emotional reactions. They could tell that something had happened in the part of them that writes reviews for *Time* and *Newsweek*, and they say that. In the *New Republic* the guy was honest about how viscerally affected he had been and you could see it in the language. "Aha," I thought, "Something magical *did* happen." I didn't control *it*, but there was *something* in those narratives that just forced *itself* to be told through me. (Silko, "Narratives of Survival" 108; my emphasis)

Silko has talked at some length about this unnamed "something" and about feeling as if she did not consciously control what she was writing. She vacillates between portraying herself as "controlled by a spirit, not by spirits, but by a spiritual storyteller and narrator" (Silko, "The Past Is Right Here and Now" 104) and likening herself to a messianic voodoo priestess ridden like a horse by multiple multicultural spirits:

> I began to lose control of the novel and to feel that all the old stories came in, and I felt the presence of *spirits*. *It* was taken over. I meant for *it* to take only two years to write, and pretty soon after the years went by and *it* just went on and on. And

I began to remember reading about Zora Neale Hurston, who has a wonderful book, *Tell My Horse,* and this title is a reference to voodoo religion, a new religion that was born in the Americas. African slaves ran away in the Caribbean and met the Caribbean Indians. Together they made a new, indigenous American religion. Zora Neale Hurston's book talks about when the spirits come they ride you, you become their horse. They use you. And so I began to realize that from the time I was a little girl and the old folks at home had told me little stories about the loss, the hurt, and the anger of five hundred years that I had been always groomed—I had not realized it—but for generations they have been waiting for somebody. And now *it* seemed *it* came down upon me, but not just for me, or for the Native American people, but to think about all people. So the novel had to be bigger.

That's why I had to bring in Germans and to talk about Japanese. A *burden* that had come down to me over hundreds of years, I believe. I was the one that had to serve these spirits. (Silko, "An Interview with Leslie Marmon Silko" 154; my emphasis)

In the beginning of this passage, the pronoun *it* refers to the novel. Toward the end of the passage, *it* appears to refer to Silko having been "groomed" at Laguna by the "old folks," to the "burden" that had come down to her, and to exterior forces or spirits. Silko does not name these spirits. She does metaphorically construe them as informing *Almanac* with a messianic "burden" that she, as the non-white woman, has been destined to bear.[1]

Silko's feeling of being controlled by "a spiritual storyteller and narrator," or of being ridden like a horse by multiple spirits, can be used to help understand the mode of narration found in *Almanac.* One could say that the writing storyteller, in whom Western writing culture and Pueblo oral culture are melded, shows up here similarly to the way Aunt Susie's voice showed up when Silko was reading the story of Waithea to her audience at the English Institute at Harvard, or similarly to the way Coyote shows up in the anonymous protagonist of "Coyote Holds a Full House in His Hand." Thus, the spiritual storyteller and narrator could be presences from Cliff House, where Aunt Susie went to finish writing out the stories she did not have time to write while she was living. At Cliff House, it would seem, Aunt Susie is together with other writers from pre-Columbian Mesoamerican cultures as well as with writing and nonwriting storytellers from many other pre-Christian cultures.

There is a dicey *mise en abîme* of irony at work here that seems almost to defy grasp. I have argued that in "Coyote Holds a Full House in His Hand," Silko gives a special twist to the *style indirect libre*.[2] This narrative twist reverses the cold, patronizing, and condescending irony generated by the gap between the subjective point of view of the character and the so-called objective point of view of the third-person narrator and the interpretive community. The irony produced by the traditional Anglo-European *style indirect libre* easily lends itself to discrimination against race, class, and gender. Silko's matronizing irony in the Coyote story produces the erotic and warmly self-debunking humor characteristic of stories in which the trickster is both fool and culture hero. This irony warms, equalizes, and reduces discriminatory exclusion to a minimum. In *Almanac,* however, the gap between her own scribal point of view and the absolute knowledge that Silko implicitly ascribes to the "spiritual storyteller and narrator" (or to the multiple voodoo riding spirits), produces an irony that is even more dizzying than the ironizing of irony found in "Coyote Holds a Full House in His Hand." This is vatic irony. It turns the warm, matronizing, and equalizing irony of the looping Coyote narrative until it becomes frighteningly dry and dizzying, like the massive whirlwind that the Ghost Dance prophet, Wovoka, foretells carrying away all things non-Indian in *Gardens in the Dunes.* Silko, the scribe, like a character reading the prophetic book in which she figures, experiences the irony produced between her "subjective" point of view and the total perspective of the third-person "spiritual narrator and storyteller." Silko, who has compared the readers of *Almanac* to "bad kids" whom the Pueblos scare into correcting their behavior with an "ogre kachina" ("Narratives of

Survival" 111), scares herself with this massive book in which she can now read dicey things *it* wrote through her.

This vatic irony dries up the power of most of the male characters in *Almanac*. It does not equalize, but turns linear agency upon itself, dehydrating the corrupt, perverse, principally male oppressors, who are white, like Bartolomeo, the Cuban marxist, or who pretend to be white, like Menardo, the mestizo with the tell-tale Indian nose. Menardo, who denies his Indian blood, and thus refuses the power of the spirits and the stories told by his full-blood grandfather, shows signs of his dryness in his sexual life. His ejaculations are felt by Alegría to be "feeble" and "dry" (485). He ends up sacrificing his blood to the bulletproof vest that has been given to him by the Tucson mobster Max Blue. In sections entitled "Work of the Spirits" (502–4), "Miracle of High Technology," and "How Capitalists Die" (507–12), Menardo's story comes to an end that is pathetically bloody, humorous, and allegorical. He insists that his chauffeur, Tacho, El Feo's twin, shoot him in front of fellow members of his gun club. Menardo is wearing the bulletproof vest. Meant to be a joke to impress his powerful friends, this gesture of hubristic belief in Western technological potency both allegorizes the vulnerability of the narrative of Western superiority to the spirits and ironically mirrors the Ghost Dancers' pathetic belief in the allegedly bullet-proof shirts that they wore at Wounded Knee. Tacho has no need of special medicine as he carries out Menardo's blindly suicidal wish with his master's own pistol. The weave of the vest—the ultimate of contemporary Western technology—is penetrated by the 9 mm bullet, just as the weave of the Western narrative of Manifest Destiny is penetrated by the words of the old almanac. Menardo's blood, however, not only soaks the bulletproof vest but miraculously appears in Tacho's bundle as he is preparing to return to the mountains: "Tacho packed his clothes. As he prepared the canvas for the bedroll on the floor, he knelt in something wet and cool on the floor. Blood was oozing from the center of his bedroll where he kept the spirit bundle" (511). Spirit macaws communicate to Tacho the meaning of this blood: "Tacho felt he might lose consciousness, but outside the door hanging in the tree upside down, the big macaws were shrieking. The he-macaw told Tacho certain wild forces controlled all the Americas, and the saints and spirits and the gods of the Europeans were powerless on American soil" (511). Menardo's unintended self-sacrifice becomes an emblem of the coming disappearance of the white man in the Americas: "Tacho recalled the arguments people in villages had had over the eventual disappearance of the white man. Old prophets were adamant; the disappearance would not be caused by military action, necessarily, or by military action alone. The white man would someday disappear all by himself. The disappearance had already begun at the spiritual level" (511).

Power reversals in categories and roles belong to the ironic rhetoric and paradoxical logic of messianic and revolutionary writing in many cultures.[3] For Silko, the discerning reader should realize the impossibility of maintaining a politically liberal, humanist, individualist, and aesthetically modernist position similar to that of Sven Birkerts when faced with her text. In his review, Birkerts is not entirely unsympathetic with Silko's ideological antipathy toward the imperialist, capitalist individualism of the USA today and yesterday. But he offers only measured praise for her gifts as a storyteller, while judging both her crafting of this novel and the ideological vision that informs it to fall short. He objects in particular to the manner in which Silko has made the novel unreadable by putting in too many things and by stitching them together with quotations from the old book and notebooks that Yoeme passed on to Lecha and Zeta: "And running like a jagged stitch through these chapters are the extracts—many of them non-sensical—from the Almanac: 'Eight is the day called the Dog. Bloody pus pours from the ears of the dog,' etc" (352). Appealing to common sense and stylistic clarity, Birkerts refuses to imagine that, even with the counsel of spirit macaws and the visionary powers of a magic opal that bleeds, sweats, or urinates in Tacho's spirit bundle, the twin brothers' army could overthrow the U.S. government and Anglo-European culture: "[Silko's] premise of revolutionary insurrection is tethered to airy nothing. It is, frankly, naïve to the point of silliness. The appeal to prophecy cannot make up the common-sense deficit. While it is true that a great deal of fiction is an enactment of wish-fulfillment scenarios, it is also true that little of it is of the first order" (352). Ultimately Birkerts is probably looking for a stylistic minimalism and a secular ideology that does not leave him feeling as if he had stepped into a revival of multicultural Pentecostals handling snakes and speaking in tongues. Thus, he cannot but patronize Silko, condescending ironically to her revolutionary and allegedly apocalyptic worldview and telling her what she should do in order to see as he thinks she had seen in *Ceremony:* she should "prune and prune until her tree of the apocalypse stands in clear outline against the sky" (353).

Silko is aware that *Almanac* grew out of control during the ten years she spent writing it. She has suggested that the original English text is still stylistically in need of the loving editor's hand it found in her German translator: "[I]n 1994, I went to Germany to promote the German translation of *Almanac of the Dead,* which is more copyedited and more technically correct than the English version, because for my German translator, Bettina Munch, it was a labor of love" ("Listening to the Spirits" 165). This German woman is not a *traduttore/traditore* (translator/traitor). Perhaps it is ancient Germanic love of *Blut und Boden* that turns this Italian aphorism on its head. As a loving translator, Munch is not a traitor but a loyal discerning reader, disciple, copyeditor, and exegete who brings the text closer to that universal and aboriginal perfect language of which the book dreams and for which Silko more and more strongly yearns as her literary career unrolls. This is the language of the old almanac that Lecha and Zeta keep, transcribe, gloss, and translate.[4]

In *Almanac* Silko shows a growing awareness of the complex philosophical problems and rhetorical strategies involved in writing a book that she envisages as a translation and interpretation of prophetic pre- and postcontact Mayan writing. *Almanac* is the enactment of a wish-fulfillment scenario not only insofar as it prophesies the drying up from the inside of Western culture in the Americas and the retaking of the land by American Indians, but also insofar as it dreams of a pure and universal language that is material and spiritual truth itself. This language is not the language of justice; it is justice. *Almanac* is a gift to the reader that contains the encoded command that it be lovingly translated and passed on again and again. *Almanac of the Dead—Gardens in the Dunes* even more so— lends itself to being read not just as a novel about American culture, but as a text destined to produce not the apostasy but the syncretic melding of monotheist, individualist cultures of exclusion and hierarchy with pagan and animist cultures of inclusion and equality everywhere. This syncretism would effect a carnal and spiritual reversal of the exorcism performed by the orthodox Christ on the demoniac. Rather than casting out the "unclean spirit" (Mark 5:8), Silko calls out to that spirit, whose name is Legion, to enter into herself and her readers. She sees herself as a peer to the alternative Christs whom orthodox patriarchal Christianity suppressed and rejected as heretical. She is a messianic scribe, a mixed-blood Mary Magdalene figure whose writing functions as heretical gospel. Her novel of translation, glossing, and transcription is to be translated and glossed in all cultures and all languages, leading not to the end of time, but to the end of the Reign of Death-eye Dog. This novel is not apocalyptic in the Christian sense, for it does not point to the Last Judgment at the end of time, but to the recognition that time has no end.

Lecha's notebooks are first mentioned in the opening chapter entitled "Unanswered Questions." It would appear in this chapter that some of these questions, which are also for the most part only implicitly asked, could concern the notebooks that are very briefly described in third-person narration from the point of view of Seese. Seese, a sometime exotic dancer, prostitute, cocaine addict, and aggrieved mother, whom Lecha has hired to type her transcription of the notebooks into the word processor, does not appear to understand much about them. Nor does she understand the weird crew in the ranch house outside of Tucson where Lecha has brought her:

> Zeta runs the sink full of cold water to rinse the clothes she's dyed. She has been dyeing everything she wears dark brown. No reason, Zeta claims, just a whim. But Lecha had warned Seese not to be fooled. *Nothing happens by accident here.* The dark brown dye stains the white grout between the Mexican tiles patterned with blue, parrot-beaked birds trailing serpent tails of yellow flowers. Lecha's mysterious notebooks have drawings of parrot-beaked snakes and jaguar-headed men. Leave it to Zeta to have the kitchen counters redone with the Mexican tiles only two weeks before Lecha returned to transcribe the notebooks. (21; my emphasis)

Lecha's warning to Seese also serves to warn the readers that they should be on the lookout for significance in this and similar passages. If it is no accident that Zeta is dyeing everything brown, it is also no accident that she had the Mexican tiles installed shortly before Lecha returned. Likewise, it is no accident that the white grout is being stained brown. It is tempting to read this passage as a prefiguration of the principal plot of this novel in which a brown army led by Mayan twin brothers, one of whom is counseled by yellow and blue spirit macaws, marches north from southern Mexico to reclaim the Americas. As the interconnections between contemporary societal patterns and ancient Mayan pictographs and glyphic writing are revealed, the "grout" that holds these patterns together is turned from white to brown. Silko's book not only depicts the browning of the Americas, it also symbolically and materially embodies the browning of American writing and language.

Obviously the philosophy that informs Silko's desire for this revolutionary browning of the Americas is open to the charge of ethnocentrism and of being a native reflection of the white ideology that is the enemy. Janet St. Clair has dealt lucidly with this issue not only in *Almanac* but also in the writings of Paula Gunn Allen and Joy Harjo. St. Clair attempts to define the issue in terms of an ironic dilemma or paradox that arises in the contact zone between indigenous and Anglo-European cultures:

Each of the three authors seems caught in an ironic dilemma: in order to nurture and protect a dangerously attenuated but potentially liberating spiritual philosophy founded on inclusion, they must to some degree exclude those who threaten its resuscitation and resurgence. In order to justify the exclusion, they tend to shape white people into a monolithic personification of witchery and white values and institutions into monstrous perversion of human ideologies. There is, of course, much to support their chilling interpretations of Western history and tradition: each woman knows and tells true and ghastly stories of whites' outrages against tribal people and against their own humanity. . . . Silko's characters recount atrocities of European conquest so heinous that the reader's eyes veer off the page in horror. And yet . . . such Manichean extremes are false, and serve to falsify the premises of tribal religion by merely restructuring the hypocritical and self-righteous moral hierarchies for which whites are condemned. Indians, she recognizes, tread on as hazardous a ground as whites in identifying themselves as the chosen people. ("Uneasy Ethnocentrism" 90)

Despite this paradox and despite the absolutely horrendous characters who populate *Almanac*, St. Clair still finds "the novel is by no means without hope" ("Death of Love/Love of Death" 153). That hope, it turns out, is partly embodied in the old almanac, kept by Lecha and Zeta. This almanac, according to St. Clair, is "an ancient collation of sacred story abstracts" that "serves as a metaphor for the importance of memory—one of the central themes of Silko's first novel, *Ceremony*" (153). This is to say, the hope that readers found in Silko's first highly praised and widely read novel can be glossed in the Mayan writing and in the gloss on that writing. *Almanac of the Dead* glosses these imaginary texts that are alleged to contain prophecies of the arrival and the disappearance of the Europeans in the Americas: "But the prophecies of the Almanac are explicit: the blood-maddened male Death-Eye Dog will die; a renewed era of active spiritual and social community in the Americas

will ultimately prevail" (155). Whether the meaning of the prophecies is explicit is not as clear as St. Clair ultimately contends. The
paradox she signals as "uneasy ethnocentrism" may defy being
made perspicuous.[5]

One of the features of the notebooks and of the old book that
can be discerned in Yoeme's narrative (128–32) is that it is difficult
to know their true meaning. This is partly due to the code that has
been used to write or to explain the old book. It is also partly due
to the physical condition of the old book itself. As it and the notebooks have been passed from person to person for a period that
seems to span nearly five centuries, the book has become riddled
with lacunae. Yoeme tells Zeta that "the work that faced Lecha had
been made more difficult because from time to time, weakhearted
keepers of the old almanac had sold off pages here and there for
frivolous reasons" (128). When Yoeme received these writings, she
was requested to fill one of these lacunae that was quite recent.
This task is made more difficult because of the *code:*

> I have kept the notebooks and the old book since it was passed
> on to me many years ago. A section of one of the notebooks
> had accidentally been lost right before they were given to
> me. The woman who had been keeping them explained what
> the lost section had said, although of course it was all in *a
> code, so that the true meaning would not be immediately clear.* She
> requested that, if possible, at some time in my life I should
> write down a replacement section. (128; my emphasis)

It is not clear from her story whether Yoeme succeeds in fulfilling
the woman's request to write down a "replacement section" before
she passes the book and notebooks on to her granddaughters. This
lack of clarity is subtly increased by the unclear reference of the
pronoun *it* Yoeme uses: "I have thought about *it* all my life. The
problem has been the meaning of the lost section and for me to
find a way of replacing *it*. One naturally reflects upon one's own
experiences and feelings throughout one's life. The woman warned
that *it* should not be just any sort of words" (129; my emphasis).

To what does *it* refer in this passage? Is *it* anaphoric, referring back to the previous linguistic context, namely, writing down a replacement section? Is *it* cataphoric, referring ahead to the problem entailed in finding the "true meaning" of the lost section and writing a passage in code that conceals this meaning? Is *it* exophoric, referring outside the text to a situation or an object? This passage itself seems to be written in a code or a riddling mode that intentionally renders the referent of *it* ambiguous. Whatever the exact referent of *it* may be here, Yoeme connects her own life experiences with it.

Already the writing storyteller, as a third-person narrator in the opening chapter of *Almanac,* has stated that Lecha's task includes transcription. It would seem that Yoeme is unsure whether she has fulfilled the task passed on to her. Nevertheless, this task is passed on to Lecha and described in terms of exacting and encoded repairs: "I am telling you this because you must understand how carefully the old manuscript and its notebooks must be kept. Nothing must be added that was not already there. Only repairs are allowed, and one might live as long as I have and not find a suitable code" (129). Here, it appears that the code is necessary for encoding. Earlier, however, we saw that encoding and decoding seem to be entangled in the glossing and translation that the keepers of the almanac are requested to perform. Later in this chapter, after the narrative returns to the third person of the writing storyteller, it will become clear that the task is one of writing down what Yoeme has said, as well as translating and transcribing the old book and notebooks. This brings up the intriguing possibility that the lacuna about which Yoeme spent her life thinking includes the story of Indians having been chased and hanged from cottonwoods, as well as the Geronimo story that she tells Zeta and Lecha, as well as the story of her telling these stories to her granddaughters. Perhaps passing the old book and notebooks on to Zeta and Lecha as well as telling them stories connected with these writings fulfills the request to fill the lacuna, but at the same time produces another lacuna to be filled. An analogue to this textual lacuna shows up in the inner emptiness of some of the characters.[6]

Having mentioned the problem of repairing the lacuna, Yoeme seemingly digresses to the image of Indians bloodlessly massacred by the Mexican army. This image obsesses her: "I must always return to what the white men kept hanging in all the lovely cottonwood trees along the rivers and streams throughout this land. Swaying in the light wind, rags of clothing flapping the shrunken limbs into motion. They try to walk, they try to walk—the feet keep reaching long after the neck is broken or the head has choked" (129). In this grotesque scene reminiscent perhaps of a mural by Diego Rivera, skeletal Indian mummies march in airy nothing, perhaps prefiguring the twin brothers' brown army that is marching north through the novel.

Then, as if by free association—but nothing is an accident in this novel—Yoeme goes on to a Geronimo story: "They [the American soldiers who accidentally were killed by Mexican soldiers] were all hunting the Apaches running with the man they called Geronimo. *That was not his name.* No wonder there has been so much confusion among white people and their historians. The man encouraged the confusion. He has been called a medicine man, but that title is misleading. He was a man who was able to perform certain feats" (129; my emphasis). This story, and a longer version of it told (in chapters entitled "Mistaken Identity" and "Old Pancakes" 224–32) by multiple narrators to Zeta's partner in the smuggling business, Calabazas, take up and toy with not only the U.S. Army expeditions led by Generals Crook and Miles with the purpose of capturing Geronimo and putting an end to Apache raids, but also the story of Silko's Marmon ancestors who led the Marmon battalion in the Apache campaigns of the 1880s. In these Geronimo stories Silko is rewriting in a postmodernist mode "A Geronimo Story" from *Storyteller*.[7]

I would like to turn to the story of Yoeme's mixed-blood marriage and the Indians hanging in the cottonwoods and weave this narrative thread back around to the old almanac. The imagery in this mixed-blood family story links Western writing and science with meaninglessness, imbecility, weakness, blood, disease, emptiness, desiccation, and cannibalism. In other words, the lacunae that riddle

the old almanac and notebooks have as counterparts the emptiness described in some of the characters. The father of Lecha and
Zeta, the German mining engineer who remains unnamed in the
narrative, Amalia, their mother, and Zeta herself all experience an
emptiness.

Amalia's inner emptiness manifests itself as consumptive pain:
"'Yes, she [Yoeme] is my mother, although I do not remember her
very well.' Amalia had clasped both hands to her stomach because
the pain had come again. The twins had jumped back, in awe of
the pain. Yoeme had told them the pain was actually a jaguar that
devoured a live human from the inside out. Pain left behind only the
skin and bones and hair" (115–16). This pain devouring Amalia's
innards can be read from a Western cultural point of view as consumption, or more precisely in the terminology of modern medicine,
as tuberculosis. Told from Yoeme's point of view, this pain is a
ravenous jaguar.[8] Amalia's being consumed by this jaguar from
inside out is associated here with the mixed feelings that she, the
daughter of a white man and an Indian woman, has about her mixed
blood. The pain makes itself felt when Amalia avows what she has
hidden from her twin daughters before the arrival of old Yoeme,
namely that the old Indian is their grandmother, and thus that she
and they are part Indian.

It seems that blood will tell in this tale, but what it will tell is
maddeningly hard to tell. After her arrival, Yoeme has been taunting
her feeble mixed-blood children by calling them her own "flesh and
blood" (115). This causes the children, who shun her and who have
locked themselves in the house, to shriek madly. She has also been
teasing Zeta and Lecha by vaguely threatening them with what
appears to be a taboo on twins in Yaqui culture.[9] The reaction she
gets allows her to differentiate both between her weak-minded
grandchildren and her twin granddaughters, and between the "identical" twins themselves:

Yoeme teased the girls, telling them she had advised their
mother to get rid of one or the other of them right away. Twins

were considered by some to be bad luck. If she had been
around then, Yoeme said she would have taken care of the
problem. She had watched both girls' faces for reactions. Zeta
had asked, "Me or her?" and Lecha had said, "You kill me
when I'm a baby and they'll hang you!" which had caused
Yoeme to clap her hands together and laugh until their mother
had come out to see what was the matter. (115)

Yoeme's clapping and laughter might seem to be signs of her madness, but they also point to the old woman's method that allows her
to discern how Lecha and Zeta differ. On the one hand, Zeta's question, "Me or her?" could be read to suggest indecision, vacillation,
even weakness, traits that seem to characterize her kinfolk in the
Guzman family. Or, Zeta's either/or question could also be read to
suggest an attitude that is more coolly objective, exclusionary, and
intellectual than emotional. On the other hand, Lecha's unequivocal
threat, which incidentally folds the past and the present together,
as if Yoeme still had the power to kill her granddaughter as a baby,
demonstrates intelligence, decisiveness, and emotional strength.
Yoeme laughs because she has detected this strength in her granddaughter, because it so contrasts with the Guzmans and because
it will enable her granddaughter to stand out from the rest of her
old white grandfather's weak-willed, feeble-minded, and cowardly
breed.

Yoeme wins the attention of the twins. Rather than shunning her
like their dim-witted cousins, they are attracted to her. Having heard
from their mother that their grandmother left her children because
of "cottonwood trees," Lecha and Zeta ask their grandmother to
explain. Yoeme relates a story of how "the fucker Guzman, your
grandfather, sure loved trees" (116). Her story not only illustrates
the incompatibility between herself and her husband and his family,
it also suggests a fundamental incompatibility between Yaqui tribal
culture and the legal system that was transplanted from Europe
into the Americas. At the root of this cultural incompatibility lies
the concept of justice. For the Yaqui, at least as Yoeme exemplifies

her people, justice cannot be dissociated from the earth, which is conceived as a loving mother, who nurtures her creatures, who in turn nurture her. White justice, it can be argued, is not only blind, it is desiccating and indifferent. It does not nurse or mother. It is not loving. It is analytic and unemotional. It is structured somewhat like Dante's *contra-passo*, whereby the sinners in Hell configure their sins as punishment. Take the example of cannibalism, a "sin" that is figured in *Almanac* in the episode of the spiderlike woman at "The Mouth." Count Ugolino, who ate his own children while imprisoned and starved in a tower, is punished in the *Inferno* (canto 33) by being made to gnaw on the skull of his enemy who had him imprisoned. Ugolino's punishment both repeats his sin and serves eternally to punish the sinner who forced him to indulge in cannibalism. This act of the damned furthermore is a parody of the Eucharist, the sacrament whereby the divine judge offers salvation to those sinners whom he also finds guilty. Thus, white justice is both otherworldly and this-worldly, both secular and religious. It is a matter of using words referring to words to manipulate things so that one might be able to give nothing, or next to nothing, in return for everything. White justice, from Yoeme's point of view, is identical with injustice.[10] I will support this reasoning in the reading of the motifs of desiccation and emptiness that follows.

At both the beginning and the end of this story, the question is asked why Guzman had his thirsting Indian slaves uproot cotton-wood trees from the banks of the Rio Yaqui, transport them for hundreds of miles, and transplant them around his mines and his house. As a child Yoeme had seen hanging in these beautiful cotton-woods the desiccated bodies of Indians, her clanspeople, she was told, though she could not recognize the faces because "'[t]hey had all dried up like jerky'" (118). When Yoeme decided to leave "that fucker Guzman and his weak children" (118), she had all the cottonwoods cut down or girdled by three Indian gardeners who fled with her and whom she had paid off with the silver she took from Guzman's safe.

Yoeme's story is not related in a strictly linear mode. It snakes around, moving from place to place, time to time. It is helpful to a reading of this story to construct from it a historical as well as a personal progression. The periods in both of these progressions are marked by different legally defined states: First, there is the historical period of legal slavery, which, of course, began with conquistadors such as Nuño de Guzman, the genocidal butcher who is a possible literary namesake if not the ancestor of Yoeme's husband. This period is followed by another in which slavery is no longer legal. Overlapping these two historical periods there is a personal progression marked by Guzman's life. Within it there are three periods: bachelorhood, matrimony, and separation. The legal status of this last personal period remains unclear. Guzman's marriage also marks a regional, historical subperiod in which Yaqui tribal culture and white legal culture are interwoven by an agreement.

Before slavery was made illegal, the Guzmans, on economic grounds alone, might have been expected to take care of their Indian slaves, but they were not legally bound to do this. Thus, if the slave masters wanted to remain indifferent to their Indians' most basic needs, this was a matter of personal choice, perhaps economically unsound but not legally actionable. Guzman's indifference to these needs emerges in the story of the cottonwoods. This indifference can be characterized as dry, insofar as he literally refused to give the slaves water in return for their labor: "The heat was terrible. All water went to the mules or to the saplings. The slaves were only allowed to press their lips to the wet rags around the tree roots" (116).

In the hierarchy of beings that implicitly informs this colonizing culture of the New World, Guzman's aqueous parsimony places the Indians below beasts of burden and suggests that they might even be considered inferior to the uprooted trees whose rag-wrapped roots they must nurse for water. Like the legal system, like Guzman, the trees have been transplanted. Just as the Indians are forced to suck water from the barely moist rags covering the tree roots, so they are forced to suck justice and life from the fabric of a desiccating legal system. Like Guzman, who gives nothing in return to his slaves for their labor in the mines and nothing in return to the earth for the silver taken from it, the transplanted trees give nothing in return for the water they take from the earth. Some of those slaves "did nothing but carry water to those trees" (116).

After slavery has been made illegal, which would suggest that the status of Indians should have been raised in the hierarchy of beings at least to just above the status of beasts of burden, Guzman gives even less to the Indians in return. Unless one could consider the beauty of the trees and his words praising that beauty to be what he gives in recompense: "'What beauties!' Guzman used to say. By then they had no more 'slaves.' They simply had Indians who worked like slaves but got even less than slaves had in the old days" (116).

Needless to say, from Yoeme's point of view, the injustice in the second period is even greater than in the first, since slavery, despite having been outlawed, continues de facto, now masquerading as freedom, and the former slaves nurse at even drier roots.

When more white men start to come into the area of Guzman's mines and hacienda, the peace deteriorates. The Yaqui seek an agreement with Guzman whereby both parties would benefit in an exchange. Zeta and Lecha have just asked again why Yoeme and the Guzmans fought over trees: "'Hold your horses, hold your horses,' Yoeme had said. 'They had been killing Indians right and left. It was war! It was white men coming to find more silver, to steal more Indian land. It was white men coming with their pieces of paper! To make their big ranches. Guzman and my people had made an agreement. Why do you think I was married to him? For fun? For love? Hah! To watch, to make sure he kept the agreement'" (116). This agreement, for which Yoeme is supposed to be the "security" that the Yaqui give in return for being protected against the warring white land thieves, enables the establishment of a mixed culture, in which white law and tribal custom overlap, with the apparent goal of coming up with a concept of justice compatible to both parties. From the perspective of white law, Guzman and Yoeme's family become in-laws. From the perspective of Yaqui custom, Guzman and Yoeme's tribe are bound within the tribal kinship system. In a sense, since Yoeme is the Yaqui word with which the Yaqui name themselves, Guzman becomes the spouse and the in-law of the tribe. For this agreement to work, Guzman must enforce the law that ensures that he is the proprietor of the land that his ancestors and he had already taken from the Yaqui and mined. This enforcement would require litigation: the white men who pour in are said to have "pieces of paper" that are probably grants or deeds to the ranch lands they want to grab. Even if Guzman could win decisions in court rendering the white men's pieces of paper null and void, he would still have to resort to armed force to keep these white men from breaking the law by taking his and his Yaqui in-laws' land. At this point irony twists the character given the name of Guzman. Yoeme's husband does not have the brutal and aggressive character of his bloodthirsty conquistador namesake, yet his lack of desire to inflict suffering results in suffering.

The law can be understood as cleverly designed to make some of the human traits that it attempts to regulate (e.g., greed, aggressiveness, sexual desire, desire for power) also the source of the energy that drives its application and enforcement. Guzman, however, despite having been a slave owner, is apparently neither aggressive nor greedy. He wants neither power nor wealth. He is basically a nonviolent, order-loving, beauty-loving, peace-loving, and law-abiding weakling. Within him there is none of the vital energy, curiosity, and belligerent spirit of competition that drove many of the conquistadors; rather, there is an emptiness. This emptiness is expressed in terms of cowardice, physical and sexual weakness, and, paradoxically, living death:

> But Guzman had been only a *gutless*, walking corpse, not a real man. He had been unwilling to stand up to the other white men streaming into the country. "He was always saying he only wanted to 'get along.'" "Killing my people, my relatives who were only traveling down here to visit me! It was time that I left. Sooner or later those long turds would have ridden up with their rifles, and Guzman would have played with his wee-wee while they dragged me away." (116–17; my emphasis)

Guzman's weakness appears to be passed on to most of his children. For that reason, says Yoeme in answer to Zeta's question about how she could leave her children, she easily made up her mind to leave them, and also because her in-laws hated her because she was an Indian:

> "But your children," Zeta said.
> "Oh, I could already see. Look at your mother right now. Weak thing. It was not a good match—Guzman and me. You understand how it is with horses and dogs—sometimes children take after the father. I saw that." (117)

Lecha brings the story back to the trees, which is to say back around to the question of why Guzman had the trees transplanted in the first place and why Yoeme had them destroyed. From Guzman's point of view, the purpose of the trees seems to be mainly aesthetic. From Yoeme's teleological perspective, despite their beauty the trees were transplanted to be gibbets. These trees occasioned Guzman's cruel and dry indifference to the Indian slaves' thirst when they were transplanted, thereby interrupting the motherly relationship between trees, people, and water:

> Oh yes, those trees! How terrible what they did with the trees. Because the cottonwood suckles like a baby. Suckles on the mother water running under the ground. A cottonwood will talk to the mother water and tell her what human beings are doing. But then these white men came and they began digging up the cottonwoods and moving them here and there for a terrible purpose. (117)

The trees serve as bullet-saving gibbets on which the empty Guzman allows his Indian in-laws to be hanged and "dried up like jerky" (118). Here, the term "jerky" reflects the theme of cannibalism, which will be taken up below. The great chain of being, in which the Indians are positioned by whites like Guzman only to nourish beautiful cottonwoods, can also be rephrased as the economic metaphor of the food chain in which it is, as the capitalist aphorism has it, a dog-eat-dog world.

Already, from Yoeme's story, it is apparent that Guzman values the trees more than the lives of the human beings hanging from them. Likewise, it should be obvious from a postmodern liberal perspective, as well as from Yoeme's perspective, that legal justice is problematic, if not impossible, in a culture in which a white man can decide the life of a tree is more valuable than human life and remain legally unimpeachable. For this reason, Yoeme's having Guzman's beloved trees killed by three gardeners rather than killing Guzman and his feeble brood allows her to obtain something that resembles justice in some ways, yet in other ways bears the marks of vengeance. There is a clever ironic twist within Yoeme's perspective: it is just that she should take the silver that Guzman has robbed from the earth and give it to the three Indian gardeners who help her kill the trees and then flee to their villages:

> Fortunately, while the foreman was rushing to the big house to question the orders, the gardeners had been smart enough to girdle the remaining trees. Yoeme had paid them to run off with her, since in the mountains their villages and her village were nearby. She had cleaned out Guzman's fat floor safe under the bed where she had conceived and delivered seven disappointing children. It was a *fair exchange,* she said, winking at the little girls, who could not imagine how much silver that had been. Enough silver that the three gardeners had been paid off. (118; my emphasis)

This "fair exchange," about which Yoeme histrionically winks to her granddaughters, is at least double: First, the silver pays the three gardeners not only for killing the trees, but also for the uncompensated labor they and other Indians have been performing for Guzman. Second, in taking the silver from the "fat floor safe" under the marriage bed where her "seven disappointing children" were conceived and born, Yoeme can be read as taking recompense for the time, sex, and labor she gave as Guzman's wife. Just as Mother Earth gave up silver without being paid back, so Yoeme gave up children. By robbing the safe, she recompenses herself and changes her status from that of legal wife to that of concubine or whore. The wink she directs at her granddaughters signals her amusement, her lack of shame or guilt at revealing the marriage to be merely a "business" arrangement in which she played/turned a "trick" on/ for "that fucker Guzman."

Thus, in doing "one of the best things" (118) that she has ever done, Yoeme inflicts on Guzman a vindictive loss that—assessed from his perspective—is greater by far than the loss of human life and greater than the loss of silver. For him, the latter loss is easily forgiven owing to the ongoing plunder of the earth. The loss of the trees, however, is expressed by a verb usually employed metaphorically to designate human massacre and literally to designate the bloody slaughter of animals for food. It would appear that as far as Guzman is concerned, such a loss can be neither recompensed nor forgiven:

> Guzman had later claimed that he did not mind the loss of the silver, which a week's production could replace. But Guzman had told Amalia and the others their mother was *dead* to them and forever unwelcome in that house because she had *butchered* all the big cottonwood trees. He could never forgive that.
>
> The twins were solemn. (118; my emphasis)

In some ways Guzman's reaction helps accomplish Yoeme's curious combination of justice and vengeance. In declaring Yoeme "dead" to her children, Guzman only "kills" her in words, not in fact. It is not even clear that he can legally set aside his wife; thus, the verbal act whereby he banishes Yoeme ironically fulfills her own intention of turning herself into his former concubine, thereby problematizing post hoc the legitimacy of his children. Furthermore, by "killing" Yoeme in words, he paradoxically achieves one of the goals of justice, which is to prevent aggrieved parties from entering into a growing spiral of reciprocal violence and vindictive bloodshed. From the point of view of the Western jurist or judge, Guzman's indifference to the hanging of his Indian in-laws is no cause to indict or to forgive him. Quite literally, he did *nothing*. In the case of Yoeme's having "humanely" wreaked just vengeance on her weak husband by "butchering" the living gibbets he loved and by cleaning out his floor safe, his inability to forgive will not result in the spiral of increasing reciprocal vindictive violence, but will only serve to make the gutless nonviolent nonresister to violence even weaker. Hiding in Guzman's love of trees, in his "'always saying that he just wanted to 'get along'" (117), is a love of abstract order and *nothingness*.

Having told this story to the twins, Yoeme is asked by Lecha to clarify her having teasingly threatened them with the taboo on twins. In this passage the themes of blood lineage, justice or the impossibility thereof, and inner nothingness are woven together in the image of birth as Amalia vomits blood on hearing that she has lost her daughters to her mother:

> "But you wanted to get rid of one of us." Lecha had let go of Yoeme's hand in order to say this.
> The old woman had stopped and looked at both of them. "I wanted to have one of you for myself," she said.
> "But you didn't get one of us."
> "No." Yoeme had let out a big sigh. "I didn't even get *one* of you. Your poor mother was too dumb for that. And now do you see what I have?"
> The twins had looked at each other to avoid the piercing eyes of old Yoeme.
> Yoeme laughed loudly. "I have you both!" she said in triumph, and from the bedroom inside they could hear their mother fumble for the enamel basin to vomit blood. (119)

Here symbolically and literally Yoeme "gets" twins who will bring her concept of justice closer by keeping, transcribing, translating, and glossing the old almanac. Amalia's consumption, her self-consumption from the inside out, the emptiness left as the jaguar devours her, her pain, results in the birthlike regurgitation of blood as Lecha and Zeta are "rebirthed" as Indians by their midwiving old granny. In this tale of Yoeme's return—her name is the name by which the Yaqui call themselves—it is Yoeme's blood that tells. There are muted echoes here of human sacrifice, which was practiced by the Maya and which could be encoded in the old almanac that Yoeme passes on to her granddaughters.

Lecha and Zeta's father, unlike their grandfather, is never called by his name. He is a geologist, but unlike his father-in-law, "that fucker Guzman" who "really loved trees," he appears to end up loving nothing. Not rocks, not science, not his daughters, not his wife, not even himself. As a geologist he is a scientific reader of the land, but this reading, which he has transcribed into geological maps, designates nothing: "The rumors and reports had arrived in Canenea that while the mining engineer could still name the formations and the ore-bearing stones and rocks, and could recite all of the known combinations for that particular area, his calculations on the maps for known deposits had been wrong; he had directed the miners to *nothing*" (120; my emphasis). Curiously, rather than being an undiscerning reader, he seems to be among the most discerning. His scientific method and knowledge appear accurate as verified by other readers of this map and of the earth: "When other geologists had been called to evaluate his projections and the samples and assay results, they could find no fault with his work. They could not account for the absence of ore in the depths and areas he had designated. They had of course been reluctant to pass judgment upon a 'brother'; the geologists had discussed at length the 'scientific anomaly'" (120). Yoeme, however, has an explanation for this "scientific anomaly," for this arid geologist without a name whose map designates nothing and who belongs to a brotherhood who find themselves reluctant to judge, to decide. For her it is no anomaly at all; rather, it follows rules of teleological cause and effect that any discerning reader should be able follow. From her perspective there is no undecidability: the mapmaker and mapped have become identical to the map: "Yoeme said the veins of silver had dried up because their father, the mining engineer himself, had dried up. Years of dry winds and effects of the sunlight on milky-white skin had been devastating. Suddenly the man had dried up inside, and although he still walked and talked and reasoned like a man, inside he was crackled, full of the dry molts of insects. So their silent father had been ruined and *everybody* had blamed Yoeme" (120; my emphasis).

Well, nearly everybody had blamed Yoeme, except Zeta and Lecha who have been intuitively reading by Yoeme's rules since they were young. According to these rules, the discerning reader foregrounds the emotional rather than the intellectual in order to sense the truth: "But Lecha and Zeta had *sensed the truth* years earlier. They had both felt it when they walked with him and he had lifted them into his arms: somewhere within him there was, arid and shriveled, the *imperfect vacuum* he called himself " (120; my emphasis). Here, sensing "truth" is synonymous with feeling the "imperfect vacuum" that is the self of this anonymous geologist. Other readers of this scientific anomaly, the nonscientists who blame Yoeme, are even less discerning. Yoeme debunks their readings with even more contempt than the discussions of the undecided geologists: "Yoeme had been contemptuous of the innuendos about witchcraft. What did these stupid mestizos—half no-brain white, half worst kind of Indian—what did these last remnants of wiped-out tribes littering the earth, what did they know?" (121). Similar to Tacho, who shoots Menardo at his request, Yoeme need neither speak spells nor use medicine here. What happens to her daughter's husband can be described in terms of Western scientific knowledge or by a knowledge of natural telluric justice that comprises and transcends scientific knowledge:

> Yoeme had not wasted a bit of energy on Amalia's ex-husband. The geologist had been perfectly capable of destroying himself. His ailment had been common among those who had gone into caverns of fissures in the lava formations; the condition had also been seen in persons who had been revived from drowning in a lake or spring with an entrance to the four worlds below this world. The victim never fully recovered and exhibited symptoms identical to those of the German mining engineer. Thus, Yoeme had argued, witchcraft

was not to blame. The white man had violated the Mother Earth, and he had been stricken with the sensation of a gaping emptiness between his throat and heart. (121)

Here an apparent form of radiation sickness, caused by exposure to radiation from underground, is understood as Mother Earth's justice on the rapists. The geologists' Western scientific reading, however, which arrives at undecidability, is depicted as meaningless. Without the teleological Indian reading, the Western understanding of this phenomenon is similar to the lack of understanding and of knowledge that characterizes the consciousness of the damned in Dante's Hell. The scientific reading simply describes in redundant terms the just aridity and gaping emptiness. Meaning can come only from understanding this empty aridity through Indian eyes as the justly dry injustice that Western culture has called on to define itself.

At this point the writing storyteller, who does not follow a linear progression but snakes around temporally, mentions that Zeta, but apparently not Lecha, shares this inner emptiness with her father, mother, and grandfather: "Zeta could feel an empty space inside her rib cage, an absence that had been growing even before their mother died. She felt a peculiar sadness when she remembered their father, the detached white man who smiled and spoke and who was a dead man already" (121). This empty space within Zeta, like the question she posed to Yoeme in regard to the teasing about getting rid of one of the twins, suggests that, like her mother, she could also consume herself over her mixed-blood status. Her self-consumption, however, does not so much overlap with her mother's pain caused by tuberculosis and coinciding with her desire to vomit up her Indian blood, as with her father's metaphysical emptiness. When first sent to Tucson after her mother's death, Zeta appears to want to study her father: "Zeta had hoped she might be with her father long enough to learn something more about the emptiness inside her" (121). This geologist, who rather than being an erudite of the earth is an erudite of nothingness, has already made meaningless arrangements to send his daughters to a boarding school in El

Paso run by Catholic nuns. He regrets this, for, as he tells his daughters, "he thought God was of no use" (121). How "fitting" for the man riddled by nothingness to send his daughters off to be schooled by those who believe in God, that is to say, from his point of view, those who believe in nothing.

While waiting three days for the train, Zeta and Lecha have a chance to observe the strange behavior of their quiet and almost emotionless father, who leaves them as their inheritance a piece of earth. This small ranch, he tells them, is "worth next to *nothing*" (124; my emphasis). He leaves undecided whether this ranch is something or nothing: "I did not buy it for ranching. Eighty acres isn't enough to raise anything. But, I suppose, it is something. Or maybe it isn't" (124). To be understood, this piece of earth that Zeta and Lecha inherit from their nameless geologist and father must be read through their inheritance from Yoeme, the old almanac and the notebooks that are infused with their Indian blood, but which, as Yoeme repeatedly points out, are also riddled with lacunae.

Zeta and Lecha's attempt to understand their father's behavior is informed by images in which fullness and emptiness fluctuate. Zeta, owing perhaps to her own inner emptiness, is ultimately better able to detect the nothingness that she and Lecha had taken for fullness in their father:

> Zeta had tried to guess what it was that *filled* their father's head so *full*. She began to awaken before dawn and hear small muffled sounds—the creak of a chair, the opening of a drawer—sounds of a man who no longer slept. He had not invited them to his room. Lecha wanted to see because she thought the clues might be there. She had ruled out women and love affairs immediately, but confided that strange philosophies or religions might be responsible. Zeta had felt a surge of anger in her chest at Lecha's stupidity. "It isn't *anything*. There's *nothing*. You won't find *anything*," she snapped as Lecha had started for his room. (122; my emphasis)

Rather than strange philosophies or religions, the nothing that Zeta suddenly realizes "fills" their father's thoughts will turn out to be the alienation and dryness that inform Western philosophy and science. Zeta's feelings, which center in her chest, are contrasted with Lecha's vision, or rather with her failure to see what is going on in this scene. Lecha continues to want to see what can only be "seen" paradoxically as nothingness. She starts walking in circles, symbolic perhaps of the philosophical whirligig in which her father's and her thoughts turn at this moment:

> When he had opened the door, Zeta saw he did not recognize them immediately. Lecha was looking past him into the room and did not see this. Zeta felt her heart fall in her chest. The bed had not been slept in. The pillows and spread had not been touched since the hotel maid. The black wire hangers in the closet nook were empty. He had been sitting at the small desk. The desk top was bare, although for an instant Zeta had mistaken cigarette scars along the edges for a pattern of decoration. "Where is *everything*?" Lecha said, walking around and around the small room impatiently. Their father had turned as if he suffered from stiffness in the neck and shoulders. He had begun to hunch under long, unkempt white hair. They had always spoken English with him since he had never been able to learn Spanish. But Lecha had had to repeat the question twice before he could answer. "*Everything?*" he had said in a steady voice. "I am trying to think about *it*," he had answered. (122; my emphasis)

This scene of questions and apparently confused answers can be interpreted from Yoeme's perspective or from a Western scientific point of view, or from a dialectical combination of the two. From the Indian point of view, the father's death is natural telluric justice; having believed in nothing and understood nothing, like the rest of the white men who came to the Americas, he becomes nothing. Using the diagnostic of medical science, Zeta and Lecha's father can be diagnosed both as suffering from radiation sickness and as being incipiently senile, possibly in the early stages of Alzheimer's disease. One need not be a physician to recognize the signs. They are there for the discerning reader who has been around the aging: He has difficulty recognizing his own daughters. His desires are attenuated. He registers minimal affect. He is beginning to forget to eat and drink. He stares into empty space. He wants only to sit silently in his nearly empty room, doing nothing, thinking about everything, that is, about nothing, becoming more and more confused all the time: "The farewell at the train station had been brief. Staring past them into the distance their father had announced, 'You will never see me again. I am going to die. My life has never interested me much. I think about myself and this room. The longer I think the less I understand'" (121–22).

The text can also be read as a dialectic, the dialectic that Larry McMurtry signals in his review of the novel: In the life of the dying and demented mining engineer, Western culture meets Indian culture. The father arrives at the logical, epistemological, and ontological conclusion of modern Western thought. His desiccation and emptiness testify to how the Anglo-European analytic philosophy of rugged individualism, empiricism, logical positivism, and arid scientific objectivity—the philosophy that informs the secular side of Manifest Destiny—when put into contact with holistic, spiritual, telluric Indian culture, leads to a subversion of Western knowledge: "The longer I think the less I understand." The father's sitting in the hotel room thinking about everything until there is nothing left but dry dust figures the deconstruction of the Cartesian cogito: "I think, therefore I am or maybe I am not," are the silent words to be read in the father's hotel room.[11]

The description of the father's death is a very strange passage:

The note he left had said simply, "*This* should have been done years ago." He had done "*it*" in *this* room. The mother superior refused to give them any details. The relatives at the big house in Potam had known nothing of his death until months later when Lecha told them. Zeta had to smile at the mystery. Her father had not used a necktie or belt. Zeta had searched old county records to know. The report said he had simply sat at his chair not eating or drinking. *It had been as if he had consumed himself.* When he had been discovered by the hotel maid, he was not a swollen corpse, nor was there a terrible odor. He had been as dry and shriveled as a cactus blown down in a drought. Zeta had laughed: "He sounds like one of those saints that don't decay!" The report noted the condition of the corpse had been *somewhat unusual.* The corpse had begun to mummify, possibly, the coroner had theorized, because of the dry summer heat and the circumstances of the death. The report included autopsy results. *Zeta could not make much of the technical notations,* but the coroner's assistant had noted the deceased's body weight. "All that was left of him was fifty pounds," Zeta told Lecha later. (123; my emphasis)

To begin with, the exact cause of death appears to be left undecided. From the point of view of Western science, this paragraph seems to turn endlessly in undecidability. The pronoun "this" in the note left would appear to refer to the note writer's "suicide," if this is the just term to designate what occurred. The word "suicide" does not appear anywhere in the text. The pronoun "it" also would appear to have the same referent in this second sentence. The pronoun "this" modifying "room" in this second sentence is somewhat odd. One would expect to find "that room" rather than "this room." The use of "this" to modify "room" suggests that the sentence is thought, spoken or written by a person in the room in question. This person could be the third-person narrator. Or this person could be Zeta, since in the two paragraphs that precede the paragraph quoted above, Zeta is said to have repeatedly returned to rent "this" room in which she appeared to imitate her father's odd behavior:

Zeta had never forgotten the room. She had gone back, years later, to the desk clerk at the Santa Rita Hotel, to ask if she might look at a certain room on the third floor. She had been dressed in her business suit, hose, and heels carrying her briefcase. She could not remember the room number and had to take the elevator up to find it. The desk clerk had informed her the room was already taken.

But she had returned, and from time to time she rented
Room 312. She did not care what the clerk or bellboy thought.
She spent afternoons sitting at the desk. The wall behind the
desk had been plastered and painted many times. *She sat and
stared at it and was soothed by the emptiness.* (123; my emphasis)

It would appear that in "this room" Zeta is attempting to figure
out the "mystery" of this death. In other words, she is attempting
to perform an autopsy, that is, to see for herself and in herself the
cause of death. Why does she smile at this mystery? How and why
does the emptiness sooth her? In a sense she is letting the soothing
emptiness "father" her. She is carrying out her earlier project of
learning more about the emptiness inside herself.

The mother superior's refusal to give the sisters details could be
interpreted as motivated by propriety or decorum: It would have
been improper to refer explicitly to the "insanity" or the "suicide"
of the bereaved orphans' father, as well as to go into the details of
such a shameful sin. Or the mother superior may not have had
any details. Or the mother superior may have known details that
suggested that this "mystery" was not a suicide but something
occult about which a God-fearing nun dare not speak.

Why is Zeta said not to care what the "clerk or bellboy thought"?
What do they think? That the room is in some way polluted by the
odd death or suicide, that the room is haunted, that it is "dicey" to
rent this room? One can only speculate about the answers to these
questions. That speculation resembles staring at a blank wall.

Zeta researches the mystery of her father's death. She learns he
"had not used a necktie or belt" to do it. Indeed, it would seem
that the verb "to do," which is used in the past tense in the first
two sentences of the description, is not exactly apposite, for paradoxically "to do it" he appears to have *done nothing:* "The report
said he had simply sat at his chair not eating or drinking" (123).
So, if there is an act involved in this strange death, it is an act to
negate itself as act. It is an act of will neither to eat nor to drink, an
act of will to negate desire, an act of will to negate volition, and

thereby to negate one's self. This "self" has already been likened to the "imperfect vacuum he called himself" (120). In a sense, "to do it" the father made a gibbet of his self, which is to say, of almost nothing.

Thus, the pronoun "this" in the father's note refers to an aporia similar to that of a cartoon dragon sucking up its own tail and impossibly passing from this self-consumption into imperfect nothingness: "It had been *as if* he had consumed himself" (123). This aporia points questioningly at two acts the taboos of which inform Judeo-Christian culture: cannibalism and suicide. Does one violate both of these taboos by consuming oneself in such a fashion? Does one violate the taboo on suicide by dying by doing nothing?[12] And yet this most minimal act of will imaginable is an act of nearly total asceticism, of nearly total self-denial, self-sacrifice. There are no signs of carnality, such as the terrible odor of rotting flesh. There are even hints that this may be a miracle, rather than the unspeakable work of the Devil that can be inferred from the mother superior's refusal to give details: "Zeta had laughed: 'Sounds like one of those saints that don't decay!'" (123). There are hints that this, like the deceased father's geographical map that designates nothing, could be another example of a scientific anomaly: "The report noted the condition of the corpse had been somewhat unusual" (123). The coroner cannot determine, cannot decide the cause; he can only theorize in a way that hints at mysterious non-Western burial practices: "The corpse had begun to *mummify*, possibly, the coroner had theorized, because of the dry summer heat and the circumstances of the death" (123; my emphasis). Ultimately the autopsy is comprised of writing that is meaningless to Zeta, including a measurement of a seemingly puzzling empirical fact that Zeta repeats to Lecha: "The report included autopsy results. Zeta could not make much of these technical notations, but the coroner's assistant had noted the deceased's body weight. 'All that was left of him was fifty pounds,' Zeta told Lecha later" (123). These ciphered notations, as well as the "cipher" giving the deceased's body weight, are meaningless unless read from the perspective of Yoeme's telluric justice.

In this passage, Western science, technology, and analytic philosophy, which cannot but ultimately arrive at a dry imperfect nihilism, is mocked as a metaphorical mummy.

Peeking between the lines of this scene of self-consumption is the theme of cannibalism, which shows up in other chapters entitled "Journey of the Ancient Almanac" (245–53), "Village of Sorcerers and Cannibals" and "The Opal" (476–81), and "Mr. Fish the Cannibal" (533–35). As "Journey of the Ancient Almanac" quietly makes clear, cannibalism is one of the notorious behaviors found in the Reign of Death-eye Dog. In *Almanac* persons of both indigenous and European blood indulge in it. Indeed, indigenous cannibalism is said to pre-date the arrival of the Spaniards in the Americas:

> In the old days the Twin Brothers had answered the people's cry for help when terrible forces or great monsters threatened the people. The people had always feared the Destroyers, humans who were attracted to and excited by death and the sight of blood and suffering. The Destroyers secretly prayed and waited for disaster or destruction. Secretly they were thrilled by the spectacle of death. The European invaders had brought their Jesus hanging bloody and dead from the cross; later they ate his flesh and blood again and again at the "miraculous eternal supper" or Mass. Typical of sorcerers or Destroyers, the Christians had denied they were cannibals and sacrificers. Tacho had watched enough television and movies to realize those who secretly loved destruction and death ranged all over the earth. (475)

It is through this story of the Destroyers, the clan of cannibalistic witches to which Kochininako is said to belong in "Estoy-eh-muut and the Kunideeyahs" (*Storyteller* 140–54), that Tacho explains for himself a universal taste for blood and human sacrifice. The human sacrificial rites that the Spaniards found upon arriving among Mesoamericans have long been one of the major moral and logical obstacles to be overcome by European friends of the Indians who would like to declare indigenous American culture morally superior to non-American cultures, whether Western, Eastern, or whatever. Silko attempts to take care of this obstacle, which is a version of the problem of evil with which Western philosophers and theologians have wrestled, by drawing up two sides in a precontact conflict that resulted in a migration of noncannibals from Mesoamerica northward to the area around the Pueblos:

> The old parrot priests used to tell stories about a time of turmoil hundreds of years before the Europeans came, a time when communities had split into factions over sacrifices and the sight and smell of fresh blood. The people who went away had fled north, and behind them dynasties of sorcerer-sacrificers had gradually taken over the towns and cities of the South. In fact, it had been these sorcerer-sacrificers who had "called down" the alien invaders, sorcerer-cannibals from Europe, magically sent to hurry the destruction and slaughter already begun by the Destroyers' secret clan. (475)

Cannibalism can be construed as a metaphor for the ravenous greed hidden beneath the pious story of Manifest Destiny.[13] Zeta and Lecha's father is not a cannibal in the usual understanding of this term. He does not and did not eat other human beings, as does the old hunchbacked Indian woman in the village called "the Mouth." He does, however, consume himself, paradoxically by not eating and drinking. By completely renouncing—or forgetting about—hunger and thirst—he accomplishes materially in person what the logical end of the last cannibal in the world would be. He does this, however, not of necessity, but of his own will.

In the chapter entitled "Journey of the Ancient Almanac" (245–53), preserving oneself, preserving one's people, and preserving the ancient almanac are raveled in possible conflict in a strange story that is informed literally and metaphorically by cannibalism. In this narrative, eating pages of the almanac, after one has memorized them, becomes the only way the four children can avoid cannibalism and continue to transport and preserve the old manuscript as well as themselves. In a sense, their lives depend on eating and preserving what they cannot read and write. Writing, as it begins to emerge in

Almanac, is both a metaphorical and a literal self-consumption directed toward a "rebirth" of truth and justice as a perfect language.

The story of the journey of the ancient almanac is narrated as being remembered by Lecha as she holds the old manuscript and notebooks in her hands. The chapter begins with imagery that associates the almanac and the notebooks with bullets: "Lecha reached under the pile of pillows beside her and found the wooden ammunition box with the notebooks and fragments of the old manuscript. . . . She seized the wooden ammunition box full of notebooks and the loose squares of the old manuscript; the *strange parchment* got drier and more curled each season until someday the old almanac would reveal nothing more to an interpreter" (245; my emphasis). This "strange parchment" that is getting drier and on which the writing will eventually "reveal nothing more" can be read to recall thematically Lecha and Zeta's father, the unnamed geologist whose maps designated nothing and whose strange death consisted of drying up into virtually self-consuming and self-signifying nothingness.

Perhaps more of what is "strange" about this "parchment" is not mentioned explicitly here, but can be found by comparing this passage with information Silko has catalogued in "Books: Notes on Mixtec and Maya Screenfolds." In these notes, which contain Silko's account of the argument between Grandmother A'mooh and Aunt Susie over *Stiya,* Silko states that the old book of which Lecha and Zeta are the keepers is a fourth Maya codex: "There are three known surviving Maya screenfold books: the Codex Dresden, the Codex Madrid, and the Codex Paris. They are named for the cities where they are now kept. Of course, those two old Yaqui women in my novel *Almanac of the Dead* possess large portions of a fourth Maya book, which survived the five-hundred-year war for the Americas" (*Yellow Woman* 158).

In this passage, without any overt sign of tongue in cheek, Silko puts Zeta and Lecha and their old book and notebooks on the same plane as the three surviving Mayan codices, and presents these three manuscripts as pre-dating the Spanish conquest, if not the arrival of the conquistadors:

Codex refers to European illuminated manuscripts consisting of pages bound on one side. The Nuttal painted book and the other surviving picture books from preconquest southern Mexico, as well as the surviving Maya preconquest manuscripts (Dresden, Madrid, Paris) are actually screenfolds of animal skin or *amatl,* agave bark paper. The animal skin or paper was covered with a thin coat of lime plaster, on which was painted in various colors (jade green, ochre yellow, black, white, light red, and medium red), encased in black outlines, the images of the picture book. (156)

Until recently, Mayanists and epigraphers have considered all three of these codices to be of precontact provenance. Ironically, there is an alleged fourth codex, named the Grolier, which Michael Coe, relying on a radiocarbon dating of the bark paper on which it is painted, dates at A.D. 1230 plus or minus 130, "just about perfect for the style and iconography, which is a kind of hybrid Maya-Toltec" (228). If the fourth codex possessed by Zeta and Lecha is equally ancient, then it is strange that Yoeme tells her granddaughters that the "strange parchment" is made of *horse* stomachs. Certainly Yoeme must have been aware that horses were "transplanted" to the New World by the conquistadors. It would appear that Yoeme's old book is made from a combination of precontact and postconquest materials. Stranger still, it appears that Silko has vaguely "foretold" the discovery that Michael Coe made about the Madrid Codex after the appearance of *Almanac:*

> Looking closely at the Madrid Codex, he [Michael Coe] noticed that European paper had been incorporated into its first and last leaves, not as a repair but as part of the original manufacture of the book. Upon this paper there appear traces of Spanish writing, in a seventeenth-century hand. The Itzá had access enough to European texts, religious writings left behind for their use and other materials captured from Spaniards. Thus there seems a very good chance that the Madrid Codex was composed at Tayasal, the only place where the ancient tradition would have been maintained, at some point between the 1620s and 1697. (Drew 392)

Furthermore, it might be perceived as strange that the keepers of these pages of manuscript ritually fed blood to them in the same manner that Silko claims priests and scribes fed blood to the remaining Mayan codices, as well as to the books burned by Bishop Diego de Landa: "For the people, these images were more than images are for Europeans. Certain aspects of the divine world were actually present, at least for a while, in these images. Thus the people ritually fed the books with sacrificial blood. The universe of the gods came to life through the coupling of the brush to the bark paper" (157).

If the pages of the old almanac that Yoeme gives to Lecha and Zeta were ritually fed with sacrificial blood, as Silko contends, it is understandable that the old Yaqui granny might have been disinclined to talk much about it to her granddaughters. Also, if this were the case, then the story of the journey of the ancient almanac with the four children is a story in which eating human flesh and blood and eating the "strange parchment" of the old manuscript are immixed in a strange whirligig. To eat the manuscript is to consume human blood; though it may be dried out, it is still there. And to eat a human being who has eaten the old manuscript is to consume human flesh and blood that have been nourished on human blood. Indeed, in this strange story, the oldest girl's putting a page of the old book into the hunchbacked woman's stew staves off the hunchbacked woman putting one (or all) of the children into the stew. Furthermore, the younger girl, who, against the advice and pleading of the oldest girl, returns to have a bowl of the second stew only to be slaughtered and eaten by the old hunchbacked woman, is the first to give in to the temptation to eat the strange parchment. Thus, in eating the younger girl the old hunchbacked woman also consumes, for a second time, part of the page the oldest girl threw into the stew and part of the margins of the pages the younger girl had nibbled in secret.

The three girls and one boy who set out to carry to the north the pages of the ancient almanac in their clothing know that the future of their people depends on the survival of some of these pages: "The people knew if even part of their almanac survived, they as a people would return someday" (246). Thus, to a certain extent, when the four children find themselves "on the edge of this stern motherland" (247), that is, in the Sonoran Desert where there is practically nothing to eat, eating pages of the almanac would loom just one step before eating one's companion. When the oldest girl discovers that the youngest girl has yielded to her ravenous hunger and eaten some of the almanac, it seems the only thing left for them to do is to shed tears: "While the other three had slept, the younger girl had lain next to the others secretly chewing and sucking the edges of the brittle horse-gut pages. The eldest led the others, and they began slapping and kicking the younger girl until she collapsed on the ground in tears. But they were weak from hunger, and soon they stopped and sat on the ground beside her and cried too" (247).

Sown throughout this short narrative are signs that are linked to the theme of eating: The point on the river where the children encounter the old hunchbacked woman is "where the village known as 'the Mouth' is now located" (248). The old woman moves "along the ground like a spider" (248). Spiders, of course, are known in the insect world not only for spinning webs in order to catch edible prey, but also, in the case of the black widow, a native of the Americas, for devouring their own mates. The spiderlike woman's cooking pot is filled with bulbs and roots that "floated in the water like the severed arms and heads the children had seen in a lake near their home in the South" (248). The old woman is extremely happy to see the children, and, of course, the reason for this happiness is not hard to see: she plans to eat them.

One could continue a close reading of this passage and of other passages to which it is thematically linked. One would not, however, be able to end the reading, as there are questions to which the answers remain speculative and problematic, and that point only to more passages in an endless web. For example: Why does the youngest girl go back to the hunchbacked spiderlike woman? In order to get another bowl of stew? Or perhaps in hope of eating her? How can the older girl know what is on the pages of the almanac if she cannot read? "Although she could no more read the writing than she could understand the language of the hunchbacked woman, she looked carefully at each stiff, curled page" (249). Later she contends that she had heard the stories told: "I remember what was on the page we ate. I know that part of the almanac—I have heard the stories of those days told many times. Now I am going to tell you three. So if something happens to me, the three of you will know how that part of the story goes" (250). Why is the story of what was on the page eaten not included? Does this belong to the "strangeness" of this old book? How can the oldest girl, without being able to read, know that what is "written" on the page that she put into the stewpot *is* the story she had heard told many times? Is she capable of looking at the glyphs and understanding them not as writing but as truth? The girls agree that they can eat the pages they have memorized. Carnally and metaphorically they become the manuscript they are consuming. Finally, we can return to the question of the strange parchment that Yoeme speculates to be made of horse stomachs. If it is of precontact origin, it cannot be made of horse. Is it possible that the strange parchment is made from human skin?

After the old book and notebooks have been described, an "earlier" scene is recounted in which Yoeme differentiates between the twins by their attitude toward snakes. Lecha cannot stand to look at snakes, much less to pick them up. Zeta, however, likes snakes. Having been introduced to a big bull snake by Yoeme, Zeta learns that she can communicate nonverbally with this telluric being. Although she cannot exactly put into words what is going on here, there are signs that this snake helps her to cut emotionally and intellectually the ties of kinship to her white grandfather. It would seem that this snake helps her to fill the lacuna that is inside herself. It does this by affording her a vision in which justice is served on the weak, cruel, and unforgiving old man by one of his weak, cruel, and unforgiving children:

> Zeta had never mentioned any of this [handling the bull snake] to Lecha because she could not exactly explain how it

worked. Certainly the snake didn't talk. But looking at the
snake as it curled in Yoeme's arms and thinking how beauti-
fully the light brown spots were with the pale yellow under
it, Zeta had for no reason thought of Grandpa Guzman not
as her grandpa, but as the "old white man," which was what
others, outside the family, called him. She had thought of
him overturned and moaning feebly for help. And her aunt
Popa was ignoring him because she figured there would be
something dirty to clean up. All Zeta had ever thought was
that she knew how it worked, how one talked to snakes. But
it had never impressed her. (131)

Zeta's ability to "talk" to snakes, although differentiating her from
Lecha, also serves to bind her to her sister when Yoeme gives them
the book and notebooks. Yoeme tells her that her gift, that is, the
ability to talk with snakes, and the portion of the notebooks are the
key to filling the lacunae of this text. It should also be the key to
filling the emptiness in herself, but Zeta seems to vacillate, reading
her grandmother's talk and writing as mad rather than prophetic:

Old Yoeme had given Zeta the smallest bundle of loose notebook pages and scraps of paper with drawings of snakes.
Yoeme had warned Zeta not to brag to Lecha, but the notebook of the snakes was the key to understanding all the rest
of the old almanac. The drawings of the snakes were in
beautiful colors of ink, but Zeta had been disappointed after
she began deciphering Yoeme's scrawls in misspelled Spanish.
This did not seem to be the "key" to anything except one old
woman's madness. (134)

But, then, in a world of transitions, whether between boulders and
bears or between uranium mine tailings and Quetzalcoatl, the
Plumed Serpent, madness and the words of the prophet are written
on the wall of a lawyer's building in Tucson where Silko painted
her controversial mural (discussed in ch. 7).

Before setting *Almanac* back on the Babelian library shelf, I would
like to comment briefly on the irony of Birkerts's judgment that

the passage quoted from the old almanac in which bloody puss pours from the ear of the dog is nonsensical and that Silko has tethered her vision of revolution to airy nothing. This passage can be given meaning by reading it as a nexus of the thematic threads of blood, disease, and dogs that snake through this text. The Reign of Death-eye Dog suggests the fundamental "law" that is in force in the modern world. In the boardroom, on the golf course, in the rocky arroyos where drugs and arms are smuggled, on the battlefield, in the village called "the Mouth" where the four children carrying the pages of the old almanac meet the spiderlike woman, it is a "dog-eat-dog world." This saw that epitomizes rugged individualism echoes through the novel. It can be heard in dog-loving Judge Arne's bedroom where he ejaculates into his basset hounds. It is whispered in the cribs of babies suffocated with stuffed toy dogs. It can be read in the Spanish slave-catchers' dogs and through the packs of wild dogs to which the conquistadors tossed Indians to be torn apart. It is metaphorically incarnated in Zeta and Lecha's coyote years. It can be felt in Paulie's "Dobermans with ears cropped so short their heads looked more snake than dog" (38). Sterling reflects on these Dobermans, named Cy, Nitro, Mag, Stray, and so forth, which guard the ranch, and on an article about a woman having suffocated her babies with a stuffed toy dog. By far the most sympathetic character in the novel, Sterling "had never liked dogs of any kind—stuffed or alive. He got chills each time he remembered those poor babies and the ugly glass eyes of the stuffed toy dog" (37). One may disagree with Silko's critique of "the dog-eat-dog world," of the canine vision through which contemporary capitalist culture sees itself, but depicting this vision through canine imagery is not nonsense; it is saying that such a world is sick, bloody, chillingly robotic, and lethal. Spiritually such a world has tethered its vision to arid and imperfect nothingness. Pragmatically the Western world's vision is tethered to the aporia of the top dog eventually consuming itself as it waits either for the Second Coming or for what entropy has in store for the planet: the empty, dead earth meaningless in black nothingness.

Silko contends in interviews and essays that the Mayan writings predicted Cortés's arrival down to the exact day. It is the envy of contemporary mathematicians that keeps them from recognizing the accuracy of the Mayan calculations, she says. If we accept this premise, then the ancient Maya were capable of predicting what chaos theory demonstrates contemporary scientists cannot. They had a system capable of foreseeing an occurrence even as "trivial" as the beat of a butterfly's wing that could eventually cause a hurricane that could delay or even prevent the arrival of the Spanish in Mexico (in 1519 or 1520). Furthermore, if we contend, as Silko does, that past, present, and future coexist in instantaneity, that time is round "like a tortilla," then the arrival of the Spanish, like everything else that "has occurred" in Western linear time, is reversible. Of course, if the Mayan calculations amount to prophecies or divine forecasting of history, then there is no way a human mathematician could do what the "divine" Mayan astronomers did, short of becoming divine themselves. Silko's conception of Mayan mathematical skills does not distinguish between numerology and mathematics. In the former, numbers provide a paradoxically unmediated means of knowing. Numbers not only prophesy, they are reality. In the latter, numbers are only one of the humanly constructed symbolic means whereby humanity can construct hypothetical models of the cosmos. In this chapter, I have argued that Silko has conceived her writing as a gloss and translation of the Mayan writings. Those books, the Dresden, Paris, Madrid, and Mexico City codices, which survive in incomplete form, like the engraved stones in Middle America, still pose problems for epigraphers who have been trying to translate them. Silko's writing aspires toward a special ontological status, like that she attributes to the codices. For the numerologist, reality is numbers. For the Kabbalist mystic, words are being. For Silko ridden by the spirits, her own writing, tethered to Mayan writing, is reality, and all else is almost airy nothing.

Silko has repeatedly told stories about how she got lost in the composition of *Almanac*. Perhaps the ten years she spent writing this vast book were "a laborious and impoverishing extravagance"

(Borges 15). Perhaps, however, she did follow the Argentine master's advice in pretending that Yoeme's old almanac and notebooks did exist. But instead of a fifteen-minute commentary or résumé, she got caught up in a ten-year gloss. She did, however, put this book down before consuming herself in writing an endless Babelian library. It can be argued that *Almanac* has no end. Or perhaps it has neither a closed nor an open ending. Like the giant stone snake that Sterling contemplates on the last page, *Almanac* can be understood to point to the retaking of the Americas by the brown army from the south. As a book about a book of prophecy, however, it points to the book it glosses, like a snake eating the tail of another snake that is eating its tail. Or, and this is where I find hope in *Almanac,* it can be said to point to another book, *Gardens in the Dunes,* which, despite the tears that fill its pages, offers characters and a worldview in which it is somewhat easier to glimpse hope than in *Almanac.*

CHAPTER 7

TOLLE, LEGE

Glossing Glossolalia in Gardens in the Dunes

Il faut cultiver son jardin.

—VOLTAIRE,
Candide

"Raphèl maÿ amecche zabì almi," *the fierce mouth, to which
sweeter psalms were not fitting, began to cry. And my leader
towards him, "Stupid soul, keep to your horn and with that
vent yourself when rage or other passion takes you. Search at
your neck and you will find the belt that holds it tied, O soul
confused: see how it lies across your great chest." Then he
said to me, "He is his own accuser: this is Nimrod, through
whose ill thought one language only is not used in the world.
Let us leave him alone and not speak in vain, for every language is to him as his is to others, which is known to none."*

—DANTE,
Inferno

Before her marriage to Edward Palmer and her trip to England, Italy, and Corsica, which amounts to a version of the
Grand Tour,[1] Hattie Abbott, the main Anglo-American protagonist in *Gardens in the Dunes,* had been interested in alternatives to
orthodox Western religion and thought. While auditing a graduate

seminar on heresy at Harvard, she read about Gnosticism. Eager to "read more, but from the pens of the Gnostics themselves" (99), she gained permission from a scholar of Gnostic texts to read his translations and to work in his library. On her first visit to this library she takes up volume one of the old scholar's translations of Coptic and Latin texts and reads at random the following passage: "Abandon the search for God and other matters of a similar sort. Look for him by taking yourself as the starting point. Learn who is within you who makes everything his own and says: My God, my mind, my thoughts, my soul, my body. Learn the sources of sorrow, joy, love, hate. If you carefully investigate these matters you will find him in yourself" (99–100). Although Hattie does not yet know it, in reading these lines she has taken the first step in a "conversion" to a syncretic culture in which pre-Christian and so-called heretical Christian beliefs coexist. Pleased and excited, she leafs through manuscripts and comes upon another passage that provides her with the topic for her thesis project:

> After a day of rest, Wisdom, Sophia, sent Zoe, Life, her daughter who is called Eve, as an instructor to raise up Adam. . . . When Eve saw Adam cast down and she pitied him and said, "Adam, live! Rise up upon the Earth!" immediately her word became deed. For when Adam rose up, immediately he opened his eyes. When he saw her he said, "You will be called the mother of the living because you are the one who gave me life. . . ." It is she who is the Physician, and the Woman and She who has given birth. . . . the Female Spiritual principle came in the Snake, the Instructor, and it taught them, saying, "You shall not die; for it was out of jealousy He said that to you. Rather your eyes shall open and you shall become like gods, recognizing evil and good. . . ." And the arrogant Ruler cursed the Woman and the Snake. . . . (100)

These two citations, the second of which is actually a conflation of two separately cited passages, can be found nearly verbatim in Elaine Pagels's *The Gnostic Gospels* (xix–xx, 30, 31). Their inclusion in *Gardens in the Dunes* contributes to the difficulty the critic has when describing this book and trying to fit it into canonical literary categories.[2] It is a neo-Victorian novel of education and adventure. It is also an open pancultural text that playfully embodies intertextuality in order to subvert Western history, bringing together differing historical, ethnic, philosophical, religious, economic, ideological, and aesthetic perspectives, including Native American, African American, Gypsy, Gnostic, Catholic, non-Christian feminist, and modern scientific. Central to its main plot is a tension between writing, embodied in the thesis project Hattie never completes, and the "language of love" that Silko depicts spoken at the Ghost Dance and which, I argue, also is implicit in the narration of the apparition of the Holy Mother on a schoolhouse wall in Corsica. It is this apparition that finally brings about Hattie's "conversion" to the syncretic system of belief informed by the "Female Spiritual Principle [that] came in the Snake, the Instructor." In *Gardens in the Dunes* Grandmother Spider's web is spun through ancient and modern gardens and libraries, and the normative voice of the Pueblo in *Ceremony* and *Storyteller* becomes the universal voice of Maternal Serpentine Wisdom, as Silko rewrites history, theology, and philosophy. The citations taken from Pagels give Silko's text an explicit exegetical or metalinguistic status and invite a philosophical or theological reading. Not only do these passages work within the plot, motivating Hattie to come up with "The Female Principle in the Early Church" for a thesis topic, they also beckon the reader to *take up and read* Pagels's writings on Gnosticism and the host of texts that she cites.

The second citation comprises a nonorthodox telling of the story of Adam, Eve, and the Serpent in the Garden (Gen. 3). From an orthodox point of view this story is a gloss that not only informs Hattie's heretical thesis project, but also supports the major thesis or grand narrative that emerges in Silko's thought and writings. This thesis can be summed up as the principle of aboriginal serpentine matriarchal spirituality. It construes the earth as Mother and Serpent, treats time as predominantly nonlinear, prioritizes syncretism, openness, sexual and social equality, tolerance of diversity, and metamorphosis. It depicts all humans as yearning for life in a garden of natural love and nonmediated communication with creation. This thesis is intimately interwoven with three serpentine American mother goddesses, Tonantsi, Coatlicue, and the Virgin of Guadalupe, who join the Gnostic Serpent in informing Silko's text.

Opposed to this thesis is the orthodox Christian gloss on the Fall in the Garden of Eden. This gloss informs the dominant grand narrative of Western culture that Silko debunks and indicts on every occasion. This is a narrative of sin and salvation or damnation; it is exclusionary, patriarchal, sexually and culturally repressive, primarily linear, intolerant of difference, diversity, and metamorphosis. It prioritizes guilt, progress, destruction, death, and writing. The perspective of the narrator of this narrative is embodied by the male academics on Hattie's thesis committee. They reject her thesis project with the same arrogance that the "Ruler cursed the Woman and the Snake" and the early church fathers rejected as heretical, apocryphal, and marginal the writings Hattie wants to write about.

Caught in a conflict between these two narratives, Silko's principal characters experience a desire to embrace all, but also a realization that this is not yet possible. This desire can be seen not only as welcoming diversity but also as potentially producing confusion in the same manner that early interpretations of the Galilean's life and teachings produced diverse cults that the church fathers excluded and wrote off as heresies. The problem is an old one in world thought: If an all-embracing culture of love, tolerance, diversity, and equality embraces the members of an exclusionary, intolerant, hierarchical culture, it risks destroying itself. If it excludes the members of the antithetical culture, it takes the first step toward becoming like the culture it excludes. In an interview with Ellen Arnold, Silko toys with her growing realization of this problem as she acknowledges the role Pagels's writing played in the gestation of *Gardens in the Dunes:*

> There are many different Jesuses. That was another thing I started reading about, the Gnostic Gospels—Elaine Pagel's

[*sic*] wonderful book, *The Gnostic Gospels.* [. . .] Well. I was deep in the middle of writing *Almanac of the Dead,* and that book sat on my shelf for years. So recently I wrote her a letter and thanked her for it, and I said, oh, and by the way, I wrote a whole novel partly because of your book. I started to realize that there are lots of different Jesus Christs, and the Jesus or the Messiah of the Ghost Dance and some of the other sightings of the Holy Family in the Americas were just as valid and powerful as other sightings and versions of Jesus. ("Listening to the Spirits" 164)

Implicit in this talk about Gnosticism, heresy, and the powerful validity of "different Jesuses" is a scene in which Silko, like Hattie, took up Pagels's book and read it. In it she found a grand narrative that embraces the diversity of "different Jesus Christs," but nevertheless seeks a way to deal with the exclusionary and arrogant Ruler of Eden and those patriarchs who anathematize the Serpent. They and their writings figure the punishment Silko associates with her great-grandmother A'mooh's Presbyterianism. They embody the desire to punish people and books by burning them. Silko's including the two Ghost Dance scenes in *Gardens* and the scene of the apparition of the Holy Mother on the schoolhouse wall in Corsica can be read as her having arrived at a syncretism that does not exclude Christ, but instead embraces diverse glosses on his teachings along with so-called pagan culture. Thus, by not explicitly excluding Christianity, she avoids becoming like the orthodox church fathers who exclude themselves by writing their patristic exegesis, by insisting on the one rather than the many, and who in the long run will be no more than the dry leaves on which they wrote. They and their straitlaced converts will blow away in the great swirling wind of the Ghost Dance. In short, reading Pagels's "wonderful book" provided for Silko something akin to a Gnostic and pan-Indian version of Saint Augustine's famous *tolle, lege,* "take up and read."[3]

Let us take up *Gardens in the Dunes* and read a passage near the end of the narration of the first Ghost Dance.[4] Indigo and Sister Salt are said to remember a curious linguistic phenomenon that occurred during the fourth and final night of this gathering, after the Messiah and his family have appeared. The Holy Mother and the Messiah's wife have opened up their shawls, blessing the dancers with "plump squash blossoms."[5]

> Now it was so quiet only the fire's crackle could be heard; no one spoke as they waited their turn to take a squash flower. Later, when Indigo and Sister Salt discussed that night, *they remembered with amazement that whenever the Messiah or the Holy Mother spoke, all the dancers could understand them, no matter what tribe they were from.* The Paiutes swore the Messiah was speaking Paiute, but a Walapai woman laughed and shook her head; how silly, the Messiah spoke her language. When Grandma Fleet and Mama knelt to pick up blossoms, the Holy Mother blessed them in their Sand Lizard language. When the Mormons approached the Messiah, Sister Salt stayed nearby to listen for herself; she was amazed. As the Messiah gave his blessing to the Mormons, Sister Salt distinctly heard the words he spoke as Sand Lizard, not English, yet the Mormons understood his words and murmured their thanks to him. (31–32; my emphasis)

An attempt to conceptualize a language that is simultaneously understood by speakers of many different languages as their own language leaves one facing multiple paradoxes. In this language one is also many, the identical is the other, the homogeneous is the heterogeneous, the known is the unknown, the speakable is the unspeakable, and the comprehensible is the incomprehensible. Such a linguistic phenomenon can be likened to what Walter Benjamin postulates to be the "pure language" whose release "in his own language" is the "task of the translator" (80), or to what Umberto Eco calls a "parameter language," a *"tertium comparationis* which might allow us to shift from an expression in language A to an expression in language B by deciding that both are equivalent to an expression of a metalanguage C" (346). It can also be said to resemble what took place when the Holy Ghost descended upon the apostles at Pentecost:

And suddenly there came a sound from heaven as of a rushing mighty wind, and it filled all the house where they were sitting. And there appeared unto them cloven tongues like as of fire, and it sat upon each of them. And they were all filled with the Holy Ghost, and *began to speak with other tongues*, as the Spirit gave them utterance. And there were dwelling at Jerusalem Jews, devout men, out of every nation under heaven. Now when this was noised abroad, *the multitude came together, and were confounded because that every man heard them speak in his own language*. (Acts 2:2–6; my emphasis)

This particular phenomenon is usually referred to as the gift of tongues, or speaking in tongues. It is also called *glossolalia*.

In *The Search for the Perfect Language*, Umberto Eco provides a gloss of this linguistic phenomenon, as it is mentioned by Saint Paul and by the author of Acts 2. Eco attempts to distinguish *glossolalia* from a related phenomenon, *xenoglossia*:

What was the exact nature of the gift of tongues received by the apostles? Reading St Paul (Corinthians 1:12–13) it seems that the gift was that of *glossolalia*—that is, the ability to express oneself in an ecstatic language that all could understand as if it were their own native speech. Reading the Acts of the Apostles 2, however, we discover that at the Pentecost a loud roar was heard from the skies, and that upon each of the apostles a tongue of flame descended, and they started to speak in *other* languages. In this case, the gift was not *glossolalia* but *xenoglossia*, that is, polyglottism—or failing that, at least a sort of mystic service of simultaneous translation. (Eco 351) [6]

Similar to the term *gloss*, which has come to designate both a valid interpretation that clarifies the meaning of an obscure or foreign word or passage and a purposefully misleading interpretation, *glossolalia* is used to designate paradoxically not only an ecstatic speech that all can mystically understand "as if it were their own native speech," but also babble, speech that no one can understand. The *American Heritage Dictionary of the English Language* gives two definitions of *glossolalia*. In the first, which is secular and clinical, *glossolalia* is explicitly placed in a causal relationship with mental illness and is related to babble in the etymological gloss on its Greek roots: "glos.so.la.li.a . . . 1. Fabricated and non-meaningful speech, especially such speech associated with a trance state or certain schizophrenic syndromes. 2. See gift of tongues. [New Latin: Greek *glossa,* tongue + Greek *lalein,* to babble.]" (4th ed.). The second definition found under "gift of tongues" is theological, but it does not exactly coincide with Eco's definition, as it still leaves open the problem of how one can interpret what is said in tongues without "a sort of mystic service of simultaneous translation": "gift of tongues *n.* The ability or phenomenon to utter words or sounds of a language unknown to the speaker, especially as an expression of religious ecstasy. Also called *glossolalia, speaking in tongues.* [From the Apostles' speaking in tongues in Acts 2:4.]" There is in these definitions the subtle assumption that religious ecstasy and abnormal physiological and psychological states, like schizophrenia and mystic trances, produce babble, languagelike confusion, a language known to no one, rather than the perfect language. How does "a language unknown to the speaker" differ from "[f]abricated and non-meaningful speech"? Such a question could be said to arise from the narrative perspective of the objective scientist, the skeptic who would exclude from linguistic study a "pseudo-linguistic" phenomenon like glossolalia. This is the point of view of someone like Edward in *Gardens in the Dunes,* but it is not the point of view of Hattie or Indigo or the Ghost Dancers.

There is in Eco's theological definition of *glossolalia* the assumption that when the Holy Spirit descended on the apostles, they spoke the language that was spoken by Adam in the Garden of Eden and, according to Genesis 11, ceased to exist at Babel. Thus, from a historical or linear temporal perspective, this language is unknown, but from the total or mystic perspective brought on the speakers by the Holy Ghost, it is known again to all.[7] Eco is aware of the paradox inherent in a Pentecostal language that is simultaneously both one and many. He implicitly takes it up in his discussion of the disparity between Genesis 10, in which different languages are said to be in the world before the erection of the Tower of Babel, and Genesis 11, in which the confusion of tongues is recounted as a cataclysmic punishment inflicted on humanity by God the Father in one swirling curse.[8] Eco does not resolve the disparity between the two accounts in Genesis. Indeed, he translates it into questions and crises of interpretation that have repeatedly arisen in the history of the search for a perfect language: "How are we meant to interpret this evident plurality of languages prior to Babel? . . . If the languages were already differentiated after Noah, why not before? . . . If languages were differentiated not as a punishment but simply as a result of natural process, why must the confusion of tongues constitute a curse at all?" (9–10). If not a curse, then is the plurality of tongues a blessing? "Yes," many writers have answered in diverse tongues.

Rhetorically speaking, in the first Ghost Dance, Silko, Wovoka, the Messiah, and his Mother are not so much opposing Genesis 10 to Genesis 11 as they are suggesting that an aboriginal diversity of tribal languages is no curse. Especially if there is a great prophet like Wovoka who can bring them together in a whirling powwow comprising an egalitarian and loving speaking in tongues rather than a hierarchical and arrogant curse of linguistic confusion. Nimrod, rather than being the great hunter and the type for schismatics, as Dante and preceding exegetes portrayed him, is implicitly interpreted as the type for the hunters of the Great Plains, descendants of a lost tribe of Israel. The potential results of such a movement were perceived by most Anglos as devastating for their exclusionary narrative of Western culture.[9] The U.S. government banned the Ghost Dance and, convinced of its own exclusionary vision of godly moral clarity, sent U.S. troops to Wounded Knee to liberate Indian men, women, and children.

In the scene of the first Ghost Dance in *Gardens in the Dunes*, a Paiute is said to gloss the curious linguistic phenomenon: "When Sister Salt excitedly told Mama and Grandma what she had heard, a Paiute man standing nearby smiled and nodded his head. *In the*

*presence of the Messiah and the Holy Mother, there was only one lan-
guage spoken—the language of love—which all people understand,* he said,
because *we* are all the children of Mother Earth" (32; my emphasis).
The Paiute appears to understand Sand Lizard. It is not made explicit, however, in what language he speaks this gloss, which apparently
helps Indigo and Sister Salt to understand why they are understanding. However this may be, this gloss in English can be read
as Silko's inserting her principle of matriarchal spirituality into the
gap between Genesis 10 and Genesis 11, the chink in the armor of
Western patriarchy that informs the orthodox narrative of divine
punishment for diversity. For those who wish to include themselves
in the referent of first-person plural pronoun *we* that shows up
here in the indirect discourse of this third-person narrative, this
chink becomes endless transition, total perspective, loving inclusion in a world in which spatial and temporal boundaries and
inequality are erased in an embrace that is earthly, maternal, spiritual,
and writerly.[10]

At the Ghost Dance before the Messiah and his Mother appear,
dancers are said to fall into trances, sometimes to moan and to
writhe, then to remain silent. Such behavior was referred to as
"dying" in the language used to describe the Ghost Dance. On one
occasion this behavior in a white man is described in such a way
that it could be specifically identified as glossolalia: "Early on the
final night, Indigo got to see for herself what happened to a Mormon visited by his ancestors. The young man suddenly fell to his
knees with his face in his hands, *babbling* and weeping before he
slowly sank to the earth and lay quietly on his side, no different
from any of the other dancers who visited with the spirits" (30; my
emphasis). Here, Indigo does not appear to understand the young
Mormon's babbling. On the one hand, his babbling could be interpreted as "[f]abricated and non-meaningful speech, especially such
speech associated with a trance state"("glossolalia" *American Heritage,* 4th ed.). Thus, the young Mormon's babbling would be speech
in a tongue that is unknown both to Indigo and to himself. This
could mean that he is not speaking the same language that Indigo

and Sister Salt, in the presence of the Messiah and his Mother, will hear and understand as Sand Lizard and that the Mormons will hear and understand as English. He is babbling nonsense. On the other hand, from a nonskeptical, spiritual point of view, it is possible to understand that the young Mormon, having entered into a trance, is spiritually in the presence of the Messiah and his Mother, and is speaking "the language of love" with the spirits of his ancestors. The trance itself could be interpreted as a form of *gnosis* through which the young Mormon individually regains the "lost" perfect, unmediated language of love that lies waiting to be reknown within all beings, human and other. Silko suggests that this language extends not only to nonhuman animals, but also to plants and to rocks. Indigo, however, has not yet "died." She cannot yet understand this language, since she is not in the presence of the Messiah and his family. She cannot yet even understand the meaning of the words to the songs sung by the dancers. In other words, depending on the point of view taken by the reader, this Mormon's babbling and weeping could be either an occurrence of glossolalia as the perfect language or as meaningless babble.

Eco's problematic distinction between the two terms, *glossolalia* and *xenoglossia*, is not only a distinction between Saint Paul's interpretation of what happened to the apostles at Pentecost and the interpretation of the author of the Acts of the Apostles. It is also a sketch in a nutshell of two historical ways of viewing cultural diversity and linguistic differences:

> The question of which interpretation to accept is not really a joking matter: there is a major difference between the two accounts. In the first hypothesis [that of Saint Paul], the apostles would have been restored to the conditions before Babel, when all humanity spoke but a single holy dialect. In the second hypothesis [that given in Acts 2], the apostles would have been granted the gift of momentarily reversing the defeat of Babel and finding in the multiplicity of tongues no longer a wound that must, at whatever cost, be healed, but rather the key to the possibility of a new alliance and of a new concord. (351)

Saint Paul, as might be expected, belongs to the exegetes whose vision is informed by a logic of exclusion; the author of the Acts of the Apostles appears to belong to those writers whose vision is informed by a logic of inclusion. Seen in light of the opposition of *glossolalia* to *xenoglossia,* how might we interpret the Ghost Dance as portrayed in *Gardens*? Well, not quite either way, as both are predominantly patriarchal. The "language of love" spoken at the Ghost Dance can be glossed not only as an intertextual link to the apostles speaking in tongues at Pentecost, but as a gloss of Genesis 3 and 11. What Silko and the Ghost Dancers are doing is spiritually rewriting the Tower of Babel in the spirit of loving maternal syncretism.

Silko is usually more inclined toward syncretism, openness, and multicultural tolerance, although she can be strident in her denunciation of capitalism and Christianity. When talking with Ellen Arnold about the possible reaction of different communities to *Gardens in the Dunes,* Silko represents the original position of the Laguna Pueblo "old folks" as being open and tolerant. This openness and tolerance to non-Pueblos, especially to Europeans, however, "got them into trouble, because they welcomed these newcomers" ("Listening to the Spirits" 172). Silko reasons that those persons who now attack her work have internalized the "behavior of Europeans" (172). This behavior is informed by a logic of exclusion, racism, and intolerance of diversity. There is a messianic fervor in Silko's insistence on not excluding the exclusionary: "the old prophecies tell us that it still doesn't matter, and it's all going to be okay. That's the only way it can be, including everybody. That's the only way that the kind of peace and harmony that this earth of the Americas wants is going to happen" (172). This voice of the "old folks" emerges as the normative Pueblo voice for Silko as she and her text cross more and more boundaries.

In her espousal of syncretism, Silko is returning the Serpent to its role as wise motherly teacher of diversity and writing. This is figured in the end of *Gardens* where the "Old Snake's beautiful daughter moved back home" at the spring in the garden (477). This spiritual, maternal, and serpentine Babel embraces all but those who willingly exclude themselves and who will dry up and blow away like leaves in whirling winds. This spiritual Babel as figured by Silko embraces the Gnostic view that favors an individual spiritual inwardness that leads to a multiplicity of mystical experiences of the self as Christ and of God as both Mother and Father, and, aboriginally, as Mother and Serpent-Instructor. Such a philosophical system, Pagels has argued convincingly, was perceived to undermine Church hierarchy, leading to schisms and cults, inviting compromise with pagan beliefs in syncretism and other "abominations" such as social and religious equality among men and women, which the church fathers pronounced to be anathema. In other words, Silko has made room for Pagels's host of Gnostic heretics to dance with the Messiah, his family, Wovoka, Mary Magdalene, the Mormons, and all the others at the Ghost Dance who accept diversity. The Ghost Dancers, when they visit with their ancestors, have knowledge of matriarchal spirituality and the language of love. This knowledge has no need of the entire canonical and exegetical structure by which the authority of Saint Peter, the church fathers, and officials of orthodox Christianity, whether Protestant or Roman Catholic, is founded. Rome, incidentally, is not a stop on Indigo's and Hattie's version of the Grand Tour.

The importance of dancing to the Messiah and his followers is not just something that Wovoka first envisioned and incorporated into his syncretic pan-Indian ceremony. A passage from the *Acts of John,* a Gnostic text quoted by Pagels in her discussion of Christ as a spiritual rather than a material being, depicts Jesus teaching his friends to dance in a circle around him as he chants in the Garden of Gethsemane:

> The *Acts* goes on to tell how Jesus, anticipating arrest, joined with his disciples in Gethsemane the night before:
>
>> . . . he assembled us all, and said, "Before I am delivered to them, let us sing a hymn to the Father, and so go to meet what lies before (us)." So he told us to form a circle, holding one another's hands, and himself stood in the middle. . . .

Instructing the disciples to "Answer Amen to me," he began to intone a mystical chant, which reads, in part,

> "To the Universe belongs the dancer."—"Amen."
> "He who does not dance does not know what hap-
>   pens."—"Amen." . . .
> "Now if you follow my dance, see yourself in Me who
>   am speaking . . .
> You who dance, consider what I do, for yours is
> This passion of Man which I am to suffer. For you
>   could by no means have understood what you suffer
> unless to you as Logos I had been sent by the Father . . .
> Learn how to suffer and you shall be able not to suffer."
>   (74)

Just as the Roman soldiers arrive to arrest Christ and sow confusion among his dancing disciples in the Garden of Gethsemane, so the U.S. soldiers and Indian police arrive to arrest and disperse the Ghost Dancers in *Gardens in the Dunes*.

The Ghost Dance, as conceived by Wovoka, stirs together Christian myths and Native American culture. Silko subtly adds readings in Gnosticism to this swirl. The goal of the Ghost Dance, as it is described by Silko, is not only to restore the land to what it was before the arrival of European settlers, but also to heal the wounds inflicted on tribal cultures by the totalitarian, urbanizing, analytic, and linear narrative of Western culture. This is accomplished by winds that seem to far exceed in power the wind described descending from heaven in Acts 2:4–6:

> Jesus promised Wovoka that if the Paiutes and all the other
> Indians danced this dance, then the used-up land would be
> made whole again and the elk and the herds of buffalo killed
> off would return. The dance was a peaceful dance, and the
> Paiutes wished no harm to white people; but Jesus was very
> angry with white people. As the people danced, great storm
> clouds would gather over the entire world. Finally, when all
> the Indians were dancing, great winds would roar out of clear
> skies, winds the likes of which were never seen before; the

winds, for weeks without end, would blow away all the top-
soil and strip the trees of all leaves. The winds would dry up
all the white people and all the Indians who followed the white
man's ways, and they would blow away with the dust. (23)

In describing the Ghost Dance Silko uses metaphors that echo both
Acts 2 and the story of the confusion of tongues at Babel (Gen. 11):
"The voices of the dancers rose above the river. Indigo closed her
eyes: the sound of the hundreds of voices was not human but
mountain, as if out of the depths of the mountains a great hum-
ming rose" (30).

If the Messiah and his family came to stay with the buffalo and
the elk, it would appear that in their restored form the "children of
Mother Earth" would have no need for writing or for translation.
We would all speak the perfect and universal "language of love"
in the presence of the Messiah and his family. *They,* that is, those
who had excluded syncretism in their patristic writing, would dry
up and blow away as writing. If this were the case, then, writings
like Hattie's thesis project, or even like Silko's novel, could be
among the things that would be blown away. Hattie's burying her
thesis project and notes can be read as a thematic nod to the end of
writing, a nod to the return of perfect orality, which Silko paradoxically yearns for and dreams of as she writes what amounts to her
thesis project.[11] Yet, the Ghost Dance is interrupted twice. The second
time Hattie is carried away by her parents, the Abbotts. She ends
up in England, living with Aunt Bronwyn and communicating
with Indigo by written letters.

The twice-interrupted Ghost Dance emblematizes the paradoxical narrative goal of *Gardens.* Silko's and her characters' yearning
for an aboriginal serpentine matriarchal spirituality and for the
perfect language of love manifests itself as a dream of a text that
both depicts and effects nonmediated communication. This yearned
for communication would be effected as a perfect language, an
ontologically privileged aboriginal "writing" that neither signifies
nor represents, but coincides with being, with creation as a gift of

tongues. Since no such perfect language exists, except as the "pure language" mentioned by Benjamin or as the "parameter language" postulated by some translators, or as the "supreme language" conceived by Mallarmé as "thinking [that] is writing without accessories or even whispering" (Mallarmé 363–64), the dream cannot but be interrupted; the yearning turns to textuality, or secondary orality.

It is my contention that the narrative of the apparition on the schoolhouse wall in Corsica approximates or simulates this goal of nonmediated communication. In my reading of this scene, I shall attempt to show that there are oblique narrative glimpses of Indigo, Hattie, and their Corsican host experiencing traces of *glossolalia* or of *xenoglossia* or of "a sort of mystic service of simultaneous translation" (Eco 351). Threatening to interrupt this scene, rather than the U.S. Army and the Indian police, is exclusionary writing. From the religious perspective, exclusionary writing is embodied by the menacing representatives of Roman Catholic patristic exegesis, the cross-brandishing monks. From the scientific, objective, and skeptical perspective, exclusionary writing is embodied by Edward, the thief in the garden who so clearly needs and unconsciously desires, yet refuses, the Serpent's instruction. Also threatening to interrupt the scene is the old exclusionary tendency in Silko's own writing, in which Indigo risks becoming a double to Marion Burgess's Stiya. Both characters are simulacra, caught in a book between orthodox Western literate thought and the oral matriarchal principle of spirituality. Smoldering in this scene is the tension between Grandma A'mooh's desire to throw *Stiya* into the fire and Aunt Susie's clever salvation of this book in Pueblo textuality. Every time Indigo sulks or sullenly rejects a syncretic, inclusionary point of view, Grandma A'mooh's desire to burn the simulacrum flares up in Silko's writing. Instead of burning her own simulacra, however, Silko has Hattie bury her thesis notes and burn down half the town of Needles.

In the scene of the apparition in Corsica, as in the rest of the novel, there is very little direct dialogue. The mode of narration can be described as a version of *style indirect libre* similar in some ways to that analyzed in chapter 5 in "Coyote Holds a Full House in His

Hand." As in Silko's other texts where I have described the relation between irony and narrative point of view, there is not a clearly *condescending* and *patronizing* gap between the supposedly objective point of view of the third-person narrator and the subjective points of view of the characters. Rather there is what I have called a *matronizing* and *equalizing* effect that closes the gap. Thus, rather than constructing a cold and intellectual irony, in the manner of Flaubert's narrator in *Madame Bovary,* Silko's narrator warmly and sentimentally ironizes paternal irony. She problematizes the concept of narrative objectivity by shifting back and forth among the points of view of the characters involved (Indigo, Hattie, Edward, and maybe their host and his sister-in-law) and a point of view that, rather than being informed by directness and objectivity, embodies refraction and obliqueness. This third-person point of view that is multiple creates an effect that can be likened to what Roland Barthes calls the writerly when he describes the difference between the work and the text. Any attempt to posit an objective point of view shared by the third-person narrator and an interpretive community is undermined by this indirect narrative discourse.[12] Nevertheless, a spiritual community that does not need to interpret is projected to share with the writing storyteller what can best be described, not as a point of view, but as a total perspective. It is this total perspective that the discerning reader can glimpse within herself or himself and that the ecstatic reader can share with the world.

This oblique telling in the third person is radically allusive and symbolic. It is constructed to defer interpretive closure. Since the third-person narrator putatively translates what is said by characters not only into indirect discourse from direct discourse, but also into English from the Corsican patois in which the characters speak, particular problems in cross-linguistic communication tend to be glossed over. Such is the case, for example, in the paragraph in which Hattie and Indigo, having finished their meal with the Corsican villagers, are said to learn of their host's after-dinner plans: "After wedges of cheese and ripe soft pears, their host announced that they would all walk together to the little schoolhouse at the edge of the village where the image of Jesus' Blessed Mother recently began to appear on the front wall above the door" (316). In this scene, as in many of the other scenes in Corsica and Italy, the question of how the Corsican or the Italian characters and the American characters communicate can be raised. If, as Ellen Arnold has claimed, *Gardens in the Dunes* "returns to a kind of literary realism in the tradition of Henry James," is it unrealistic for the reader to expect a realistic account of the characters' linguistic skills?[13] If we assume that the host speaks in Corsican dialect, it is not clear whether Hattie understands the language the host is speaking or whether she just makes out the general meaning of his announcement by understanding some of his words and gestures. Since Hattie has attended Catholic elementary and secondary schools, has completed undergraduate work at Vassar, and has audited graduate courses at Harvard, it is plausible that she has received instruction in Latin and French, and perhaps even in Italian.[14] If she has a gift for languages, she might be able to understand a few words in Corsican dialect, though most native speakers of French and Italian find the dialect rather difficult to understand. Thus, the narrator's glossing over the question of cross-linguistic understanding at this point in the scene is puzzling, since at a few other points in the text problems of cross-linguistic communication are alluded to. This is the case when Edward and Hattie talk with the Corsican mayor, who is said to have lived in the United States (312), and at a crucial moment in the scene of the apparition, when the mayor's brother's sister-in-law, who "once traveled to the United States" (318), explains to Hattie what is being said in the dispute between the monks and the villagers.

Indigo also appears to have understood the host's announcement about the plan to visit the schoolhouse wall: "Indigo was wide eyed as she whispered to Hattie; *this was it!* Indigo could hardly sit still while the others finished eating. Had the Mother of God come alone, or were the other family members and dancers with the Messiah, camped higher in the mountains? Maybe the Blessed Mother could look across the sea and find Rainbow perched in a potted lemon tree on the ledge of a splashing fountain" (316; my emphasis). Indigo certainly understands that the host has spoken of the appearance of the "Mother of God." The short phrase, "this was it," is replete with echoes from other passages in Silko's texts where the referent of the pronoun "it" is ambiguous and seems to be, among other things, some exterior force or spirit that can enter into a character. Here, insofar as Indigo is concerned, the goal of her journey to see the Ghost Dancers again is near. Just that morning Hattie awakened her as she was dreaming that she, Linnaeus, and Rainbow were approaching the Sea of Galilee where they would see the Messiah and his family (314).

Indigo's understanding of the host's announcement and her questions about who will be with the Messiah's Mother appear to be informed by her experience at the Ghost Dance. This experience included the linguistic phenomenon that has been likened to glosso-lalia above. Her interrupted dream psychologically primes her, so to speak, for a repetition of this experience in the apparition. This and her preoccupation with her lost parrot lend psychological real-ism to the scene, but also gloss over the question of tongues. Is it "realistic" that Indigo, who speaks Sand Lizard and English, maybe some Spanish, and plausibly some other Southwestern Indian languages, but who, unlike Hattie, could not have even a rudiment-ary knowledge of French or Italian, could understand the Corsican patois? Is Indigo gifted here with polyglottism? Is she a literary cousin of Baudolino, Umberto Eco's protagonist in the novel of that name, who has the gift of learning a language unknown to him after having heard two persons speak only several sentences? Or, is the narrator performing what Eco refers to as "a sort of mystic service of simulta-neous translation," for the characters as well as for the reader (351)?

In the scene of Hattie's and Edward's initial attempt to talk with Indigo, there is the suggestion that the Indian child is more gifted for tongues than the stiff and learned white scientist:

> Edward returned with a volume of linguistic surveys of
> various desert Indian tribes. He stood with Hattie at the door

of the cage and began to attempt to pronounce words in
Shoshone and Paiute to see if the child responded. All this
time she had not moved from her place on the monkey's pal-
let inside the cage. Edward went through the Agua Caliente
and Cocopa words and was just beginning to struggle with
words from Mojave when a big smile spread across the girl's
face and she laughed out loud. The monkey chattered excitedly
and climbed to the cage top. The girl stood up and looked
down at them confidently.

"I talk English," Indigo said. "I talk English way better than
you talk Indian."

All morning Indigo had listened closely whenever the man
and woman spoke, and she realized she understood English
better than ever; there were only a few big words now she
didn't recognize. The monkey made it clear the woman was a
friend of his. The appearance of the length of rope had
alarmed Indigo, but the woman's words caused the man to
drop the rope; the woman's words gave Indigo the confi-
dence to speak. (108)

In this passage not only does Indigo appear to have a gift for tongues,
but she can also understand the monkey. Juxtaposing Edward's
labored mispronunciation of Indian words with the chatter of the
monkey is a nice touch of irony. Named Linnaeus after the eighteenth-
century Swedish botanist, Indigo's chattering simian friend is nomi-
nally linked to his namesake's having devised the modern binomial
system of classification for plants and animals that constituted a
scientific attempt to repeat in Latin Adam's mythical naming of all
the animals in Eden.[15] When she first approaches Linnaeus and
lets him out of his cage, Indigo is said to have the impression that
he understands her speech: "Out he came, chattering his gratitude.
He wrapped his long curling tail around the bars of the cage to
steady himself as they studied each other closely. He had shining
golden eyes and *he seemed to understand the language of the Sand
Lizard people* when she spoke to him" (104; my emphasis). Indigo
and Linnaeus, unlike Edward, seem to have a gift to communicate

across borders, not only between languages but also between species. Of course, there is the possibility that the Sand Lizard language, which Silko has made up but which never appears inside the text, is akin to a perfect language once spoken by all living beings.[16]

As I said earlier, the oblique third-person narrator glosses over these problems concerning cross-linguistic communication among the characters by acting as translator. In Italian, and probably also in Corsican patois, translators are reputed to inspire distrust. *Traduttore, traditore!* Is the third-person narrator-translator a traitor? Or is the close reader who asks questions from a realistic point of view a traitor to a text that is constructed around the dream of unmediated communication and epistemological communion?

The following paragraph appears to be told from Hattie's point of view. Once again psychological realism is lent to the narrative by the subtle suggestion of differences in Hattie's cultural perspective and the behavior of the Corsican villagers: "Hattie expected their host and perhaps his *immediate family* might accompany them to the site of the *miraculous* wall, but the *entire family came along in a procession* of sorts. The *sun was still blazing hot* as they set out. Edward refused offers from the young boys to carry the camera case and the tripod, although his leg was beginning to bother him" (316; my emphasis). Hattie's immediate expectations concerning the actions of the host's family appear to be informed by her own experience at home, which leads her to conceive the family more as nuclear than as extended. This can be inferred from her surprise at the "procession of sorts" formed by the extended Corsican family and other villagers.[17] It is also possible to detect in Hattie's vocabulary signs of her Catholic education and residual faith: the wall is said to be "miraculous." Of course, given the obliqueness of the third-person narration, Hattie may be repeating the word used by their host. There are other details that allow one to distinguish Hattie and Edward's cultural background from that of Indigo and the Corsicans. For example, Hattie and Edward seem to experience the heat as a source of physical discomfort, which does not seem to be the case for the Corsicans or for Indigo. Edward's past leg

wound makes itself felt. This wound was incurred during an expe-
dition to collect, name, and categorize "unknown" plants in South
America. Of course these plants were only "unknown" and unnamed
from the point of view of the thieving explorers. To the Indians the
plants are known and named, a fact to which Edward is blind and
deaf, so to speak. This pain from a wound incurred during an earlier
uncomprehending foray into a region where indigenous tongues
are spoken provides an occasion for Edward to reduce the distance
that separates him from Corsican culture. He has only to let the boys
assist him. The wound functions like a metonymy for the cogni-
tive and emotional gap created by Edward's scientific and exclusionary perspective between him and people like the Indians in
South America or the Corsican villagers. The theft he has planned,
however, which is as inseparable from his camera as it is from his
character and his wound, motivates his remaining aloof from the
Corsican community in which he could possibly be healed. While
Hattie's point of view approaches that of the Corsican villagers
during this scene, Edward's point of view becomes increasingly
distant from that of Hattie and their host.

Within Hattie's point of view, feelings vacillate with observations,
observations with interpretations and evaluations. The dialogue of
other characters is obliquely referred to, but the points of view of
the other characters are not clearly distinguishable from Hattie's
point of view. The third-person narration with minimal dialogue
in direct discourse makes it difficult to distinguish between what
is spoken by Hattie or by other characters and what Hattie observes,
feels, interprets, evaluates, imagines, thinks to herself, or mentions
to Indigo or Edward. In the following passage not only does the
distinction between her inner feelings and her outer perceptions
remain ambiguous, but the confusion of the two with what is being
said by the host casts doubt on the validity of Hattie's assumptions:

> Hattie *felt an odd energy,* a mood of excitement, among their
> host's family as they walked along, despite the heat, and she
> *assumed* it was due to their visit. Their host explained the

miraculous wall brought a steady stream of visitors to their village. The mayor's brother tugged at the edge of his neatly trimmed beard as he explained that recently a disagreement between the townspeople and the church officials sprang up. Since the apparition of Our Lady on the schoolhouse wall, the visitors and pilgrims who used to visit the gold and silver portrait of Mary in the Abbey Shrine seldom went there anymore. Who could blame them? If they knelt or stood long enough in front of the schoolhouse wall, they might get to see the Blessed Mother herself! (316–17; my emphasis)

Once again, it is not mentioned in which language the mayor's brother is speaking. Earlier, when he explained details about the way citron trees were "trained to grow in a vase form," he was explicitly said to "speak in an odd mixture of Italian and French" (315). How much of this odd mixture Hattie and Edward understood is not stated. Whether this Corsican can speak English, like his older brother who years before had "lived in the United States and never grew tired of greeting visitors from his adopted country" (312), remains unclear. Furthermore, whether the "odd energy" that Hattie "felt" is within herself or outside in the procession is possibly clarified by the paraphrase of this energy as a "mood of excitement," the signs of which she could *observe* in the villagers' actions, facial expressions, tone of voice, and gestures.[18] But Hattie's assumption that the Corsican family's excitement is due to Edward's, Indigo's and her visit is implicitly put in doubt by the host's mentioning that the "miraculous wall brought a steady stream of visitors" and his specifically mentioning the conflict that has arisen between the townspeople and the church officials. The visit of outsiders has become a common occurrence. As will become clear later, the family would more likely be excited because, in going to the schoolhouse to see the "Blessed Mother," they are risking an encounter with the church officials who have declared such a procession anathema.

Finally, the contrast between seeing the "portrait of Mary" and the "Blessed Mother herself" reflects a theological and interpretive problem that can be raised in this scene as well as in the scene of the first Ghost Dance. The portrait kept in the abbey is clearly a representation, an icon, crafted by human hand in gold and silver. The "Blessed Mother herself," at least as described in the above passage, would be the real thing. It is not clear if the mayor's brother is saying that "Our Lady" is physically present, or if Hattie is assuming that he is saying this. A precise translation of the direct enunciation in Corsican dialect is needed to know. Earlier, when the host—who presumably is the same person as the mayor's brother—spoke, presumably also in the Corsican patois, it was "the *image* of Jesus' Blessed Mother" (316; my emphasis) that was said to have begun to appear on the wall. Nor is it clear if the mayor's brother is vacillating between saying, perhaps hyperbolically, that the "Blessed Mother herself" appears and saying that her image appears. This adds to the ambiguity in the narrative. But even if he is just saying that her image is present, he would probably be assuming that it is present not as the result of human craft or art but as the result of divine intervention. The image of the "Blessed Mother" on the wall would not be, strictly speaking, a mimetic representation. Seeing it would constitute something like an unmediated vision of spirituality. The inward perception of the image itself would coincide ontologically with the "Blessed Mother." The theological problem raised here is similar to the one raised in Hattie's thesis between the difference in Mary Magdalene seeing "Jesus' resurrected spirit" and Peter seeing "Jesus' resurrected body" (261).

The narrative ambiguity in this scene can be read as intended or as accidental. Even if it is accidental, it still results from the difficulty posed by articulating theological concepts like spiritual and corporal resurrection or spiritual visions. One cannot deal with such theological problems without rendering paradoxical not only narrative point of view but also language itself. The underlying paradox becomes increasingly obvious in the following passage in which the narration seems to mix direct and indirect discourse, beginning from a point of view shared by Hattie, Edward, their host, and the third-person narrator: "Dawn and sunset *were* the best times to look for Our Lady's image; *you must close the eyes,* pray, and then slowly *open the eyes* only a little as *you focused* on the rough stone wall, their host explained" (317; my emphasis). In this passage, the verbs in the past tense would belong grammatically to indirect discourse. The second-person pronoun as well as the modal verb combination "you must close . . . open" are in the present tense and give the effect of being reported directly (without quotations marks) by the narrator. The final clause, "their host explained," also suggests a direct report. The past tense used in the expression "as you focused," in contrast to the preceding second-person subject-verb phrases, gives the effect of being reported indirectly by the narrator. Furthermore, the nonidiomatic use of the definite article "the" in English—"you must close *the* eyes . . . open *the* eyes"—could be read either as a direct rendering of the host's non-native English or as the third-person narrator's rendering in an indirect discourse that translates an idiomatic usage similar to that of French literally into nonidiomatic English, giving the effect of a language in which the rules of grammar, of linguistic orthodoxy, so to speak, have been relaxed.

The ambiguity of the narrative points of view is also reflected in the themes related to vision, closing and opening one's eyes, special lighting, photographic representation, and the hidden theft Edward intends to commit. At the end of the paragraph, the narration passes to Edward's point of view, which Hattie does not share. This is signaled by the repetition—"quick-quick-quick"—which, in the following passage, would most probably be uttered in Edward's mind or muttered under his breath:

> While the group stood with their eyes closed in front of the schoolhouse, Edward set up the camera behind them. After he made the photograph of the group in front of the miraculous wall, he planned to politely excuse himself to make photographs near the citron groves that surrounded the village. He was relieved to have attention focused on the large group gathered at the schoolhouse wall shrine so he could go among the citron trees unnoticed. Then, he would watch for a moment when no one was watching him, to seize the twig

knife and *quick-quick-quick* cut the best citron twig specimens. (317; my emphasis)

From a realistic perspective, dawn and sunset offer atmospheric conditions that are more conducive to odd prismatic light effects on the wall. These light effects could be caused by refraction of the sun's rays owing to the angle of the sun, changes in atmospheric humidity, and formation of clouds that could also reflect refracted light at oblique angles.[19] From a metaphysical and mystical perspective, these two liminal periods between night and day can be construed as times when ontological and spiritual "transitions" are more likely to occur.[20]

In the following paragraph, Edward's point of view becomes difficult, if not impossible, to distinguish from the narrator's point of view:

The faithful watched the wall, lips moving in silent prayer as he completed preparations. He put his head under the camera cloth to begin to compose the picture when behind him a distance away he became aware of a low sound growing steadily louder, as if a giant swarm of flying insects were approaching, but soon he heard voices raised in anger. As he turned, he saw a strange sight down the road at the schoolhouse: their host with his family standing behind him was in a face-off with another, smaller group of villagers, led by what appeared to be Catholic monks who brandished large crucifixes. (317)

The effect is one of an apparently objective perspective, the objectivity of which is undermined as the reader attempts to tell who is thinking what. Does Edward perceive the prayers of the persons before the wall as silent, or does the third-person narrator objectively report them to be silent? Would the distance between Edward and the praying faithful make it difficult if not impossible for him to hear the mumble in which prayers to the Virgin are often recited? Likewise, the distance between the approaching group and Edward apparently causes him first to perceive their voices as the sound of a swarm of insects. This perception entails an unflattering comparison, which one can attribute to Edward, who generally scoffs at religion. However, in Edward's first taking the sound of angry voices for the sound of swarming insects, one can also detect possible allusions to biblical passages, which Edward would be unlikely to intend, notably to the confusion of tongues at Babel (Gen. 11:7) or the "sound from heaven as of a rushing mighty wind" heard as the Holy Spirit came upon the apostles as Pentecost (Acts 2:2–3). The angry vocal confrontation between these two "Catholic" points of view, which Edward does not appear to understand or to take much interest in, reflects and adds to the theme of ambiguity and confusion of tongues in the narrative.

Primed by American yellow journalism, Hattie at this point appears to be thinking less about the Blessed Mother than about Indigo's and her own safety. Her first reaction is to look to Edward for male protection: "Hattie became alarmed and took Indigo firmly by the arm to stay close to Edward in case violence erupted. Bloody Corsican feuds were regularly reported in American newspapers" (317). Indigo watches attentively, refusing to take her eyes off the wall, but thinks that the "Blessed Mother probably would not come now that she heard the angry voices" (317).

Edward, whose point of view literally coincides with his looking through the viewfinder of his camera, appears to be completely detached from what he is seeing. He is in the perfect position to record through the camera's *objective lens* both the dispute and the possible apparition on the wall. However, he has brought the camera along not owing to a desire to record the truth objectively, but rather owing to his plan to hide his intended theft. Thus, the so-called objectivity of this technological point of view is entwined with deception, mendacity, and desire for monetary gain as well as with Edward's seeming lack of concern for Hattie's and Indigo's safety. He takes two photographs of the dispute, thereby recording images of anger, lack of understanding, and confusion, but then, rather than staying to record the apparition that is the issue of the debate between the two groups of Corsicans, he heads for the orchard where he will sate his desire to steal from fruit trees:

Edward kept watch through the viewfinder and made one good exposure of their host arguing nose to nose with another man as the monks and the others formed a semicircle around them. Hattie tried to follow the argument as both men gestured at the old schoolhouse and then at the abbey on the hill beyond, but she couldn't make out more than a few words.

Edward seemed unconcerned as he moved the camera and tripod to get another view of the altercation. When the second plate was exposed and safely stored, Edward looked up the road for the best grove of the citron trees, branches arched gracefully over the low rock walls easily within his reach. He carefully balanced the camera and tripod on his shoulder and carried the camera box up the road toward the orchard he'd chosen for its robust trees. (317–18)

Ironically, Edward's leaving the scene of the religious dispute leads to him unwittingly assuming a role in a "heretical" gloss on the story of the Fall. His theft from fruit trees in an orchard can be construed as an intertextual link to the story of Adam and Eve in the Garden. Adam and Eve's theft from the Tree of Knowledge is interpreted in the orthodox patristic tradition as the felix culpa whereby they and their descendants originally lost immortality and clarity of vision in the earthly Garden but prepared the way for themselves and part of mankind to ultimately gain the heavenly City of God. This original sin thus felicitously opens the long-suffering wait for the Messiah and his Blessed Mother in the Western narrative of sin, salvation, or damnation. In this narrative, God the Father curses the Serpent, curses Eve with sorrow in childbirth, and curses the earth, which man will henceforth be obliged to cultivate with great toil. This same God curses mankind at Babel with the confusion of tongues. The narrative in Silko's text obliquely glosses the stories from Genesis, undoing the misogynic patristic interpretation and reattributing and redefining the culpa as infelicitous male blindness. In this Corsican orchard, at the moment that the townspeople, Indigo, and Hattie are awaiting the reappearance of the Blessed Mother on the schoolhouse wall, it is not the woman but the man who is responsible for the theft in the garden. Furthermore, Edward is not seduced by the Serpent, who offered knowledge to Eve, but by his blinding desire for wealth, a desire mediated by his modern Western worldview, which is capitalist, scientific, and scholarly.

Silko's story of Edward in the garden is obliquely and ironically exegetical. It is a parable that turns on its head the orthodox tradition of patristic exegesis. Her third-person narrator tells the story from a confusion of points of view, but at the same time obliquely casts a light on why Western culture, and capitalism in particular, is, in Silko's own words, "absolutely irredeemable"[21] and its perspective one of blindness. In pretending to be making an objective photographic record of the configuration of the citron trees, when he really is hiding the cupidity that is the sole motivation for his trip to Corsica, Edward links scientific objectivity with deceit. For readers with a perspective similar to Edward's, perceiving the oblique luminous glow that this parable casts should lead them to question their own worldview. By persisting in that worldview, such readers identify with Edward, who winds up infelicitously inculpated back in Italy and eventually dead from quack science in the desert. For readers with a postmodern or deconstructive worldview, perceiving this oblique luminous glow should reinforce their questioning of all theoretical perspectives, leading them to the paradoxical understanding that nothing can be understood. All is ultimately babble. For readers who aspire to the worldview of Silko's writing storyteller, this babble, when perceived in the right outer and inner light, is the perfect language of love. This is the language that provides a total perspective.

Hattie, of course, is unaware of what Edward is up to. She is confused by the dispute. On a realistic level, as said above, her being able to make out only a few words can be attributed either to her inability to understand the Corsican dialect or to her distance from the disputants. Figuratively, however, her not being able to understand this dispute can be read as a thematic link to the theological debate she raised in her thesis proposal. Just as she does not understand what is taking place before the schoolhouse wall, so she did not fully understand what took place between the professors at Harvard and herself. Nor did she understand the dispute between the Gnostics and the church fathers whose writings defined orthodoxy. Just as the Harvard professors did not even deign to engage in a scholarly debate with a woman, so the misogynic church fathers dismissed the matriarchal spirituality of the Gospel of Mary Magdalene, declaring it anathema. The Harvard professors, relying on the authority of the writings of the church fathers, rejected as inauthentic the text that Hattie had read in translation and interpreted to be central to her thesis.[22] Now, on the wall, Hattie will experience the authenticity of her thesis topic and of the Gnostic heresy.

Before that experience, however, the dispute before the wall is glossed for Hattie, not by a father figure, but by a woman:

> After a time, a friendly woman, their host's sister-in-law, who once traveled in the United States, joined Hattie and Indigo to explain. Recently, church officials contacted the town mayor to order him to put a stop to the devotions at the schoolhouse wall. The mayor replied there was nothing he could do; the image of the Blessed Virgin could not be washed off or painted over—the monks and other church authorities already tried to expose the apparition as a hoax. But the beautiful colored light that formed the image was only enhanced by the whitewash splashed over the wall. Truly this was a miracle, and the people who once went to the abbey for miracles now came here to the street in front of the schoolhouse, *where no offerings were required to see the Mother of God*. (318; my emphasis)

This friendly woman's being with her in-laws before the wall indicates that she has taken sides against the abbot in the dispute. Although the narrator does not explicitly specify in what language the host's sister-in-law speaks to Hattie and Indigo, it would appear that her having "traveled in the United States" not only motivates her to be more friendly, but also makes her more likely to have some knowledge of English that would aid her to explain and translate.

That this dispute is about the equivalent of heresy and about excommunicating heretics becomes more apparent when the abbot's interpretation of the apparition on the wall as well as the measures he has taken to make his interpretation official Church doctrine are recounted: "The abbot alleged the image on the wall was the work of the devil because the miraculous appearance overshadowed the monks' shrine to the portrait of Mary in *silver and gold.* Still, the people flocked to see the lovely image of Our Lady until the abbot contacted Rome and a monsignor came all the way from Rome and forbade its veneration on pain of *excommunication*" (318; my emphasis). Even though Hattie may now have an oral translator and explicator with whom she speaks directly, the reader still has only the third-person narrator. The reader remains at a remove from the direct discourse either of the friendly woman or of the abbot. In other words, the third-person narrator leaves ambiguous not only whether the woman is explicitly speaking in English but also whether she is explicitly saying or just implying that the abbot and the monks are motivated by love of money rather than by love of the Blessed Mother. Likewise, the third-person narrative leaves ambiguous whether the abbot has explicitly accused the villagers of being motivated by avarice rather than by love of the Blessed Mother (since they no longer make charitable offerings to the portrait of Mary in silver and gold), or whether he has just declared them to be taken in by the Devil's works.

Of course, the entire scene does depict the host's friendly sister-in-law and her family as more sympathetic than the anathematizing angry abbot and the crucifix-brandishing monks. Furthermore, the abbot's reasoning as it can be glimpsed in indirect discourse appears patently self-inculpating. It is easy to read the abbot's and the monks' point of view as grounded in cupidity. If they see this, they are mendacious hypocrites. If they do not see this, they are blinded by their love of money and power, which, in this scene, is the same as a desire for orthodoxy. Thus, the abbot relies on the patriarchal authority of the Church, which is based on the written tradition of patristic exegesis and validated by the pope and his College of

Cardinals, to whitewash his and the Church's love of money as love of God. Their motivation in this dispute is the religious version of what has sent Edward into the orchard to steal. Furthermore, the abbot has interpreted the source of the luminous apparition to be the Devil, in the same manner that the church fathers interpreted the Serpent in the Garden of Eden to be Satan. In other words, Hattie is witnessing a dispute between the orthodox patriarchal Church and a group of Corsican heretics who are beginning to worship the principle of spiritual motherhood. Ignoring Church dogma, the heretics are taking the luminous image on the wall to be the Blessed Mother. Seen through the orthodox prism of patristic exegesis and Catholic dogma, what they are seeing on the wall is an image of the same Serpent that seduced Eve.

It may not be entirely coincidental that Silko chose to figure the apparition of the "Blessed Mother" on a wall in a scene that figuratively indicts the greedy patriarchy of Western culture, both secular and religious. In a controversial mural, painted during 1986 and 1987 at 930 North Stone Avenue, Tucson, Arizona, Silko pronounced a similar indictment in Spanish words and American Indian images. The principal image in the mural was a huge rattlesnake whose body contained skulls. Also depicted was a spider on a web and a hummingbird. The words on the mural, "La gente tiene hambre. La gente tiene frio. Los ricos han robado la tierra. La gente exige justicia. De otra manera Revolucion,"[23] echo the reasons that the "Blessed Mother" showed herself to the Corsicans in the small village: because the "people were poor; their lives were a struggle" (320).

In an interview with Ellen Arnold, Silko tells how she came to paint the mural while she was writing *Almanac of the Dead* and how it was covered over, first with whitewash and then with thick paint, owing to the owner of the building, a "wretched dickhead of a rich man . . . against the wishes of the people" ("Listening to the Spirits" 176).[24] According to Silko, the whitewash was not thick enough to keep the snake and the words, which people repainted, from showing through. At the time of the interview (1999), according to Silko, the thick paint was already peeling off. Thus, one can liken the treatment of the mural to the treatment of the schoolhouse wall, which Church officials, with little success, had tried to cover with whitewash. Despite attempts to cover them over, the teachings of the Instructor-Serpent show through like earlier writing in a palimpsest. When viewed through the prism of the scene of the apparition in *Gardens,* and in conjunction with the passage to which Hattie just happened to open when she took up and read Dr. Rhinehart's translation of the Gnostic Gospels, the story of Silko's mural can be interpreted as an uncanny retelling in American Indian images and concepts of the Gnostic version of the Serpent and Eve in which "the arrogant Ruler cursed the Woman and the Snake" (*Gardens* 100). This passage is cited by Pagels to support the argument that the Gnostics saw the god of Eden as a "jealous master" who insisted on his patriarchal authority. In this passage the "arrogant Ruler" is analogous to the "wretched dickhead" who had Silko's educational snake painted over. Whether in Mexico or in Eden, this insistence on patriarchal authority leads to drawing borders, to cursing snakes, to subjugating woman to man, poor people to the wealthy Church hierarchy, Indians to whites.

Ironically, when read from an orthodox Catholic point of view in connection with the above passage, as well as with the scenes in Italy where Hattie and Laura view stone statues of ancient snake-mothers, the abbot's interpretation is on target. The villagers are seeing on the wall the "Female Spiritual Principle [that] came in the Snake, the Instructor." From an orthodox point of view, the monks and the abbot have every reason to be disturbed. The villagers are already receiving religious instruction at the schoolhouse, rather than at the abbey. Now, without knowing it, the excommunicated Corsican villagers have established communion with a foreign visitor, Hattie, the "heretic of Oyster Bay," and a "pagan" Sand Lizard, with whom they have broken bread and to whom they are telling stories of the disputed miracle:

> By this time other women joined them, curious to hear what their kinswoman told the foreign tourist. Yes, it was true. The

abbey was built to house the precious picture of hammered
silver on gold. Pilgrims crawled on their knees up the abbey's
marble steps to leave offerings. The paralyzed walked; the
deaf and blind heard and saw again. When the Greek king
lay seriously ill, the abbot himself carried the precious picture
to the bedside of the king, who kissed the picture; instantly
the illness receded and in a few days the king was well again.
Over time, however, the miraculous power of the picture
slowly got used up; but now the blessed Mother herself had
come to them. (318)

Once again, the narrator does not make explicit whether Hattie
understands the tales these women are telling in Corsican dialect,
or whether the women's kinswoman is acting as a simultaneous
translator in both languages. Whatever the means, Hattie the heretic
and the excommunicated are communicating, while Edward and
his camera, allegedly in search for knowledge among the citron
trees, recede into the distance where he becomes more and more
ex-communicado: "With Edward barely visible in the distance, bent
over his camera, Hattie was grateful for the friendly conversation;
at the time she thought his behavior a bit odd, even rude, but he
did want to learn all he could about the citron groves while they
were there" (318; my emphasis). In this passage, there is an indication
not only of the distance between Hattie's point of view and Edward's
point of view "at the time," but also of the distance between Hattie's
point of view "at the time" and her point of view at a later time
after Edward's arrest. As the distance between Edward and Hattie
increases, both physically and figuratively, the distance between
Hattie and Indigo shows signs of decreasing: "Indigo gripped Hattie's
hand tightly as she felt the excitement all over her body" (318).

Hattie does not appear to understand the "loud words exchanged"
(319) as the dispute between the monks and the villagers is broken
off. Indigo also does not appear to understand the literal meaning
of these loud words. She does, however, understand that they are
ugly and therefore that they are an impediment to seeing the "colorful image of blue, green, yellow, and red" (319): "The Blessed Mother

was not likely to appear so soon after ugly words were exchanged" (319). She is remembering the need for the people both to speak and to act harmoniously in the language of love in order to be in the presence of the Messiah and his Mother.

Hattie's wait before the wall is said to contrast with Indigo's. As Indigo pays close attention, both to the wall and to the villagers, assuming they might be able to see something that she cannot see, Hattie chats with the host's sister-in-law. When the apparition occurs, Indigo and Hattie are not said to see the same thing. This could suggest that what is narrated in this religious experience is an inner vision, mediated by each character's worldview, previous experiences, and current desires and expectations. These combine to inform their individual perception of the light on the wall. The language used to depict Indigo's perception and feelings suggests that her vision is interior and that in it remembered experience merges ontologically with present experience to create what could be called an instant of eternity in which ontological, temporal, and epistemological boundaries are erased:

> As the light changed, Indigo began to see tiny reflections glitter on the surface of the whitewashed plaster that *she recognized as* the flakes of snow that swirled around the dancers the last night when the Messiah appeared with his family. *She could make out the forms* of the dancers wrapped in their white shawls and the Messiah and his Mother standing in the center of the circle—all were in a beautiful white light reflecting all the colors of the rainbow, lavender, blue, red, green, and yellow— and in that instant Indigo *felt* the joy and the love that had filled her that night long ago when she stood with Sister Salt, Mama, and Grandma to welcome the Messiah. In that instant joy swept away all her grief, and she *felt* their love embrace her. (319; my emphasis)

From a so-called objective point of view, it is highly unlikely that Indigo is looking at snow flakes falling on a hot summer day. It is much more likely that she is watching an odd prismatic light effect caused by refraction in the atmosphere or reflected refraction from the "quartz pebbles" she is said later to have "picked up near the schoolhouse with the miraculous wall" (323). From the point of view of psychological realism, this light effect triggers in her an involuntary affective memory.

As mentioned above, Hattie is not said to see the same thing as Indigo. When she first sees the light on the wall, a question is posed that signals the possible presence of a scientifically objective point of view in Hattie:

> A murmur rose from those closest to the wall, interrupting their conversation, and when Hattie and the others turned to look, the faithful were on their knees in the dirt. *Was it an odd reflection off metal or glass nearby?* A faint glow suffused the whitewashed wall and Hattie felt her heart beat faster as the glow grew brighter with a subtle iridescence that steadily intensified into a radiance of pure color that left her *breathless*, almost *dizzy*. (319; my emphasis)

The rapid pulse, breathlessness, and dizziness can be read both as physical signs that Hattie is nearly in a trance and as possible impediments to the objectivity of her observation. In the passage that follows, she is said to reason that the presence of witnesses proves that the luminous glow on the wall is real, in contrast to the one she saw in Aunt Bronwyn's garden, which might have been part of a somnambulist's dream. This, however, does not prove that what is on the wall is any more than an odd light effect. Furthermore, her conclusion that she has witnessed a miracle, based on her own and the villagers' tears of joy and on their excited speech, which she is not said to understand, is easily contestable. For all Hattie and the reader know, the Corsicans may also have seen only an ephemeral prismatic refraction of light. Nevertheless, the possibility of a scientific explanation for what Hattie, Indigo, and the "faithful" are seeing is associated with the point of view of Edward, whose having distanced himself from the scene leads to Hattie "perceiving" him unflatteringly as a distant dark speck, beyond communication:

The strange light in Aunt Bronwyn's garden might have been a dream, but here she was with dozens of witnesses! *Where was Edward? He must see this! Hattie turned and saw him, a dark speck in the distance, too far to call;* but when she looked back at the wall again the light was already growing faint. She was surprised to feel tears on her cheeks and saw that the others—men as well as women—wept though their faces were full of joy. Yes, yes, they all spoke excitedly with one another, they had seen her. Yes, Hattie nodded her head, yes! So this was what was called a miracle—she felt wonder and excitement, though she saw the glow of colored light on the wall for only an instant. (319–20; my emphasis)

Hattie is not said to see more than "the glow of colored light," nor is she directly told what the villagers have seen. She appears to infer they have seen the Blessed Mother from their tears of joy and from their excited speech in the Corsican patois, the words of which she may or may not literally understand. Thus, from a scientifically objective perspective, it is possible that they too have seen only an odd light effect, but as a group of individuals who have internalized the Mariolatry that shapes their world-view, they are each having an inner vision that is mediated involuntarily by images of the Blessed Mother they have all previously seen in the abbey, as well as by stories about the miracles she has performed.

Indigo, who was earlier said to "make out the forms of the dancers wrapped in their white shawls and the Messiah and his Mother standing in the center of the circle" (319), is now said to have seen only the dancers and to hear a voice, which she interprets as coming from the Messiah: "The rocky dry hills and their people were poor; their lives were a struggle here; that was why the Blessed Mother showed herself here; the people here needed her. Although she didn't see the Messiah or the rest of the family or her mother with the dancers, Indigo was much heartened; all who are lost will be found, a voice inside her said; the voice came from the Messiah, Indigo was certain" (320). Indigo's being said "at this point" not to have seen the Messiah, but to have "heard" an interior voice, which she takes for certain to come from the Messiah, can be compared with the inner experience of the Gnostic who becomes "a Christ" (Pagels 134). The subjectivity of her certainty, however, is signaled by the disparity between the first telling by the narrator, in which Indigo "could make out the forms of the dancers wrapped in their white shawls and the Messiah and his Mother standing in the center" (319), and the second in which she is said to see only the dancers. This disparity, or vacillation, approaches the kind of narrative undecidability that characterizes the fantastic as defined by Todorov. Since the dancers are wrapped in white shawls, it would be plausible from a scientifically objective perspective to argue that Indigo too "saw" only the glow on the wall. Silko continues, however, to cast this point of view in an unflattering light by having Hattie get angry when Edward "wisecracked about religious hysteria" (320) and then realize, as he talks about "drilling machines to mine the meteor crater in Arizona" (320), that no matter what words were chosen to tell the story, they would not suffice to convince someone with Edward's scientific and capitalist worldview.

The plot, of course, proves Hattie to be on target. Edward's greed blinds him not only to the apparition that his spouse, the Corsican villagers, and Indigo have "seen," but also to the arrest that awaits him in Livorno and to Dr. Gates's scam that will lead him like a credulous fool to bankruptcy, illness, and death in the desert. Hattie, instructed by the Blessed Mother, that is, by the Serpent, has had an eye-opening experience. Silko leaves the reader with the suspicion that Edward and those readers who share his worldview are as blind as the "wretched dickhead" who had her revolutionary snake mural painted over "because he hated what it stood for" ("Listening to the Spirits" 176).

As the writing storyteller prepares to put down her pen, Sister Salt, Indigo, and her nephew, the little grandfather, are living at the gardens in the dunes. Maytha and Vedna visit, bringing a letter to Indigo from Hattie:

> The envelope was covered with strange stamps and a smeared
> postmark from England. Inside Indigo found a lovely tinted
> postcard of Bath and a folded blank sheet of paper that held
> a folded $50 bill and a glassine envelope of postage stamps.
>
> The postcard showed the big pool at the King's Bath dotted
> with the tiny figures of white men wading and swimming.
> They took turns looking and laughing at the picture before
> Indigo read the message. (474–75)

This photographic and written message, telling about white male
bodies bathing in ancient springs, love and flowers and old stones,
about returning to Laura and her gardens in Italy, is the beginning
of a correspondence between Indigo and Hattie that quietly reflects
the exchange of letters between James Wright and Silko. Stamps
and stationary are enclosed for Indigo's reply. It is not likely that
Indigo will write in the perfect language of love that she heard
spoken by the Holy Mother at the Ghost Dance. It is, however, quite
likely that in her epistle to Hattie and Aunt Bronwyn she will tell
Maytha's and Vedna's story about how love can be expressed and
reconciliation sought between strident non-Christian Indians and
staunch Indian Christians in the language of flowers:

> Remember all those gladiolus spuds Indigo planted in their
> garden and everyone scolded her for planting useless flowers?
> Guess what? Big spikes of buds appeared in the first warm
> days after Christmas, and in no time white, lavender, red,
> and yellow flowers opened. People passing by on the road
> stopped to stare—the flowers were quite a sight.
>
> When no one was around, the twins took an old bucket full
> of freshly cut flowers to the brush-covered shelter the flooded
> Christians used as a church. At first the twins weren't sure if
> their peace offering would be accepted by their neighbors.
> But the next week, they found the old bucket at their gate, so
> they refilled it with flowers. Their neighbors received all sorts
> of food donations from other churches each month; but no
> one up or down the river had such tall amazing flowers for
> their church. So those flowers turned out to be quite valuable
> after all. (475)

She might also write about how these valuable flowers provide
not only healing between the beer-guzzling twins and the Christians
but also nourishment:

> Indigo scooped up some stew with a piece of tortilla.
> "Look," she said to the twins. "Do you see this?"
> "Some kind of potato, isn't it?" Vedna fished one out of
> her stew and popped it into her mouth.
> "Ummmm!"
> Maytha stirred her stew with a piece of tortilla and examined
> the vegetable—it was a gladiolus spud! She laughed out loud.
> "You can eat them!" she exclaimed. Those gladiolus weren't
> only beautiful; they were tasty! (475–76)

Gladiolus was named by the Romans. "Its name is from the Latin
gladiolus, which means 'little sword,' alluding to the flattened, sword-
shaped leaves characteristic of the genus" (Burrows and Tyrl 720).
Similar to the little grandfather and most of the mixed-blood characters living in the desert, gladiolus are hybrids, derived from Africa.
Collectors brought them to Europe and to the Americas roughly
during the time when the slave trade was flourishing: "Collection
of these African taxa was extensive in the late 1700s, and hybrids
appeared in the 1820s" (Burrows and Tyrl 720). As word and thing
gladiolus has roots in the British Isles and in Africa. The Latin word
gladius, sword, from which the diminutive is formed, is of Celtic derivation. From *gladius* is derived *gladiator,* the captive or slave trained
to fight professionally to entertain the Romans in the arena.

Silko's language of gladiolus is rich in shushed metaphors and
tropes of healing and nourishment. But like writing, figured as a *pharmakon* by Plato, these flowers may heal or poison, whether ingested
as trope or as thing. If poor Edward's bones could speak from his dry
scientist's grave, he might warn Indigo and Maytha in the language
of botany about the possible toxicity of gladiolus "spuds," usually
called corms. He might also warn Aunt Bronwyn to keep her cattle
out of the gardens, as there are reports of cattle that have become ill
and in some cases died from eating gladiolus (Burrows and Tyrl 721).

Silko, however, appears ready to deal with the risks of writing or eating flowers, just as she is ready to deal with the potential danger of venerating rattlesnakes. The story does not end, but as we prepare to close and put down the book, the writing storyteller tells of Sister Salt's early morning bath at the spring:

> They sat so quietly the twins and the little grandfather dozed off; something terrible struck there, but whatever or whoever, it was gone now; Sister Salt could feel the change. Early the other morning when she came alone to wash at the spring, a big rattlesnake was drinking at the pool. The snake dipped her mouth daintily into the water, and her throat moved with such delicacy as she swallowed. She stopped drinking briefly to look at sister, then turned back to the water; then she *gracefully* turned from the pool across the white sand to a nook of *bright shade*. Old Snake's beautiful daughter moved back home. (477; my emphasis)

Perhaps patristic exegetes would warn this unwed whore and mother and her sister about the venomous knowledge promised by this Serpent in the garden in the dunes, but in the silent language of love Sister Salt has had a vision of the return of the matriarchal spiritual principle to the garden. It is a paradoxical vision of luminous darkness filled with grace. It is a vision of Coatlicue, the Serpent goddess. Coatlicue, the "consuming internal whirlwind . . . the symbol of the underground aspects of the psyche . . . the mountain, the Earth Mother who conceived all celestial beings out of her cavernous womb . . . Goddess of birth and death, *Coatlicue* gives and takes away life; she is the incarnation of cosmic process" (Anzaldúa 68). It is a vision of Mother Earth wrapped in a healing blanket of transplanted and indigenous flowers: "Down the *shoulder* of the dune to the hollow between the dunes, silver white gladiolus with pale blues and pale lavenders glowed among the great dark jade datura leaves" (476; my emphasis). It is a vision of renewal in which madness has been shushed as the postmodern medicine woman interweaves tropes of orality and of literacy as artfully as the Maya painted their codices and as naturally as Ayah, her mother, and her grandmother wove the bright Navajo blankets.

Some critics may find this book a difficult read in places or in its entirety owing to frequent sentimentality and long passages through many, many gardens. In my reading I have not mentioned what I find flawed. Likewise, I have not taken up the adventures of the beer-guzzling mixed-blood twins, Maytha and Vedna, Sister Salt, Big Candy, and Delena, the Yaqui Gypsy, Tarot card reader, circus dog trainer, and Zapatista, who may well be a more interesting character than Indigo, Aunt Bronwyn, or Laura. The adjective "maudlin" is apposite for *Gardens in the Dunes.* This novel is figuratively soaked in tears shed by characters. "Maudlin" is etymologically derived from Mary Magdalene, who was traditionally depicted as a tearful penitent in European iconography. In *Gardens* this author of a Gnostic Gospel neatly conflates two mother figures from Mexican and Southwestern American border culture: La Chingada, or Malinche, the raped mother and whore/traitor/translator for Cortés, and La Llorona. The flood of tears in *Gardens* could be read to signal in the perfect language this mother's incessant nocturnal wailing for her lost children, which, according to Gloria Anzaldúa, "has an echoing note in the wailing or mourning rites performed by [Aztec] women as they bade their sons, brothers and husbands good-bye before they left to go to the 'flowery wars'" (55).

Perhaps the best way to enjoy *Gardens in the Dunes* is to take it up and read a passage, letting the hybrid rhetorical flowers turn us to the goddess of the pharmakon, and then to put it down and dream with serpents of the perfect language, pen in hand.

CONCLUSION

I have argued in the introduction that Silko is not an oral story-teller. She is a novelist, a poet, and a writer of short stories in whom the voice of the storyteller is shushed, transformed into written storytelling. She has attributed not having developed her talent for oral storytelling to being a writer: "I suppose that if I didn't have the outlook of a writer, I might get better at storytelling, but I always say that I'm not good at giving off-the-cuff presentations ("A Leslie Marmon Silko Interview" 85). The writing storyteller, who is explicitly the third-person narrator in nearly all of Silko's stories and novels, is modeled on Aunt Susie. Like Aunt Susie, in the quarrel with Grandma A'mooh, the writing storyteller both liter-ally and figuratively takes the position to save the book.

In chapter 1, I have argued that Silko is a medicine woman. I have made this argument in my readings of texts in which bears figure. Silko's seeing the great brown bear lying on a boulder on Chato during her first deer hunt is a vision that she interprets to mean that she is a medicine woman. But unlike her character Humaweepi, a male who appears to be a full-blood who speaks an unspecified Pueblo tongue, Silko is a woman, a mixed blood, who knows "[v]ery little" Laguna Keresan ("Stories and Their Tellers" 19). Thus, unlike Humaweepi, she cannot literally be a shaman, living in or near a pueblo and performing oral ceremonies. Instead, she is a medicine woman who figuratively performs ceremonies when she writes. Nor can she be a "modern" shaman, like old Betonie in *Ceremony*, who consults a tattered book as he puts together a cure for Tayo. She is a postmodern medicine woman. Her bear paw is a special kind of text, the kind of text that Roland Barthes has called writerly.

For Silko, writing is not just literally writing down the voice of an oral storyteller. When Silko writes she shushes the voice of the storyteller, not killing it, not rendering it a dead letter, but glossing, translating it into a new syncretic tongue in which the oral and the written, the spirit and the flesh, cannot be unraveled. This tongue is the live letter, the letter that, rather than killing the oral tradition, quickens it.

In short stories narrated in the third person, like "Storyteller," "Lullaby," "Tony's Story," and "Coyote Holds a Full House in His Hand," Silko vacillates between a distrust of writing that is informed by a logic of exclusion and the realization that writing can both wound and heal, a position informed by a paradoxical logic of inclusion, a messianic logic of syncretic interpretation in which writing heals a lost or unknown tongue by glossing it. This can be seen in what happens to the Yupik woman in "Storyteller." The Yupik woman refuses to speak English. The old man and she repeatedly tell the story of the great white bear and the hunter. Silko does not transcribe this story and translate it into English, in the manner of Elsie Clews Parsons, the translator of the stories in Franz Boas's *Keresan Texts*. The writing storyteller glosses the oral storytelling itself, showing its relation to the literate culture that has penetrated oral Yupik culture, wounding it. This cultural wound is figured by the motif of the trace of red in the whiteness of the snow, sky, and ice. This Gussuck penetration is economic and phallic. It wounds culturally, figuratively emasculating and literally killing. This can be seen in the "murder" of the Yupik woman's parents by the storeman who sells them denatured alcohol to drink. The Gussuck penetration cuts out the Yupik tongue with education. This can be seen in the jailer and the schoolgirls who refuse to speak Yupik. That this penetration is both phallic and economic can be seen in the storeman who runs after the Yupik woman onto the treacherous icy river. The literate Gussucks sate their carnal desires in sex and pillage, figuratively raping the earth by drilling for oil. With this penetration the Gussucks are writing the death of Yupik culture. The Yupik woman, however, who is illiterate, uses her knowledge of carnality to avenge her parents. She lures the Gussuck storeman to his death in the frozen river, using the desires that inform literate Gussuck culture to do in him and, figuratively, his culture. Metaphorically she turns the Gussuck writing against itself. The logic of exclusion excludes itself.

Although the Yupik woman remains figuratively frozen in a monolingual whirligig, telling over and over again the story of the bear and the hunter, in which the roles of hunted and hunter converge, that is nowhere literally translated in Silko's text, the writing storyteller's gloss saves her, healing the cultural wound. In writing "Storyteller," Silko, the medicine woman, is performing a healing ceremony for her illiterate Yupik character.

Similarly, I have argued, the writing storyteller glosses Ayah, the bereaved and alcoholic Navajo mother who has been robbed of her children. Silko's text, like the brightly colored Navajo blankets that Ayah, her mother, and her grandmother once wove and slept in, enwraps Ayah and Chato, who lie freezing to death wrapped in an unraveling army blanket. Like the Yupik woman, Ayah is illiterate and monolingual. Figuratively Silko's text saves Ayah. Silko's text glosses Ayah as not dead, but sleeping, like the great brown bear. This gloss corresponds to the translation of the song, the lullaby, from Navajo into English by the writing storyteller. This story also offers an example of Grandmother Spider as a figure for self-reflexive textuality.

In "Tony's Story" Silko's distrust of writing is perhaps stronger than in either "Storyteller" or "Lullaby." Nevertheless, the written history of the Pueblo Revolt of 1680 becomes a model for Tony's killing and burning the big cop, implicitly glossing the now silent voice of old Teofilo, who has apparently told Tony stories of witches and witchery. Madness and its relation both to oral storytelling, visions and dreams, and to writing is also an important motif in this story. Ultimately the journalistic and legal narrative, as glossed by the writing storyteller, by the psychiatrist George Devereux, and by the literary scholar Larry Evers, is what I have glossed in chapter 4. Whether the postmodern medicine woman succeeds in curing Tony is an unanswered question.

"Coyote Holds a Full House in His Hand" is a fabulously funny story in which the writing storyteller's perspective can be described as a special kind of *discours indirect libre,* which creates an irony that is warm, matronizing, and equalizing, unlike the cold, patronizing, and condescending Flaubertian irony usually associated with this form of discourse. To a certain extent the anonymous main character in this story figures Silko. His storytelling and medicinal talents come into him like an outside force or narrative spirit, the spirit of Coyote, who plays all roles. In this story laughter and writing are the bear paw for the writing female medicine man.

"A Geronimo Story" is narrated in first person by a character called Andy. In this story Silko's distrust of writing and of literate culture is also strong, but in the end the writing storyteller wins out. The first-person narration makes it hard to find the writing storyteller, but she is there, stealthily hiding in the role of the translator of Keresan who is not a traitor. I have argued that Andy's story glosses the story of the Laguna Regulars written on the back of muster rolls by Robert G. Marmon, Silko's great-grandfather. The rhetorical battle of Pietown, in which Siteye defeats the arrogant Major Littlecock, owing to Captain Pratt's refusal to translate Siteye's rejoinder in Keresan, reverses what could be called the military "squaw man's" treason to Laguna. Treason, indeed, is a strong term, as is "squaw man," but "A Geronimo Story" suggests that Silko would see as mendacious the historical narrative of Austin N. Leiby, which depicts her great-grandfather and the Laguna Regulars as both translators and traitors.

In "A Geronimo Story," more than in the other stories collected in *Storyteller,* one can feel the cultural wound that I have argued is at the origin of Silko's yearning to become a writing medicine woman in order to heal herself. This wound, I have argued, is Silko's knowing "[v]ery little" Keresan. Out of this wound comes Silko's yearning for a perfect language, the perfect tongue in which the written and the oral are interwoven, a perfect tongue that glosses the tongue that was partially "cut out" owing to Silko's growing up in a house full of books where "absolute value was placed on speaking English" ("Stories and Their Tellers" 19) and everyone read books, even at the lunch table (*Yellow Woman* 158). This perfect tongue glosses the tongue that has been cut nearly out, heals it, supplements it, quickening rather than killing the old stories.

Silko's discovery of the Mayan codices places the perfect tongue for which she yearns not only in the future, but also in the past, in the indigenous precontact past. With *Almanac of the Dead* Silko's medicine woman persona becomes postmodern. Nevertheless, despite the now indigenous model for writing, the desire to purge oneself and one's land of the Anglo Europeans, of the writing that desiccates, that devours, that kills, is dominant in *Almanac*. No matter how much the writing storyteller glosses Zeta and Lecha and Yoeme glossing the old Mayan book and notebooks, Grandma A'mooh's logic of exclusion seems to win out in this text.

Once she has read Elaine Pagels's *The Gnostic Gospels,* Silko can finally trust writing and the paradoxical logic of inclusion. Her discovery that there are different Jesuses, different messianic storytellers figured in so-called heresies and apocrypha, as well as her interest in pre-Christian religions, gives the writing storyteller many more stories to gloss. I have argued that in the scenes of the Ghost Dance, in which the motif of glossolalia or xenoglossia is explicit, and in the scene of the apparition on the Corsican schoolhouse wall, the writing storyteller functions like what Umberto Eco calls a mystic translation service. Silko's yearning for the perfect language, which is both written and oral, becomes explicitly a theme in the story that is being written. Paradoxically, this perfect language would permit nonmediated communication and knowledge. The reader is left with figures, metalinguistic metaphors for writing and metaphor. Metaphorically, the reader is left with writing that functions like Plato's pharmakon. The flowers of rhetoric can both poison and nourish. Rattlesnakes may figure wisdom, but their "bite" is dangerous.

Scholars of American Indian literature have tended to idolize the oral storyteller. As I argued in the introduction to this book, their foregrounding of the live voice and their distrust of writing and Western culture in general have resulted in their unwitting espousal of the same logic of exclusion that informs ethnocentric Western critical discourse. In many ways, the role attributed by some of these scholars to Silko in American Indian cultures resembles that attributed to the Russian storyteller Nikolai Leskov in Walter Benjamin's "The Storyteller: Reflections on the Works of Nikolai Leskov." In this essay Benjamin sketches the decline of storytelling in Europe. This decline he attributes not to writing but to the invention of printing, the rise of the middle class, and the novel. According to Benjamin, "[w]hat distinguishes the novel from the story (and from the epic in the narrower sense) is its essential dependence on the book" (87). Benjamin distinguished Leskov's written storytelling from the writing of the novelist. He makes the relation of experience as counsel the principal criterion by which the storyteller differs from the novelist: "The storyteller takes what he tells from experience—his own or that reported by others. And he in turn makes it the experience of those who are listening to his tale. The novelist has isolated himself. The birthplace of the novel is the solitary individual, who is no longer able to express himself by giving examples of his most important concerns, is himself uncounseled, and cannot counsel others" (87). Here "counsel," as Benjamin is using it, designates words of wisdom, both cultural and personal, either figurative or literal, that the storyteller gives to his audience.

Silko, like Benjamin's novelist, does isolate herself. She left Laguna for Alaska, where she wrote *Ceremony* and "Storyteller," and then, having returned, she again left Laguna for Tucson, where she compiled, wrote, and published *Storyteller,* and where she wrote and published *Almanac of the Dead* and *Gardens in the Dunes.* What distinguishes Silko from Benjamin's storyteller is that she takes advantage of the printed book, of her so-called novels, to disseminate her and her ancestors' experience of literate Anglo-European culture's penetration into Pueblo culture and into other indigenous American cultures.

Silko has told Ellen Arnold how when writing *Almanac* she lost control of this novel, felt the old stories coming in, and felt the presence of spirits that took over the book ("An Interview with Leslie Marmon Silko" 154). In other words, although she isolated ˙ herself to write, she was joined by ancestral spirits from many tribes, who linked themselves and the old stories to her as she linked them and herself through print to the rest of the world. Silko experiences writing as being ridden by the spirits. This is the experience, the counsel, her text offers to her readers in English and in translation throughout the world. It is a counsel to know and write spiritually and carnally. It is a counsel to reject the logic of exclusion that informs so much of Western writing.

Unlike the novel that, according to Benjamin, "neither comes from the oral tradition nor goes into it" (87), Silko's postmodern text never leaves the oral tradition. It is woven around the old Mayan book that Lecha and Zeta translate. It is woven into the tradition of the writing storyteller in which Silko was born and raised. This inborn interweaving of orality and writing is already present in Grandmother Spider, the Pueblo figure who gives counsel and whose web critics have appositely shown to inform *Storyteller.* Spider, in Silko's text, figures a self-reflexive textual trope. The spider can figure the negative side of writing in this trope, or "Thought Woman, the spider" (*Ceremony* 1) can figure the positive side of writing, troping the author right out of the novel. As Louis Owens has noted, this turns *Ceremony* into a fine example of postmodernism: "*Ceremony,* more than any other novel I know of, approaches the category of 'authorless' text" (169). But whereas Owens construes Silko's text as nostalgically pointing back "toward the polyvocal oral tradition that predates the 'privileged moment of individualization' marked by the coming into being of the notion of author" (169), I have construed it as pointing both forward and backward toward a perfect language, toward the ontologically privileged Mayan text. What distinguishes the "author" of *Almanac of the Dead* and of *Gardens in the Dunes* from Benjamin's modern novelist is her dependence on the spirits to counsel her as she writes. What likens Silko to Benjamin, who was interested in the Kabbala, in Jewish writings about mysticism, and also to French poets, critics, and intellectuals like Mallarmé, Barthes, and Derrida, is her mes sianic yearning for a perfect language that makes it possible for translation to become tradition without treason.

As Silko picked up her pen to write out the stories collected in *Storyteller,* she made a gesture that duplicates Aunt Susie at Cliff House, saying that she will finally write out all of the stories "in far greater detail than [Aunt Susie] has ever been able to tell them" (*Delicacy and Strength of Lace* 48). In writing out these stories, Silko has brought a remedy to the linguistic and cultural wound left by the protestant penetration of the Laguna cultural matrix, but with that same remedy she ironically reopened the wound.

Once the wound left by the Anglo penetration has given birth to the writing storyteller, who stands with one foot in each culture, both now oral and literate, any attempt to exclude the written is also a Pauline and patristic attempt to cut out exegetically either the Indian or the Anglo, the female or the male, or both. The two are forever wedded in the past, present, and future, in Leslie Marmon Silko, the writing storyteller, the postmodern medicine woman, and in the text that is the live letter.

NOTES

INTRODUCTION: THE WRITING STORYTELLER

1. Hirsch explicitly sets out to contrast the oral tradition to the written word. He portrays Silko as conceiving of writing as mere linear representation of speech. Implicit in the organic metaphors he uses is a concept of the spoken word as life and meaning itself and of writing as associated with death, loss of meaning, and a swerve from the truth. For example, in discussing Silko's comment in *Storyteller* about "the trouble with writing" (110), Hirsch states that "in the context Silko here establishes for it, [the trouble] is twofold: first, [writing] is *static; it freezes words in space and time.* It does not allow the *living story* to change and grow, as does the oral tradition. Second, though it potentially widens a story's audience, writing removes the story from its immediate context, from the place and people who *nourished* it in the telling, and thus *robs* it of much of its *meaning*" (1; my emphasis). The tendency to grant ontological and episte-mological priority to speech over writing is by no means limited to students of non-Western oral traditions. Western culture itself has its witting and unwit-ting proponents of the spoken word and detractors of the "dead" letter and law. In "La pharmacie de Platon" (in *La dissémination*) and in *De la grammatologie*, Jacques Derrida has offered a critique of this tendency in Western thought.

2. See Susan Perez-Castillo's discussion of Silko's vituperative review of Louise Erdrich's *The Beet Queen*, in which she excoriates Erdrich for postmod-ernist, nonreferential, and fashionable writing: "Postmodernism, Native Ameri-can Literature, and the Real: The Silko-Erdrich Controversy." See also David L. Moore, "Decolonializing Critics," and Helen Jaskowski, *Leslie Marmon Silko*.

3. Gerald Vizenor and Louis Owens are notable exceptions. Owens's "The Syllogistic Mixedblood: How Roland Barthes Saved Me from the *indians*" (*I Hear the Train* 90–104) is a brilliant essay that views a photograph of his Cherokee mixed-blood great-grandfather taken in Oklahoma in 1913 in a discourse that

is informed by both Barthes and Susan Sontag. Although it is probably only a curious coincidence—and by no means am I attempting to establish a literary influence—Barthes' literary "non-autobiography," *Roland Barthes par Roland Barthes*, which paradoxically signaled at least his formal acceptance into the pantheon of French writers enshrined by the priests of French academic criticism, whom Barthes so gleefully excoriated during most of his lifetime, can be likened to *Storyteller* both stylistically and philosophically. Its decidedly non-linear discourse is interwoven with family photographs; it can be taken up and satisfactorily read on almost any page. It is the open-ended story of a marginal writer (homosexual, hedonist, agnostic Protestant, leftist, structuralist, and poststructuralist) writing his aggregation into the center of French literary notoriety. It is a liminal text that defies formalist classification by genre or essentialist classification by its relation to the Truth: it is neither autobiography nor fiction, neither historical narrative nor poetry, neither criticism nor philosophy. It is written storytelling.

4. In July 1997 Lee Marmon told me that he did not have access to Aunt Susie's writings. He also mentioned a memoir that Robert G. Marmon was dictating at the time of his death in the 1930s. This memoir ends with his arrival at Laguna. Thus, Silko's text not only rewrites Aunt Susie's absent writings, it also takes up the story where her great-grandfather's voice became silent. I have found mimeographed copies of two short essays written by Aunt Susie. In one the split between the progressives and the traditionalists is described, including some of the "jugglery" to which traditionalists resorted. In the other a Laguna wedding is described. These essays are in the private archive of Florence Hawley Ellis maintained by Andrea Dodge of Albuquerque, New Mexico.

5. In a moment of postmodern playfulness, one could liken the tricky relationship Silko portrays between herself and Aunt Susie to the relationship that arises from the curious reversal of Socrates and Plato as portrayed on the frontispiece of *Prognostica Socratis basilei*, a thirteenth-century English fortune-telling book attributed to Matthew Paris. A reproduction of this illumination, in which Plato, standing behind Socrates, appears to be dictating to his teacher, who sits writing, can be found in Jacques Derrida's *The Post Card: From Socrates to Freud and Beyond* (last page of original edition; also cover illustration of the American paperback edition).

6. This collection of letters, which was edited by Anne Wright and published as *The Delicacy and Strength of Lace: Letters between Leslie Marmon and James Wright*, is an extraordinarily moving testimony to Silko's philosophical and aesthetic curiosity at the time she was putting *Storyteller* together. In it we become acquainted with a Silko who reads David Hume and speculates about the way precontact Pueblos viewed the world, and who is told by her friend Mei-Mei Berssenbrugge that her "idea for structuring the collection (*Storyteller*) was similar to [John] Cage's book—and she's right" (37).

7. See Ellis, "An Outline of Laguna Pueblo History and Social Organization." In this essay, conversations with as well as the writings of Mrs. Walter K.

Marmon are given as sources. See also Ellis, "Laguna Pueblo," in *Handbook of North American Indians*, volume 9, in which the Marmon family figures prominently along with other whites named Gunn and Pratt who are cousins of the Marmons.

8. Silko's "salty remark" (Danielson 331) about Elsie Clews Parsons having "written off Laguna as a lost cause," which many scholars of American Indian literature noddingly quote, suggests that she has not read Parsons very carefully, or perhaps that she is relying more on rumor and the general Pueblo dislike of Parsons on account of her having "betrayed" secrets in her writings. Parsons sees Laguna as a good place for the study of exactly what Silko's *Storyteller* exemplifies, the syncretic weaving together of pre-Anglo and post-Anglo tradition: "When the town [Laguna] was first studied, twenty years ago, its ceremonial disintegration was so marked that it presented an obscure picture of Keresan culture. But, with recently acquired knowledge of that culture in mind, today Laguna and her nine colonies offer unrivaled opportunities to study American acculturation and the important role played by miscegenation" (*Pueblo Indian Religion* 890).

9. In an interview with Dexter Fisher, Silko has attributed her lack of fluency in Keresan to the importance placed on the English language in her family:

[F]: *Do you know the Laguna Language?*
[S]: *Very little.* I know very little because we're mix-blooded. I know as much as Grandma knows to get along at the store, *but there was an absolute value placed on speaking English.* I grew up with my great-grandmother, so I understood a lot more when I was small. (19; my emphasis)

10. On one level the answer to this question can be found in an interview in which, having been asked by Kim Barnes whether she "consider[s] herself to be a storyteller in the traditional sense" ("Leslie Marmon Silko Interview" 48), Silko attributes her lack of oral storytelling ability to being a writer: "I suppose if I didn't have the outlook of the writer, I might get better at storytelling, but I always say that I'm not good at giving off-the-cuff presentations" (49).

11. A curious lapse in the biographical note to *Laguna Woman* has resulted in confusion about Silko's mother's origin. Recently Silko discovered and rewrote this *lapsus memoriae matris* in a genealogical note tracing her mother's patrilineal origin to a Cherokee family. Silko notes that she wrote "mother" instead of "grandmother" in the earlier edition. It was her "paternal grandmother, Grandma Lily, who knew only that her father's family were part Plains Indian, but she never knew which tribe" (*Yellow Woman* 148).

12. The absence of direct mother-child mothering also is notable in *Ceremony*, as well as in *Almanac of the Dead*, where neither old Yoeme nor Lecha do much mothering. In *Gardens in the Dunes* Indigo's mother disappears at the first Ghost Dance, and her grandmother dies before she is shipped off to California. Sister Salt's mothering of the so-called little grandfather is an exception.

13. For an extensive treatment of these codices, see Mignolo, *The Darker Side of the Renaissance: Literacy, Territoriality, and Colonization*, and Hill and Mignolo, editors, *Writing without Words: Alternative Literacies in Mesoamerica and the Andes*. For a history of epigraphers' efforts to decipher the Mayan writing, see Coe, *Breaking the Maya Code*. For a Heideggerian reading of some of these Mesoamerican texts, see Gingerich, "Heidegger and the Aztecs."

14. Silko's interest in the Mayan screenfold books is apparent not only in this essay, but also in her novel *Almanac of the Dead*, which is plotted around "two old Yaqui women . . . [who] possess large portions of a fourth Maya book, which survived the five-hundred-year war for the Americas" (*Yellow Woman* 158). In the novel this fourth Mayan book is a special kind of writing in that it is imbued with the power of prophecy. Thus, whoever knows how to read this special kind of non-European writing is not constrained by rationalist and empirical Western notions of epistemology and linear temporality. On some levels the intricately woven plots in *Almanac of the Dead* recall apocalyptic stories from tabloids. Before the publication of *Almanac* Silko half-seriously, half-jokingly said to Kim Barnes that she wanted "this novel to be a novel that, when you shop at a Safeway store, it will be in the little wire racks at the check-out station and that I don't want to write something that the MLA [Modern Language Association] will want. I want something that will horrify the people at the MLA. Mostly, I'm teasing, but in another way I'm not. I'm sad to see that so little serious fiction gets out into the world" ("Leslie Marmon Silko Interview" 47–48).

15. My guess is that this friend is Larry McMurtry.

16. This split between progressives and conservatives, which Silko does not exactly write off as unimportant, but to which she only briefly alludes in *Storyteller* (254–56), is described by Florence Hawley Ellis (Ellis, "Laguna Pueblo" 438–49). In a conversation with the Acoma writer Simon Ortiz (June 1998 in New Orleans), I discussed the hypothesis that Silko's writing grows out of desire to heal the split between the conservatives and progressives in which the Marmons played a considerable role. Ortiz found this hypothesis both interesting and plausible.

CHAPTER 1. BEARS: WRITING AND MADNESS

1. The excerpt of this novella, *Humaweepi: The Warrior Priest*, is printed in *The Man to Send Rain Clouds: Contemporary Stories by American Indians*. In "On Nonfiction Prose" Silko has given "the spring, summer, and fall of 1971 when I was pregnant with Cazimir" as the period during which she wrote this text (*Yellow Woman* 193).

2. *Kawaik*, or *Kawaika*, is the Keresan name of the now-vanished lake after which Laguna Pueblo is said to have taken its name.

3. Mircea Eliade would probably say that Humaweepi is at the navel of the world, experiencing a "hierophany" (see *The Sacred and the Profane* 12).

This Greco-European term, while not a translation from the Pueblo, is no less apposite than calling Humaweepi's vision sacred or spiritual. It would be interesting to know what Humaweepi's experience is called in Keresan, Tiwa, Tewa, or Towa.

4. This possibly imaginary language that Humaweepi and his uncle speak is a forerunner of Sand Lizard, the language Silko "invents" for Indigo and her tribe in *Gardens in the Dunes.* The points where Humaweepi's question about the lake is suspended and where he and his uncle communicate silently foreshadow the perfect language spoken at the Ghost Dance in *Gardens.*

5. Magic realism has been described as a discourse in which the "recognizably realistic mingles with the unexpected and the inexplicable, and in which elements of dream, fairy-story, or mythology combine with the everyday" ("Magic Realism").

6. David Bohm and F. David Peat describe visual perception from the perspective of the spirit of scientific objectivity in the following passage:

> In order to see anything at all, it is necessary for the eye to engage in rapid movements which help to extract elements of information from the scene. The ways in which these elements are then built into a whole, consciously perceived picture have been shown to depend strongly on a person's general knowledge and assumptions about the nature of reality. Some striking experiments demonstrate that the flow of information from the higher levels of the brain into its picture-building areas actually exceeds the amount of information that is arriving from the eyes. In other words, what we "see" is as much the product of previous knowledge as it is of incoming visual data. (64)

Following Bohm and Peat, more information from previous experience walking with her father while he hunted deer would be flowing into the "picture-building areas" of young Leslie's brain than from her eyes, causing her to "see" a deer. Her seeing a bear, however, could suggest that previous knowledge from stories about bear country would be providing information to the picture-building area. Thus, from the point of view of Bohm and Peat, one could speculate that bear stories she had heard had primed young Leslie with an unconscious expectation or fear of seeing a bear and being lured away to live with the bears, like the young boy in one of the stories told in *Storyteller.* In *Gardens in the Dunes,* Indigo's vision of the Messiah and his family at the Ghost Dance and her vision of the apparition on the schoolhouse wall present similar interpretive problems to those posed by Silko's bear stories.

7. Just as Silko had been primed with previous knowledge from stories about bear country, so Greg Salyer, a critic who has read Silko's bear stories and "An Essay on Rocks," is primed for an ursine vision when he takes a lone walk in the country around Laguna:

While hiking on top of the mesa overlooking the 640 acres of Marmon land near Acoma, I came around a huge boulder to see a bear outlined perfectly against a rock about 25 yards away. The hair on the back of my neck stood up, and I froze. When neither I nor the bear moved for several minutes, I realized that perhaps I was misinterpreting the image. As I moved closer, I could see that this was not a bear but an incredibly lifelike formation on the rock that was a much darker color than the sandstone around it. This phenomenon occurs often when hiking in the Southwest because the landscape itself generates a variety of interpretations, just as Silko describes in this book. (129)

Salyer conflates Silko's two writings of the bear story and then reads them through the grid of his own experience, which is neither a vision of a spirit animal nor the account of a moment of madness, but the tale of a moment in which the lifelike formation on the sandstone rock produced in him a feeling of the uncanny. This allows him to reduce Silko's bear stories to an instance of joyous interpretative undecidability: Maybe it was a bear that Silko saw, or maybe it wasn't. Salyer has implicitly asked and then declared unanswerable one of the questions that Silko silences in her text: real or just imaginary? In this reading the Southwestern landscape is inseparable from the text. Salyer does not deal with the second hunting story narrated in verse in which Silko concludes that the bear was sleeping (*Storyteller* 79).

8. If one provisionally accepts the hypothesis of Bernard Hirsch, who contends that the verse passages in *Storyteller* are Silko's attempt to graphically and spatially represent traditional orality on the written page, this passage in verse would represent Silko's telling orally what heretofore she "couldn't tell": "In her own telling Silko uses poetic form with varying line-lengths, stresses, and enjambment to provide some of the movement and drama of oral storytelling" (7). Hirsch appears to find Silko's verses not only closer to the voice but also closer to the truth than the prose of the printed block-style paragraphs. He asserts that Silko's "use of poetic form here suggests that this place where she saw the great bear has become part of an inner as well as an outer landscape. Through an act of imagination she has learned a profound truth from the land which intensifies her bond to it" (18). Whether she actually did tell the story orally to anyone, however, is passed over in silence.

9. Given the size of these antlers, there is little doubt that Uncle Polly returns from Mount Taylor not only with a buck but also with a story that need not be silenced. In a sense this story is literally represented in the photograph of the deer that are dead, not sleeping. There is, however, something passed over silently in this photograph as well as in the expression "the old man of the mountain," which Uncle Polly uses to refer somewhat enigmatically to his benefactor. This is a spiritual and storytelling link between this legendary buck and Tse-pi'na, the Laguna name for Mount Taylor, which roughly translates as "woman veiled in clouds." This is similar to the link between Silko

and the giant bear, between Humaweepi and the giant bear, and between Tayo and Ts'eh, whom critics have speculated to be "the woman of the mountain." The caption for the photograph on page 78, in which one of the large mule deer is perhaps the legendary buck, also passes over in silence a story about a link between Tse-pi'na and the Laguna people that has been severed: "Bill Smith was the ranch foreman for the L Bar Cattle company, and he used to let us hunt on Mt. Taylor land the L Bar owned. There was an old cabin there we slept in. My uncle Polly and I have just finished arranging the bucks on the porch of the cabin so they can have their pictures taken" (270). This link is not dead, it is just sleeping, as Silko's writing sets out to show.

10. "Secondary orality" is the term Walter J. Ong uses to describe what Krupat ("Post-Structuralism and Oral Literature" 118) thinks poststructuralist critics have called textuality:

> Secondary orality is both remarkably like and remarkably unlike primary orality. Like primary orality, secondary orality has generated a strong group sense, for listening to spoken words forms hearers into a group, a true audience, just as reading written or printed texts turns individuals in on themselves. But secondary orality generates a sense for groups immeasurably larger than those of primary oral culture— McLuhan's "global village." Moreover, before writing, oral folk were group-minded because no feasible alternative had presented itself. In our age of secondary orality, we are group-minded self-consciously and programmatically. The individual feels that he or she, as an individual, must be socially sensitive. Unlike members of a primary oral culture, who are turned outward because they have had little occasion to turn inward, we are turned outward because we have turned inward. In a like vein, where primary orality promotes spontaneity because the analytic reflectiveness implemented by writing is unavailable, secondary orality promotes spontaneity because through analytic reflection we have decided that spontaneity is a good thing. We plan our happening carefully to be sure that they are thoroughly spontaneous. (*Orality and Literacy* 134)

Silko, like her character Humaweepi, has shown tendencies to want to live away from the center of Pueblo life. One could speculate that she has turned outward because she has turned inward, that her writerly introspection melds with her memories of Aunt Susie and Grandma A'mooh in order to turn her into the champion of cosmopolitan and syncretic spirituality. In many ways Silko's spirituality resonates with a New Age worldview.

Characters like Ts'eh, the Night Swan, Yellow Woman, the Yupik protagonist in "Storyteller," Old Yoeme and her granddaughters, Lecha and Zeta (*Almanac of the Dead*), Indigo, Aunt Bronwyn, Laura the *professoressa*, Veda and Maytha (*Gardens in the Dunes*) embody carnal spirituality. Silko's narratives are anti-orthodox in that they blend sexuality, storytelling, and textual hermeneutics, rather than attempt to separate them by metaphorically equating writing with sin, guilt, and falsehood. Gnosticism, which Silko will discover before writing *Gardens in the Dunes,* offers a way whereby she can reconcile her own eclectic and syncretic worldview with European culture and with her great-grandmother A'mooh's Presbyterianism.

11. Secondary orality, or textuality, allows Silko to maintain the secrecy about rituals and stories for which the Pueblo are known, and yet paradoxically to share these rituals and stories with an international audience. In a sense Silko could be accused of doing what Elsie Clews Parsons did by publishing in *Pueblo Indian Religion* stories and descriptions that she had promised her Pueblo informants she would keep shushed to herself. Silko can persuade herself and her readership that she does not betray the secrets (see note 16 below regarding Paula Gunn Allen's censure of Silko) because she is not writing ethnological discourse. Unlike the translations of Laguna stories by ethnologists like Parsons and Boas, which Silko thinks kill the stories, she is writing in a mode that quickens them and translates in diverse languages for diverse cultures the syncretic thought structures that inform the stories.

12. One could speculate that Lee Marmon's having learned photography in the army provided him with the "magic" he needed to avoid a fate like Tayo's.

13. I have in mind here not only Derrida's reading of Plato's metaphorical use of pharmakon to figure writing as both potion and poison in "La pharmacie de Platon," but also the similarity between the shaman's medicine and the witch's destructive power.

14. Silko tells of being driven to vacation Bible school by "Mr. Ottapopie . . . an Oklahoma Indian minister at the Presbyterian Church at Casa Blanca" (*Storyteller* 271). Although she claims not to "remember anything about religion— just the crayons and paste and the Kool-Aid they gave us at lunchtime" (271), it can be argued that Grandma A'mooh's Presbyterianism, even if it was "slowly dying out" at Laguna, left an imprint in the literate Marmons' fondness for books, for reading silently and aloud, and in Silko's syncretic worldview.

15. *Shash* is the word given for bear by Robert W. Young and William Morgan (*Navajo Language* 824). Although Silko's spelling, "Shush," could be the result of her transcribing what she had heard, this is not a reason not to read in the bear's name a cross-linguistic pun, an ursine call for the silence of writing as medicine.

16. See Allen, "Special Problems in Teaching Leslie Marmon Silko's *Ceremony.*" I suspect that Allen's censorious remarks about Silko's indiscretion in publishing clan stories spring as much from a rivalry between mixed-blood cousins as from her Pueblo cultural sensitivity. There is also the distinct possibility that Allen has not carefully thought out the cultural implications of the introduction of writing into an oral culture.

17. In an article in which he compares Silko's text with a translation from the 1930s, Robert Bell has demonstrated quite convincingly that Silko probably had access to a written source: "the hoop transformation ceremony in *Ceremony*

recapitulates, in astonishing detail, the procedures set forth in the Coyote Transformation rite in the Myth of the Red Antway, Male Evilway, recorded and translated by Father Bernard Haile in the 1930s. Simple comparison of the two texts . . .—and recalling that the oral 'texts' were always figural and symbolic—reveals a likely source for Silko's hoop ceremony at the middle of the book" (Bell 48).

18. Stories of were-bears are found in European folk legends dating back to Roman times. A French novella entitled *Lokis*, by Prosper Mérimée (1803–71), tells the story of an eccentric Lithuanian count who is possibly a were-bear, as his mad mother has been mauled and possibly raped by a bear before his birth. This text makes for an interesting ursine cross-cultural companion piece to Silko's recent interest in residual pre-Christian elements in European thought.

19. Louis Owens wittily takes up this problem in genre theory:

> By announcing in what amounts to textual superscript her own subordination as author to the story-making authority of Thought-Woman, or Spider woman ("I am telling you the story / she is thinking"), Silko effects a deft dislocation of generic expectations, placing her novel within the context of the oral tradition and invoking the source and power of language found within that tradition. She simultaneously, and self-consciously, rejects the egocentric posture of the modern author in favor of what could be defined as an ecocentric orientation and attempts a culturally determined heteroglossia in which her text serves as transmitter rather than originator of voices and meanings. As a result, *Ceremony*, more than any other novel I know of, approaches the category of "authorless" text. In response to Foucault's rehashed questions, "Who really spoke? Is it really he and not someone else? With what authenticity or originality?"—Silko's text points toward the polyvocal oral tradition that predates the "privileged moment of individualization" marked by the coming into being of the notion of author. In the oral tradition, stories are never original and always have the "duty of providing immortality"—of preventing the death of a culture; the very absence of author illuminates their authenticity. In the present age of author as icon, one can easily imagine a work such as *Ceremony* published with no author's name attached, a delightful possibility. (*Other Destinies* 169–70)

If *Ceremony* is an "authorless text," then what happens when it is "canonized" as a "novel," translated and published for an international audience, taught in English courses at every university in the United States, and its author awarded a McArthur "genius grant"? Should the revenues from this so-called novel go to Laguna? However this may be, critics and teachers alike are proclaiming: Good News! Shush and the Indians have come to save us from canonical writers and many other cranky cowboys of literary modernism.

20. See Nelson, "Rewriting Ethnography: The Embedded Texts in Leslie Silko's *Ceremony*."

21. The importance of the unsaid in effective storytelling is emphasized by comments about Siteye's knowing how to express meanings with silence that are made by Andy, the first-person narrator of "A Geronimo Story."

22. *Yupik,* according to Fienup-Riordan, means literally "a genuine person." It is derived from *"yuk* human being + *pik* genuine, real" (71). The Yupik word for foreigner is derived from the Russian word *kazakh* (*cossack* in English), which is from South Turkic, *qazaq* (adventurer). Silko gives this word as "Gussuck." Fienup-Riordan gives the phonetic approximation as *cassaq,* which, needless to say, does not phonetically suggest strong antiwhite sentiments for the native speaker of English.

23. *Solstice* is etymologically derived from the two Latin words: *sol,* meaning sun, and *stitium,* stoppage. It is not stated whether the solstice in question in this story occurs in the winter or in the summer. I am assuming it is during the summer, as the sun is visible in the sky.

24. See Jacques Derrida, "Des Tours de Babel." In chapter 6 I relate this article by Derrida to the translation and transcription of the old Mayan almanac in *Almanac of the Dead.* In the first Ghost Dance scene in *Gardens in the Dunes,* the Messiah and his Mother speak the "language of love" in a glossolalic maneuver that both brings up and suggests a way of getting around the problem of cross-linguistic communication and translation.

25. The red on white in "Storyteller" is recalled by the red Xs that designate unexplained airplane crashes on the map the insurance executive shows Lecha as she returns from Alaska, where she has met Rose and an old woman who has learned how to use electromagnetic forces and the spirit of stories in order to do in airborne petroleum geologists (*Almanac* 160).

26. The absence of *Stiya* from the house in which Silko grew up figures the absence there of the ideology of assimilation that Stiya embodies.

27. Ann Fienup-Riordan's essay "The Real People and the Children of Thunder" is an extremely informative treatment of the mix of Christian and native belief that resulted from the late-nineteenth-century Moravian missionary activity of John and Edith Kilbuck among the "Yup'ik Eskimos of the Kuskok-wim drainage"—the same location in which "Storyteller" is set. According to Fienup-Riordan, John Kilbuck, a full-blood Delaware Indian who had been taken from his parents and raised and educated by the Moravians in Kansas, was viewed by the Yupik as "blood of their blood." Despite comments that he made in his diary and letters about native immorality and despite his and his spouse's efforts to suppress overtly "pagan" ceremonies, it seems that John Kilbuck, who became fluent in Yupik, felt a strong attraction to Yupik ways: "John, especially, seemed able to enter into the spirit of what he witnessed. At the end of a detailed description of the dramatic reception of guests at what was probably a Messenger Feast (*Kerviq*), he wrote, 'Somewhere in me, there must be some of the old Injun left, for I was strangely stirred, and I could not but help thinking of my forefathers, who not so many generations back, were such proud boasters. I think it is on this account, that I feel so drawn to these

people, and helps [*sic*] me enter into their feelings' (journal to Edith, Aug. 30, 1897, MA)" (Fienup-Riordan 89–90). This attraction seems to have been quite strong when it came to carnal knowledge: "Unfortunately for John, his openness to Yup'ik morality (specifically his adulterous relations with native women) led to his dismissal from the ministry in 1899. After ten years away from the Kuskokwim, he and his wife returned to Akiak, where he continued to work as both a missionary and a teacher until his death there in 1922" (238 n. 9).

CHAPTER 2. BACK TO THE TEXT: "LULLABY"

1. Chato bewilders the white man by telling him he does not want the body back. Silko is playing on the white's ethnocentric reaction and apparent lack of knowledge about Navajo avoidance of the dead. See Witherspoon 20.

2. "One of the most startling paradoxes inherent in writing is its close association with death. This association is suggested in Plato's charge that writing is inhuman, thing-like, and that it destroys memory. It is also abundantly evident in countless references to writing (and/or print) traceable in printed dictionaries of quotations, from 2 Corinthians 3:6, 'The letter kills but the spirit gives life' and Horace's reference to his three books of *Odes* as a 'monument' (*Odes* iii.30.1), presaging his own death, on to and beyond Henry Vaughan's assurance to Sir Thomas Bodley that in the Bodleian Library at Oxford 'every book is thy epitaph'" (Ong 80).

3. "The Navajo approach to the death of a friend or kinsman is to mourn profusely for four days, then go through a rite of purification. The personal property of the deceased is buried with him or destroyed, and his name is never again mentioned for one year after his death. Even then the deceased's name is rarely mentioned" (Witherspoon 190).

4. Here again, as in the introduction, seen from a cross-cultural point of view, writing can be construed to function as medicine. Implicit in this figure is the ambiguity of the Greek term *pharmakon* that Plato uses in his critique and condemnation of writing as a remedy for memory that destroys the memory. Ong argues in a much more succinct manner than Derrida that Plato's critique of writing is beset by the paradox in that it, as well as his "philosophically analytic thought" (79), is dependent on "the effects that writing was beginning to have on mental processes" (79).

5. Ong points out that "[b]y separating the knower from the known . . . , writing makes possible increasingly articulate introspectivity, opening the psyche as never before not only to the external objective world quite distinct from itself but also to the interior self against whom the objective world is set" (104).

6. This was the reaction of my mother-in-law, who has never read Leslie Marmon Silko and knows nothing about Pueblo culture. She perceived Maria Anaya Marmon to be an *old man* crocheting, surprised and wondering what was happening. This certainly does not lend credibility to Jaskoski's contention that serenity and patience are legible in A'mooh's face.

7. In Evers and Carr's "A Conversation with Leslie Marmon Silko," Silko refers to the BAE reports as "dead and alien" (Jaskoski 97; "Conversation" 30) in contrast with the lively oral stories she has heard since she was young. Silko also talks about the mendacity of such ethnological reports that she imagines resulting from an anthropologist's informant being some "Charlie Coyote type" ("Conversation" 30) who enjoys making up "outrageous lies." In her short introduction to the early Silko interviews (91–92), Jaskoski acknowledges Silko's dual education, both Pueblo oral and Western literate, and her mixed feelings of anger and appreciation toward the Western educational institutions that inflicted suffering and racist mistreatment on Indian students like herself. Jaskoski does not, however, broach the issue of Pueblo oral culture already having interiorized chirographic and typographic culture before Silko's aunts and elders exposed her to it. Silko's innocent denial that Grandma A'mooh's being a "strong Presbyterian" had any cultural influence on her children, who were not Presbyterians, can be construed as evidence that Silko had not thought carefully about how her own literacy, which is in the Marmon tradition of Grandma A'mooh and Aunt Susie (an informant for ethnologists and historians), leaves her written fictional stories open to the charge of being "outrageous lies."

CHAPTER 3. "THE BATTLE OF PIE TOWN," OR LITTLECOCK'S LAST STAND

1. Robert G. Marmon's handwritten account on the back of a muster roll of the campaigns, military drill competitions, and military service performed by the Laguna Regulars in the 1880s was apparently prepared as part of an attempt to get governmental reimbursement for military services performed: "For field service in Apache Campaigns of 1885 this company hold Certificates of indebtedness against the Territory of New Mexico amounting $3,712.20." A photocopy of this muster roll is part of the private archives of Florence Hawley Ellis that are maintained by Andrea Dodge, her daughter, in Albuquerque, New Mexico. Florence Hawley Ellis worked with Mrs. Walter K. Marmon and other members of the Laguna community during her research on Laguna culture and history.

Ms. Kathryn Marmon recounts that for the Apache campaign of the summer of 1885 the "troops of every company in the battalion were issued certificates of indebtedness by the Territory of New Mexico" but that the "territory failed to honor the certificates, and feeling responsible for his men, Capt. Marmon [Robert G. Marmon] bought their certificates of indebtedness, a few at a time, hoping he would someday be able to collect from the territory. He never did, and the reason for the failure of the territory to settle this account has never been given" (Marmon 59). Ms. Marmon does not mention Leiby's article or the efforts Robert G. Marmon made to obtain pension certificates for the remaining Laguna scouts, who are shown in the photograph on page 224 of *Storyteller*.

2. "Much of the personal history of this work is derived from archives in the possession of Mrs. W. K. Marmon, daughter-in-law of Robert G. Marmon, of Mrs. Alice (Marmon) Day, daughter of Col. Walter G. Marmon, and of Mrs. Edith (Marmon) Lorenzo. Much of the flavor of this account derives from long discussions with Mr. Charlie Atsie of Magdalena and Laguna, cowboy, railroadman, former lt. Governor and member of Laguna Pueblo Council, and almost certainly descendent of 'Ow astie' listed on the 1882 Muster Roll" (Leiby 228).

3. "A Geronimo Story" appeared in both *The Man to Send Rain Clouds* (1974) and in *Storyteller* (1981). Leiby's article appeared in a volume of writings by members of "El Corral de Santa Fe Westerners." The goal of this volume, stated in the introduction by Albert H. Schroeder, the editor, is to gather "material that would illustrate interchange or interaction between Indian and non-Indian groups of the Southwest, or within either group and at the same time would portray a more or less significant aspect of the history of the groups or individuals involved" (xiv). A photograph (page x), under which is placed the caption "A Gathering of Some of the Corral," shows twenty-five men, none of whom has a non-Anglo-European name (page xi), and provides an interesting cross-cultural counterpoint to the photograph of the Laguna Regulars that Silko includes in *Storyteller* and that Leiby includes in his article.

4. Angie Debo, following Dan L. Thrapp's *Conquest of Apacheria*, provides the following account of Apache activity inside the U.S. border in the summer of 1885: "A hide-and-seek pursuit by the soldiers ensued through the mountains of southeastern Arizona and southwestern New Mexico, with the hostiles breaking up into small parties and dashing out to kill and rob. The soldiers seldom glimpsed them, but the bodies of at least seventeen civilians and about 150 horses and mules worn out and killed or abandoned marked their passing. By June 10 most of them had crossed the international border" (Debo 241). Austin N. Leiby, who also relies on Thrapp for movements of the U.S. Army forces under the command of General George C. Crook as well as on "archival documents in the New Mexico State Records Center in Santa Fe, in most cases from accounts written on the reverse side of muster rolls by officers in charge of companies" (229), gives more details about the Apache raiding parties in New Mexico: "The campaign of 1885 was touched off by Geronimo's foray which began on May 17, 1885. Pursued by regular and militia forces under the overall command of Gen. George C. Crook, he led raids into west central New Mexico and then fled into Mexico. But Chihuahua and his band remained in western New Mexico and eastern Arizona until late June, and both he and Geronimo raided into New Mexico in September, October, and in December" (Leiby 221).

5. Joan Myers's *Pie Town Woman* is a rewriting and retelling of Doris Caudill's stories of homesteading in the vicinity of Pie Town in the 1920s and 1930s. It includes homemade photographs, about which Caudill told the author stories, and a collection of professional photographs by Russell Lee taken in and

around Pie Town in the early 1940s as part of a depression-era federal government photographic project.

6. A photocopy of the printed document from which this excerpt is taken is among the papers of the late Florence Hawley Ellis maintained in the private archives kept by Andrea Dodge of Albuquerque, New Mexico.

7. The following is an excerpt from Robert G. Marmon's account:

"Service = April 1882[,] 83 & 84 Scout into the Datil Mountains after Apaches 6 days [initial number 3 appears crossed out and rewritten as] 500 miles—Numerous expeditions after thieves and rustlers 500 miles. Trip to Santa Fe [two illegible words] & competitive drill 2nd prize—against Santa Fe, Las Vegas and Albuquerque—Marched to Albuquerque Fair in 1883. Captured Cavalry Guidon, 1885 on scouts traveled over 1000 miles [two illegible words] as escort to Farmington—450 miles. 1886 after train wreckers. 6 days 200 miles—1887 31 men and horses by rail to Chicago to International Military Encampment was there 10 days in competitive drill 3rd prize awarded.

8. This excerpt comes from Robert G. Marmon's handwritten account on the back of a muster roll of the Laguna scouts' formation and active duty, which is among the papers of the late Florence Hawley Ellis maintained in the private archives kept by Andrea Dodge of Albuquerque, New Mexico.

9. Leiby portrays Walter G. Marmon as using "boys" to refer to the Lagunas under his command. The enclosure of this term between quotation marks may mark both Leiby's awareness of its patronizing and racist connotations and his attributing it to the commanding officer of the Laguna Regulars: "The Old Man also encouraged and assisted in the organization of other militia companies in the region, but to him his *'Laguna Boys'* were always first and always the best. He had been piqued and chagrined with the first Table of Organization and Equipment from Santa Fe. He cajoled and argued with Army and militia 'brass' until they transferred *his boys* into a cavalry unit—back in the saddles where they belonged!" (Leiby 215; my emphasis).

10. Andy's reasoning can be made explicit in the following paraphrase: I mean, Crows are Crows and Lagunas are Lagunas, what is there to say about that? Leiby includes a photograph with the subtitle "Troop F and Capt. Walter G. Marmon, 1882," in which can clearly be seen seven Lagunas mounted on small horses and one white man mounted on a large horse. All men are in full uniform. The Lagunas are holding rifles. Their hair, visibly emerging from under their military caps, is cut slightly above shoulder-length. To the extreme right in the photograph, a male figure, dressed in a civilian shirt, pants, and wide-brimmed hat, stands in a doorway, looking out at the mounted troopers. It is not possible to tell in what season this photograph was made, although the man in the doorway does not appear to be dressed for especially cold weather.

11. Given the phallic inferiority that is signified in his name, Littlecock most likely is doubly on the receiving end of this cavalier joke in which he would be mounted by his mount.

12. Kathryn Marmon, the spouse of Lee Marmon, states that a renegade Laguna was not killed, but captured: "The Apache Campaign ended with orders from the governor on June 21. The battalion had successfully warded off most Apaches from the local vicinity, returned the sick and injured to Laguna, and even captured a Laguna renegade" (59).

CHAPTER 4. DIALOGIC WITCHERY IN "TONY'S STORY"

1. "Tony's Story" was first published in 1969 in *Thunderbird*, a student literary magazine at the University of New Mexico.

2. It is not clear from Silko's text in which pueblo the procession carrying San Lorenzo back to his niche in the church is supposed to be located, nor is it clear from which pueblo Tony and Leon come. The Felipe brothers were from Acomita. In his list of patron saints and feast days for each pueblo, Joe S. Sando gives San Lorenzo for Picuris, San Esteban for Acoma, and San José for Laguna (273). It would seem that Silko's having chosen to set the opening of her retelling of the story of the Felipe brothers and Nash Garcia on San Lorenzo Day, rather than on Good Friday, sets the action in an abstract or fictionalized pueblo that resembles Laguna in its constitution and official governing structure.

3. Robert Silverberg's narrative of the Pueblo Revolt paints Popé as both a witch and a madman: "In person he was a fierce and dynamic individual who took care to give the impression that he was in league with dark powers. . . . He let it be known that demons and spirits attended him at all times; perhaps he believed it. In certain leaders greatness and madness are never very far apart, and Popé was such a leader" (114). Joe Sando plays down the importance of Popé and his leadership. He even suggests that this dark figure may be as much a creation of the Spanish view of the world as an actual person: "In explaining the Spanish view of the Pueblo Revolt, historical literature generally credits the San Juan Pueblo man Popé as the leader. However, as in most Pueblo endeavors, there were representatives from each village who helped plan and execute the revolt. Popé may have been Po-'png (pumpkin mountain), of San Juan, who was only one of the leaders" (68).

4. The Interpreter is one of the offices sanctioned in the Laguna constitution. In her account of the Laguna break of the 1870s, Florence Hawley Ellis portrays the Robert G. and Walter G. Marmon's writing of the Laguna constitution as part of the Protestants' effort to eliminate the syncretic tradition: "From their Protestant viewpoint the long-standing combination of old Pueblo beliefs and Roman Catholicism, supported by the native religious-governmental hierarchy, was stultifying. The Marmons set themselves to writing a constitution, the first to be adopted by any Pueblo, its text modeled after that of the United States. By 1872 Laguna was voting for its governor. Respect for the Marmons is seen in each being elected to serve one term as Laguna governor, an unprecedented arrangement" ("Laguna Pueblo" 447).

5. Silko's portrayal of her turn from a legal career to a career in storytelling as a quest for justice—"I decided the only way to seek justice was through the

power of the stories" (*Yellow Woman* 20)—occurs as a sarcastic parody of lawyers as "storytellers" in "Coyote Holds a Full House in His Hand" (159), which is analyzed in chapter 5.

6. Robert M. Nelson has speculated that the version of this story of the Gambler that is included in *Storyteller* shows signs of having come to Silko not only by word of mouth but also from ethnographic texts. In an article based on the hypothesis that "plenty of evidence suggests strongly that Silko's own familiarity with 'the long story of the people' derives not exclusively from having heard oral performances of it but also from having read portions of it—including portions recorded in Boas' *Keresan Texts* and in Gunn's *Schat-chen*" ("He Said/She Said" 33), Nelson cites Benedict's account of Kaup'a'ta, who "appears as a masked dancer at the Winter Solstice ceremony. He is blind and is led by his old grandmother" (46). Nelson's interpretation of Gunn's and Silko's story of Sun Man's cutting out the Gambler's eyes is ingenious: "In both cases, it seems, the protagonist not only must survive the encounter with the Gambler but must also disable him by exposing his empowering vision— literally and also figuratively—for all to see" (37).

7. Ruoff points out that the cop's high-pitched voice is similar to that of the Albino "witch" in Momaday's *House Made of Dawn*. She does not, however, broach the question of ambiguous gender figures in Keresan mythology.

8. Leon's perception of the cop as a white man is expressed as his sarcastic refusal of Tony's offer of an arrowhead to wear as protection. Tony's not being able to see the cop's eyes, even after the cop is dead, opens the possibility of his ethnic ambiguity. The unnamed cop could be white, or "Mexican"—like the real-life Nash Garcia—or a mixture of white, Mexican, and Indian. Just because he declares his hatred of Indians does not mean that he is not part Native American. Indeed, his excessive hatred could be attributed to his own mixed ancestry. Perhaps one can read this in the curious logic that emerges from his voiced bigotry: "I don't like smart guys, Indian. It's because of you bastards that I'm here. They transferred me here because of Indians. They thought there wouldn't be as many for me here. But I find them" (127–28). Where was this cop located before his transfer? One would think that the vicinity of Laguna and Acoma would be the place to send someone to be around more Indians rather than not around so many. Just as "no one ever knew where [the] witch [who wins the global witching contest] came from" (132), so it seems no one can say where the big cop-witch is coming from.

9. In chapter 6 I make the argument that, seen from old Yoeme's Yaqui point of view, which appears to resemble the point of view from which the writing storyteller views the evidence in the trial of the Felipe brothers, white justice can never be just. It is blind, dry (i.e., emotionless), analytic, linear, male, lethal, and telic. Silko's concept of justice emerges as perspicuous, loving, holistic, nonlinear, maternal, life-affirming, and open ended.

10. Within the writing storyteller resides the potential resolution of all sorts of burning conflicts, such as the "quarrel" between Grandma A'mooh and

Aunt Susie over whether the book *Stiya*, which was sent to Carlisle graduates to keep them from "going back to the blanket," should be burned. As I argue in the introduction, Aunt Susie's prevailing in keeping Grandma A'mooh from burning the book by requesting it as a gift results in its absence on Silko's side of the family. Just as *Storyteller* rewrites in its absence this sordid narrative of assimilation, so "Tony's Story" rewrites the yellow-journalistic narrative of assimilation of the now-absent Felipe brothers.

Tony's burning of the cop and his car, although it is obviously modeled on what the Felipe brothers did to Nash Garcia and his car, also recalls the ending of the story of Kaup'a'ta as translated in volume 1 of Boas's *Keresan Texts:* "Then they [the storm clouds] said, (25) "Behold," said they, "maybe it is ĸaup'a·ta´-Man who is burning the country," | thus said the storm clouds. "Enough," said they, "let us extinguish it," said they, "and | let us kill him," said the storm clouds. "Then let us do so," said the storm clouds. (I) "Hurry up," said the storm clouds. Then after a while all around | above clouds came up. Then all around it was raining. The storm clouds arrived there. | Alongside eastward they were running and mixed were flames and | water, for ĸaup'a·ta´ was surrounded (5) by flames and was ablaze" (82).

11. Ellis's account of the split portrays both the conservative and the progressive factions as accusing each other of witchery. Also according to Ellis, the leader of the progressive faction, Kwimé, brought in masks from Zuni that were associated by some Lagunas with witchery ("Laguna Pueblo" 447).

12. Linda Danielson makes an attempt, grounded in cultural sensitivity, to exorcise the Western concept of a wicked witch from Silko's Kochininako of "Estoy-eh-muut and the Kunideeyahs" (342). Within both Danielson's and Silko's understanding of witchery as "abused neutral power," there remains the metaphorical potential for writing to be an abuse of power, an ambiguous medicine.

CHAPTER 5. COYOTE LOOPS: LESLIE MARMON SILKO HOLDS A FULL HOUSE IN HER HAND

1. "Myths from many tribes begin with variants on the words used as the title of Jarold Ramsey's book *Coyote Was Going There* (1977)" (Bright 24).

2. *Canis latrans's* hunting behavior is often characterized by loops that begin where they end. The coyote may try to catch prey, say a turkey, by charging into the middle of a flock of these wild birds. Unsuccessful, it withdraws, only to run in a wide loop, allowing the turkeys to settle down, and then charge into the flock once again from the opposite direction. Silko's Coyote narrative resembles this loop, ending more or less where it begins.

3. One could liken the problem posed by the protagonist's interpretation of this Mexican postmaster's *chevaline* metaphor to the theoretical problem with interpretation posed by Paul de Man, a wily academic who in "Semiology and Rhetoric" comments on passages in which it is impossible to decide between

grammar and rhetoric. Coyote, like Archie Bunker, whom de Man reads as figuring the arch-debunkers, Nietzsche or Jacques Derrida, repeatedly poses the rhetorical question about grammar and rhetoric that is not a question: "What's the difference!" (29) When the reader of Silko's text attempts to painstakingly set out what this difference is, she/he cannot but assume a role analogous to that of Archie's dingbat wife, Edith. This is the role that the writing storyteller refuses to assume.

4. Helen Jaskoski points out that the protagonist's mother "had called him 'Sonny Boy'" (68). While sometimes used as a nickname in the same manner as terms like "Sonny," "Sis," or "Babe," "Sonny Boy" can also be used as a slightly reproachful form of address with which an adult, a parent in particular, signals his/her position of authority when admonishing a child. Jaskoski appears to place in doubt any motivated relationship between this name or nickname and the protagonist's identity: "who Sonny Boy really is and what happens to him remain enigmatic" (68). Thus, it would appear that she leaves open the possibility that Sonny Boy may be the eponymous Coyote. Nevertheless, each time Jaskoski names the protagonist "Sonny Boy," she strengthens the ironic contrast she draws between him as a "romantic" and "self-conscious, ineffective voyeur" and the "effective," "vigorous, conniving," and "powerful, appetite driven" American Indian trickster, Coyote, to whom she seems to grant in actuality the character traits that she denies the protagonist.

5. William Bright has adapted a Clatsop Chinook story in which Coyote speaks with his own "turds," receiving advice about taboos (38). Likewise Jay Miller refers to the "special power" Coyote received when his name was bestowed on him by "the leader." This power "lived in Coyote's intestines until he summoned their help. At that moment, they came out and took the form of five feces or, as polite Colvilles say, turds. Coyote called them his younger siblings and asked their advice, which they always gave wisely" (Jay Miller xii). In this failure to be repulsed by fecal matter the anonymous protagonist also calls to mind the scatological behavior of Pueblo clowns, which at times includes eating feces. Needless to say, Canis latrans shares with other canines a semiotico-olfactory fascination with feces.

6. William Bright refers to Canis latrans's capability of learning new behavior and "'developing a whole new lifestyle'" as neotony. Bright cites a zoologist, Hope Ryden, who attributes the coyote's "motivation and ability to learn" to having remained "dependent on their parents for a relatively long period" (55). The main thing the protagonist appears to have learned during his dependence on his mother for a very long period is how to tell stories to justify his lifestyle.

7. It is interesting to see what happens in this text to the referential categories of Michael McCarthy, who, in "It, this and that," distinguishes between anaphoric, cataphoric, and exophoric usages of pronouns. In the most common usage (the anaphoric), the pronoun refers back to a preceding linguistic context. In the less common cataphoric usage, the pronoun refers forward to something

that is going to be mentioned later. In the exophoric usage, which McCarthy notes is very common in spoken discourse, the pronoun points outside the text to a situation or to an object. McCarthy's categories assume that written and spoken discourse is predominantly linear and can be correctly construed as being delimited by a beginning and an end, an inside and an outside. In Silko's text, which many critics find to be organized according to predominantly nonlinear patterns such as a spider web (Danielson), the intersection of mythological temporality and narrative and the occurrence of narrative loops within narrative loops, as occurs in Coyote stories, the distinction between endophoric and exophoric tends to break down, as does the viable setting of contextual limits. The passages in which the pronoun *it* occurs are characterized by a dizzying referential whirligig that is simultaneously endophoric, exophoric, anaphoric, and cataphoric. Such is the world of a gambler on a roll or the world of discourse in a looping Coyote narrative.

8. For an excellent illustrated history of the invention of the Pueblo storyteller doll, see Barbara A. Babcock and Guy and Doris Monthan, *The Pueblo Storyteller*.

CHAPTER 6. *ALMANAC OF THE DEAD*

1. In the interview with Arnold, Silko's belief in her own postcolonial messianic role in bearing this nonwhite woman's burden is explicit in her talk about her German ancestral spirits and about the comfort *Almanac* had provided to despairing former East German women in Leipzig. For Silko in this interview, the normative Pueblo voice that earlier informed *Ceremony* and *Storyteller* has expanded to fill the world: "Yes! I wrote that novel to the world, and I was thinking about the Germans, I was thinking about the Europeans. I believe that the Pueblo people, the indigenous people of the Americas, we're not only Indian nations and sovereign nations and people, but we are citizens of the world" ("Listening to the Spirits" 165).

2. See chapter 5. I follow up on this argument in chapter 7. In effect, Silko's use of the *style indirect libre* puts the notions of narrative objectivity and literary realism in question.

3. This can be seen in the writings of Marx, who reverses Hegelian dialectic, replacing the spiritual with the materialistic, the otherworldly with the worldly, the master with the worker. It can also be seen in the sayings and parables of Christ, the exegetic logic of which could be said to inform Hegel's dialectics: "But many who are first shall be last; and the last shall be first" (Matt. 19:30). The parable of the talents (Matt. 25.14–30) is an especially interesting example of a self-reflexive, semiotico-monetary, exegetic, and apocalyptic metaphor that commands the hearer to enter into a chain of exegetes in order to avoid being among the damned at the Final Judgment. The old almanac and the notebooks passed on to Zeta and Lecha are similar to the talents of Christ's parable. The first and second servants' multiplying the talents given to them

by the Master, or passing the one talent on to the "exchangers" in order that the Master might receive "mine own with usury" (Matt. 30.27), which the third servant is told he should have done rather than burying it in the earth, is analogous to translating, glossing, and transcribing the old book and the notebooks. Silko, in this exegetic analogy, would not so much be the Antichrist as an analogue of Mary Magdalene, friend of an alternative Christ as constructed by Gnostic heretics. In *Gardens in the Dunes* Silko depicts a syncretism of Native American and Christian religion in which Gnosticism with its aboriginal matriarchal spirituality becomes a revolutionary challenge to orthodox Christianity and modern scientific objectivity.

4. In chapter 1 I have commented on Silko's speculation about her Japanese translator having made her appear Japanese in a photograph. From the interviews with Irmer and Schmidt and with Ellen Arnold (Arnold, *Conversations* 146–61 and 162–95), there emerges Silko's own vision of how she has been Germanized by the translation and by the contact with the spirits of her German ancestors. In chapter 7 the theme of *glossolalia* or *xenoglossia* in *Gardens in the Dunes* raises the question of the perfect language and its relation to the glyphic writing of the Mayas, which Silko appears to consider ontologically privileged.

5. Although St. Clair points to some of the theoretical and practical problems that arise from ethnocentrism and the attempts of these three women Indian writers to deal with them, she does not unravel the problems and paradoxes in her reading of *Almanac*. Clifford Geertz and Richard Rorty took up the problem of ethnocentrism, anti-ethnocentrism, diversity, and the paradox that anti-ethnocentrism is ethnocentric in a debate in the mid-1980s. Like St. Clair, Geertz and Rorty both refuse to give up hope completely. They believe that there can be some kind of solution to the moral, economic, political, and religious problems that arise from conflicting ethnocentric cultures, but they seem to be somewhat more pessimistic than St. Clair. See Geertz, "The Uses of Diversity," and Rorty, "On Ethnocentrism: A Reply to Clifford Geertz."

6. It is tempting for the reader of this passage of multiple and ambiguous referents to regard Yoeme's narrative as a philosophical and hermeneutic joke similar in some respects to Borges's "The Library of Babel." Silko's discourse, however, is different from that of Borges, as is her approach to the philosophical questions that Borges's text poses and toys with. Whereas the Argentine master of the short story leaves his reader trapped in an eternal and infinite linguistic labyrinth where writing never seems quite to allow access to an extratextual reality, Silko passes on to her reader a written reality riddled with lacunae, which, as it is being filled, dreams of being an absolute reality in which linguistic mediation ultimately becomes unnecessary. In other words, for Borges the universe cannot but be Babelian and any attempts to reverse the *confusio linguarum* brought about in Genesis 11 will lead only to endless chains of signifiers. For Silko, however, linguistic mendacity can be transcended in a post-Babelian perfect language. This question is taken up in chapter 7.

7. David Moore offers a postmodernist reading of these stories in which the Indian storytellers' voices metaphorically weave a polysemous text that the white military readers insist on reading as a linear narrative with Geronimo in the position of the nonproblematic signified. See Moore, "Silko's Blood Sacrifice."

8. In Mayan thought the jaguar is associated with sacred power, authority, and prophecy. Ironically, Amalia's inner pain, her consumption, is prophetic of what is to happen to white culture in the Americas. See David Drew 403.

9. In some cultures twins are not only considered to be bad luck, they are exposed and allowed to die. Yoeme here does not appear to envisage killing either of her twin granddaughters. Rather she turns out to have in mind persuading her daughter to give one of them to her. El Feo and Tacho, the twin Mayan brothers who lead the army from the south, "had been separated because twins often attracted dangers from envious sorcerers" (469).

10. Silko studied at the University of New Mexico Law School for three semesters before dropping out. It was in reading "between the lines" of Dickens's *Bleak House* that she understood that the Anglo-American legal system cannot deliver justice (*Yellow Woman* 19–20). Ironically, although Silko has declared that she "wanted nothing to do with such a barbaric legal system" (20), becoming a writer has given her something to do with it, though she only does it "between the lines."

11. The imagery of dust and desiccation used to portray the nothingness of Western culture recalls the description of the end of white people to be effected by the Ghost Dance in *Gardens in the Dunes* (23). In this novel Edward's death in the desert is also causally related to a mad scheme to mine the earth for gems in meteorites.

12. These questions are obviously related to a similar juridical question one could ask about Zeta and Lecha's grandfather Guzman: Did he commit a crime by doing *nothing* when the Mexican soldiers hanged his Indian in-laws from the cottonwood trees. The question concerning the nameless geologist is philosophically harder to answer than the question concerning the "old fucker Guzman."

13. The film *Ravenous*, directed by Antonia Bird (Fox 2000 Pictures, 1999) stages cannibalism as a metaphor for western expansion. Rather than courage, strength, respect for humanity, and a desire to found a utopian farmer's republic, the traits of the white "heroes" in this film are cowardice, weakness, cruelty, and ravenous greed. The result is literally a man-eat-man world that can logically end only with the top "dog" consuming himself after he has consumed everybody else.

CHAPTER 7. *TOLLE, LEGE:*
GLOSSING GLOSSOLALIA IN *GARDENS IN THE DUNES*

1. The Grand Tour can be said to have begun in the sixteenth century, coinciding with the rise of Renaissance humanism in Europe. By the eighteenth

century it had become fashionable for sons of English aristocracy to make a journey of two or three years through Europe in order to enrich their knowledge of the classical past and develop the socially desirable skills of a connoisseur. By the middle of the eighteenth century educated middle-class persons were also traveling. "Travellers followed a well-established route, musing—more enthusiastically as the century wore on—on the sublime landscape of the Alps, with the glories of ancient Rome and Naples as their main aim; Herculaneum was excavated from 1711 onwards and Pompeii from 1733. Travelers admired the works of the great Venetians and of 17th-cent. Bolognese painters" ("The Grand Tour"). By the Victorian age, middle-class women as well as men, from England and America, were also going on the Grand Tour. Before her marriage, Hattie has already planned to travel in Italy. By the mid-twentieth century, when European languages were still a popular academic major in American universities, study abroad took the place of the Grand Tour for educated Americans. Silko's book promotion tours to Europe have provided her with a postcolonial as well as a postcommunist version of the Grand Tour in which an enthusiasm for the suppressed matriarchal pre-Christian cultural artifacts replaces the humanist reverence of monuments of dominant Greco-Roman and Judeo-Christian patriarchy.

2. Ellen Arnold describes *Gardens in the Dunes* as a "tale of adventure, intrigue, and mystery" that "draws on elements of the naturalist tradition, American Transcendentalism, and Gothic Romance—invoking writers as diverse as James, Edith Wharton, D. H. Lawrence, the Brontes, Wilkie Collins, and Margaret Fuller" and also as a "meticulously researched historical novel set at the turn of the Twentieth Century" (101). Despite the meticulousness of her research, Silko appears to have taken certain liberties. It is unlikely that in 1900 a Catholic would have been admitted to Vassar or that a thesis committee would have been established at Harvard for an auditor.

3. Saint Augustine tells how upon hearing the voice of a child of indeterminate sex chanting the words *tolle, lege* (take up and read), he picked up the Bible and read the first words his eyes fell upon (Rom. 13.13–14). From the orthodox perspective of exclusionary logic, reading these words turned Augustine toward the true God (*Confessions* VIII.12) and away from the heresies in which he had been darkly entangled with false gods. Hattie's taking up a Gnostic text and reading words that she then relates exegetically to what, from an orthodox perspective, would be called her apostasy can be construed from a syncretic perspective informed by an inclusionary logic as the obverse of Augustine's conversion. Thus, from the orthodox and exclusionary perspective, "reading words from a Gnostic text turned Hattie to the Serpent (i.e., a false god)" could be construed as "reading words from a Gnostic text did not turn Hattie to the false God." An orthodox theologian would call this obversion a sophist's trick or declare it to be an example of Satan glossing scripture. Vedna and Maytha, who also practice this form of bibliomancy, and Sister Salt, enjoy turning tricks of exactly the kind Saint Paul's words in Romans lead Augustine to give up.

4. My exegetic role in the selection of the scene of the first Ghost Dance imitates the authorial role of Silko when she depicts Hattie opening Dr. Rhinehart's translation at random or when she depicts the bibliomancy practiced by Vedna and Maytha, the Chemehuevi-Laguna twin sisters who are friends of Sister Salt. On several occasions the twins open their Bible to passages and illustrations that they interpret, taking counsel and foretelling the future. In selecting the passages from the Bible and from Pagels's book, Silko assumes the position of an omniscient intelligence. The warning Lecha gives to Seese in *Almanac of the Dead*—"Nothing happens by accident here" (21)—is apposite as a hermeneutic principle in the web of linked themes that are Silko's text, in which the Spirit or the spirits are always at work.

5. This scene can be read as a metaphor for *Gardens,* in which the flowers, the tropes, of Silko's and the Holy Mother's rhetoric are given to the dancers, the readers, to eat. At the end of the book Indigo points out to Vedna and Maytha that the gladiolus that she brought back from her Grand Tour are edible. At the end of this chapter I point out that on occasion these flowers are also poisonous.

6. Umberto Eco's *The Search for the Perfect Language* provides an account of Western writers from antiquity until the present who have speculated about and in some cases attempted to find or construct a version of the language that Indigo and Sister Salt remember the Messiah and his family speaking at the Ghost Dance.

7. Dante depicts Nimrod in Hell as understanding no languages and speaking a language known to no one: "*Raphèl maÿ amècche zabì almi*" (*Inferno* 31:64). For Dante and the medieval exegetic tradition, this giant hunter incarnates savagery, schism, and heresy. His babble is the antitype of the gift of tongues.

8. In Pieter Breughel the Elder's painting of the Tower of Babel, a whirlwind-like cloud can be seen approaching in the sky in the upper left-hand corner of the painting as masons and other workers kneel down before a king who is in all likelihood Nimrod. Breughel, in the spirit of the Age of Exploration, has made the site of Babel a port. Ships are anchored near some of the machinery that is being used to construct the tower. No doubt some of these ships in this Renaissance setting have come from or are bound for the New World. The tower itself is an unfinished ziggurat consisting of cut stone masonry and a natural rock promontory. Its form mirrors the approaching whirlwind. It is difficult to tell whether this structure is under construction or in ruins, whether it is a natural mountain or a stone edifice. (1563. 44 7/8" × 61". Kunsthistorisches Museum, Vienna.)

9. An ideological variation on this exegetic debate about the Judeo-Christian genesis of languages can be found in the debate between Vine Deloria Jr. and his followers, who contend that Native Americans originated in the Americas, and paleontologists who hypothesize Africa to be the homebirthplace of *Homo sapiens.*

10. In Silko's third-person narration, this scheme is informed by paradox, as is most discourse concerning religious ecstasy and spiritual vision. In the

scene of the apparition on the Corsican schoolhouse wall, Silko's third-person narrator can be shown to perform for the characters as well as for the reader what Eco refers to when he glosses *xenoglossia* as "a sort of mystic service of simultaneous translation" (351). It is not unusual for a third-person narrator to perform the role of translator for the reader. For the narrator to perform this role also for the characters, however, opens the discussion of narrative point of view in Silko's text onto a theoretical abyss where orthodox patristic exegesis of Genesis 10 and 11 confronts American Indian and Gnostic syncretism.

11. This perfect orality is a myth that is approximated in the Text as described by Roland Barthes. Barthes' flowery attempt in "From Work to Text" to describe the Text as "the very plural of meaning" (902) takes the form of a stroll in a North African desert garden during which his senses open into a dreamlike glossolalia in writing.

12. J. Hillis Miller offers a demonstration of the dilemma created by indirect discourse and irony: "Since irony is a form of endless looping or feedback, this instability suggests that the interpreter can never go beyond any passage that he or she takes as a starting place, if the problem of interpreting is taken as a serious task" (163).

13. Arnold does not give much detail about what exactly is entailed in this "kind of realism in the tradition of Henry James" (review 101). J. Hillis Miller has eloquently argued in "The Figure in the Carpet" (84–105) that James's "realism" is far from simple. In texts like the short story "The Figure in the Carpet," "the story dramatizes the experience of undecidability, or, rather, since this experience can only be named in figure, it presents figures for it, not least in the recurrent pattern of interpersonal relations that forms the human base for the story's allegorizing of its own unreadability" (98). If Arnold had this "kind of realism" in mind in her review of *Gardens in the Dunes*, then she is on target.

14. Hattie is shut up in the American embassy while Edward is being processed by Italian police and officials. There she resorts to an Italian phrase book in order to know how to tell the messenger boy to keep the change as tip (323). This would suggest that her oral linguistic skills in Italian are quite limited.

15. Edward is depicted as having a reading knowledge of Latin in the scene with Aunt Bronwyn where he reads the inscription on a Roman lead curse tablet: "Edward was in a good humor as he read the inscribed curse: 'To the goddess Sulis. Whether slave or free, whoever he shall be, you are not to permit him eyes or health. He shall be blind and childless so long as he shall live unless he returns'—the next word is illegible—'to the temple'" (258). Despite his superior education and linguistic skills that allow him to read this curse, Edward remains blind, like the person on whom the curse is placed, to what Hattie, Aunt Bronwyn, Indigo, and the parrot, Rainbow, can feel.

16. There are faint echoes here of American Indian stories recounting the time when people and animals still spoke the same language. Sister Salt also shows signs of a gift for unusual communication with the developing fetus of the little grandfather: "At first she had difficulty understanding the language

her baby spoke to her from the womb, but then she recognized the Sand Lizard words pronounced in baby talk" (333). Obliquely suggested in this somewhat cutesy passage is that the fictional tongue spoken by the Sand Lizards is a natural language known through blood memory. Conceiving of such a language, to whose speakers infancy apparently would be unknown, involves logical problems similar to those that have faced "serious" linguists glossing Adam's naming the animals (Gen. 2).

17. The procession could also be interpreted as a community ritual resembling the processions led by a person carrying the saint from the church to the corn altar, which Silko must have seen at Laguna on feast day. Marcia Keegan has included two pictures of such a procession at Laguna in her photographic book on the Pueblos (*Pueblo People* 77, 81). Thus, it is possible to detect here an inkling of a theme that shows up both in this novel and in interviews with Silko after she has visited Europe: The worldview of some European folk cultures resembles in many respects that of American Indian cultures.

18. In the essay entitled "On Photography," Silko speculates about the energy registered in photographs and generated by groups of people: "The origin of waves or particles of light-energy that may give such a sinister cast to a photograph is as yet unexplained. Fields of electromagnetic force affect light. Crowds of human beings massed together emanate actual electricity. Individual perceptions of behavior are altered. Witnesses report feeling an 'electricity' that binds and propels a mob as a single creature" (*Yellow Woman* 182). Silko does not document her sources.

19. It is possible to explain "miraculous" apparitions according to the laws of physics. A divine intention can be said to coincide with the "random" occurrence of sun dogs, rainbows, crepuscular glows, will-o'-the-wisps, and other physical phenomena involving light. To debate whether or not such apparitions are miraculous is equivalent to debating whether what happens in the world is controlled by a divine power and plan or is subject to a mixture of chance and human actions. Miracles involving sudden cures or dripping blood pose other problems. The scene of the apparition in *Gardens* can be shown to conform to the definition of the fantastic as a narrative genre given by Tzvetan Todorov. Todorov distinguishes the fantastic from the marvelous. The marvelous cannot be explained by the laws of nature that are known to scientists. Children who fly, vampires, the living dead, and so on belong to this genre. The fantastic is constructed narratively in such a way that the narrator tells the event in either the third or the first person, and consequently the reader is left undecided between either a natural or a supernatural explanation (75–90).

20. This is also the case at the Ghost Dance: "Dawn was the time the Messiah and his family were expected to come" (468). "They must sing hard if they wanted the Christ and his eleven children to come down from the mountains at dawn" (30).

21. See the 1998 interview with Ellen Arnold ("Listening to the Spirits" 185), in which Silko fulminates against "laissez faire, trample-people-into-the-dirt,

destroy-the-earth capitalism," which she distinguishes from "the free market and private property" (185). She also fulminates against "giant Communism" and "Big Socialism" (186). Silko's economic ideological position appears to favor a kind of green bioregionalism, without national boundaries, with trade and markets based on principles found in American Indian cultures.

22. Hattie learns before leaving England that the Coptic scrolls translated by Dr. Rhinehart have been authenticated. Her reaction to this is conflicted between a desire to return to the debate with Harvard professors and an apparent fatigue with scholarly writing: "now she could petition the thesis committee to reconsider their decision. But almost as soon as she had the thought, she realized she had no desire to return to the committee or to the thesis, though she could not explain this reluctance" (266).

23. Silko gives the following translation of these words: "The people are hungry. The people are cold. The rich have stolen the land. The rich have stolen freedom. The people demand justice. Otherwise, Revolution" (*Yellow Woman* 149).

24. A reproduction of this mural and some of Silko's gloss on it can be found in *Yellow Woman and a Beauty of the Spirit* (149–51).

WORKS CITED

Allen, Paula Gunn. "Special Problems in Teaching Leslie Marmon Silko's *Ceremony*." *American Indian Quarterly* 14 (1990): 379–86.

Anzaldúa, Gloria. *Borderlands/La Frontera: The New Mestiza*. 1987. San Francisco: Aunt Lute Books, 1999.

———. Rev. of *Gardens in the Dunes*, by Leslie Marmon Silko. *S.A.I.L.* 11.2 (1999): 101–104.

Babcock, Barbara, and Guy and Doris Monthan. *The Pueblo Storyteller: Development of a Figurative Ceramic Tradition*. Tucson: University of Arizona Press, 1986.

Barnett, Louise K., and James L. Thorson, eds. *Leslie Marmon Silko: A Collection of Critical Essays*. Albuquerque: University of New Mexico Press, 1999.

Barthes, Roland. "From Work to Text." Trans. Richard Howard. *The Critical Tradition: Classic Texts and Contemporary Trends*. 2nd ed. Ed. David H. Richter. Boston: Bedford Books, 1998. 900–905.

———. *S/Z*. Trans. Richard Miller. New York: Hill and Wang, 1974.

Bell, Robert C. "Circular Design in *Ceremony*." *American Indian Quarterly* 5 (1979): 15–18.

Benjamin, Walter. *Illuminations*. 1969. Ed. Hannah Arendt. New York: Schocken Books, 1973.

Birkerts, Sven. "Leslie Marmon Silko." *American Energies: Essays on Fiction*. New York: William Morrow, 1992. 347–53.

Blakemore, Frances. "Yohaku, Space (on Painting) Left Intentionally Blank." *Discover Japan: Words, Customs and Concepts*. Vol. 1. Tokyo: Kodansha, 1982. 200–201.

Boas, Franz. *Keresan Texts*. Pt. 1. New York: American Ethnological Society, 1928.

Bohm, David, and F. David Peat. *Science, Order, and Creativity*. New York: Routledge, 2000.

Borges, Jorge Luis. *Ficciones*. Trans. Anthony Kerrigan. New York: Grove Press, 1962.

Bright, William. *A Coyote Reader*. Berkeley: University of California Press, 1993.

Bruner, Edward M. "Ethnography as Narrative." *The Anthropology of Experience*. Ed. Victor W. Turner and Edward M. Bruner. Urbana: University of Illinois Press, 1986. 139–55.

Burgess, Marion. *Stiya: A Carlisle Indian Girl at Home*. Cambridge: Riverside Press, 1891.

Burrows, George E., and Ronald J. Tyrl. *Toxic Plants of North America*. Ames: Iowa State University Press, 2001.

Coe, Michael D. *Breaking the Maya Code*. New York: Thames and Hudson, 1992.

Danielson, Linda L. "*Storyteller:* Grandmother Spider's Web." *Journal of the Southwest* 30.3 (1988): 325–55.

Dante Alighieri. *The Divine Comedy: Inferno*. Trans. Charles Singleton. Princeton: Princeton University Press, 1970.

Debo, Angie. *Geronimo: The Man, His Time, His Place*. Norman: University of Oklahoma Press, 1976.

De Man, Paul. "Semiology and Rhetoric." *diacritics* 3.3 (1973): 27–33.

Derrida, Jacques. "Des Tours de Babel." *Acts of Religion*. Trans. Joseph F. Graham. Ed. Gil Anidjar. New York: Routledge, 2002. 104–34.

———. *La dissémination*. Paris: Editions du Seuil, 1972.

Drew, David. *The Lost Chronicles of the Maya Kings*. Berkeley: University of California Press, 1999.

Eco, Umberto. *The Search for the Perfect Language*. Trans. James Fentress. Oxford: Blackwell, 1995.

Eliade, Mircea. *The Sacred and the Profane: The Nature of Religion*. Trans. Willard R. Trask. New York: Harcourt, 1987.

Ellis, Florence Hawley. "Laguna Pueblo." *Southwest*. Ed. Alfonzo Ortiz. Washington: Smithsonian Institution, 1979. 438–49. Vol. 9 of *Handbook of North American Indians*.

———. "An Outline of Laguna Pueblo History and Social Organization." *Southwestern Journal of Anthropology* 15.4 (1959): 325–47.

Evers, Lawrence. "The Killing of a New Mexican State Trooper: Ways of Telling an Historical Event." *Critical Essays on Native American Literature*. Ed. Andrew Wiget. Boston: G. K. Hall, 1985. 246–61.

Fienup-Riordan, Ann. *Eskimo Essays*. New Brunswick: Rutgers University Press, 1990.

Geertz, Clifford. "The Uses of Diversity." *Michigan Quarterly Review* 25.1 (1986): 105–23.

"Gift of tongues." *American Heritage Dictionary of the English Language*. 4th ed. 2000.

Gingerich, Willard. "Heidegger and the Aztecs: The Poetics of Knowing in Pre-Hispanic Nahuatl Poetry." *Recovering the Word*. Ed. Brian Swann and Arnold Krupat. Berkeley: University of California Press, 1987. 85–112.

"Glossolalia." *American Heritage Dictionary of the English Language.* 4th ed. 2000.

"The Grand Tour." *The Oxford Companion to English Literature.* 5th ed. Ed. Margaret Drabble. Oxford: Oxford University Press, 1985.

Hill, Elizabeth Boone, and Walter D. Mignolo, eds. *Writing without Words: Alternative Literacies in Mesoamerica and the Andes.* Durham: Duke University Press, 1994.

Hirsch, Bernard A. "'The Telling Which Continues': Oral Tradition and the Written Word in Leslie Marmon Silko's *Storyteller.*" *American Indian Quarterly* 12.1 (1988): 1–25.

Holy Bible. Authorized (King James) Version. Philadelphia: National Bible Press, n.d.

Jaskoski, Helen. *Leslie Marmon Silko: A Study of the Short Fiction.* New York: Twayne, 1998.

Jones, Patricia. "The Web of Meaning: Naming the Absent Mother in *Storyteller.*" *"Yellow Woman": Leslie Marmon Silko.* Ed. Melanie Graulich. New Brunswick: Rutgers University Press, 1993. 213–32.

Keegan, Marcia. *Pueblo People: Ancient Traditions and Modern Lives.* Santa Fe: Clear Light Publishers, 1999.

Krupat, Arnold. "The Dialogic of Silko's *Storyteller.*" *Narrative Chance: Postmodern Discourse on Native American Indian Literatures.* Ed. Gerald Vizenor. Albuquerque: University of New Mexico Press, 1989. 55–68.

———. "Post-Structuralism and Oral Literature." *Recovering the Word: Essays on Native American Literature.* Ed. Brian Swann and Arnold Krupat. Berkeley: University of California Press, 1987. 113–28.

Leiby, Austin N. "The Marmon Battalion and the Apache Campaign of 1885." *The Changing Ways of Southwestern Indians: A Historic Perspective.* Ed. Albert H. Schroeder. Glorieta: Rio Grande Press, 1973.

Lincoln, Kenneth. *Native American Renaissance.* Berkeley: University of California Press, 1983.

"Magic Realism." *The Oxford Companion to English Literature.* 5th ed. Ed. Margaret Drabble. Oxford: Oxford University Press, 1985.

Mallarmé, Stéphane. *Oeuvres Complètes.* Paris: Bibliothèque de la Pléiade, 1965.

Marmon, Kathryn. "Native Mission: Laguna Scouts Prominent in Apache Campaign." *New Mexico Magazine* Aug. 2002: 58–59.

Mattina, Anthony. "North American Indian Mythography: Editing Texts for the Printed Page." *Recovering the Word: Essays on Native American Literature.* Ed. Brian Swann and Arnold Krupat. Berkeley: University of California Press, 1987. 129–48.

McCarthy, Michael. *"It, this* and *that.*" *Advances in Written Text Analysis.* Ed. Malcolm Coulthard. London: Routledge, 1994.

Mignolo, Walter D. *The Darker Side of the Renaissance: Literacy, Territoriality, and Colonization.* Ann Arbor: University of Michigan Press, 1995.

Miller, J. Hillis. *Reading Narrative.* Norman: University of Oklahoma Press, 1998.

Miller, Jay. Introduction. *Coyote Stories*. By Mourning Dove. Lincoln: University of Nebraska Press, 1990. v–xvii.

Moore, David L. "Decolonializing Critics: Reading *Dialectics* and *Dialogics* in Native American Literatures." *S.A.I.L.* 6.4 (1994): 7–33.

———. "Silko's Blood Sacrifice: The Circulating Witness in *Almanac of the Dead*." *Leslie Marmon Silko: A Collection of Critical Essays*. Ed. Louise K. Barnett and James L. Thorson. Albuquerque: University of New Mexico Press, 1999. 149–83.

Myers, Joan. *Pie Town Woman: The Hard Times and Good Life of a New Mexico Homesteader*. Albuquerque: University of New Mexico Press, 2001.

Nelson, Robert M. "He Said/She Said: Writing Oral Tradition in John Gunn's 'Ko-pot Ka-nat' and Leslie Silko's *Storyteller*." *S.A.I.L.* 5.1 (1993): 31–50.

———. "Rewriting Ethnography: The Embedded Texts in Leslie Silko's *Ceremony*." http://www.richmond.edu/~rnelson/ethnography.html.

Ong, Walter J. *Orality and Literacy: The Technologizing of the Word*. 1982. New York: Routledge, 2002.

Ortiz, Alfonso, ed. *New Perspectives on the Pueblos*. Albuquerque: University of New Mexico Press, 1972.

Owens, Louis. *I Hear the Train: Reflections, Inventions, Refractions*. Norman: University of Oklahoma Press, 2001.

———. *Other Destinies: Understanding the American Indian Novel*. Norman: University of Oklahoma Press, 1992.

Pagels, Elaine. *The Gnostic Gospels*. 1979. New York: Vintage, 1989.

Parsons, Elsie Clews. "Notes on Ceremonialism at Laguna." *Anthropological Papers of the American Museum of Natural History*. Vol. 19, pt. 4. New York: 1920.

———. *Pueblo Indian Religion*. 1939. Vols. 1 and 2. Lincoln: University of Nebraska Press, 1996.

Perez-Castillo, Susan. "Postmodernism, Native American Literature, and the Real: The Silko-Erdrich Controversy." *Massachusetts Review* 32.1 (1991): 285–94.

Rorty, Richard. "On Ethnocentrism: A Reply to Clifford Geertz." *Michigan Quarterly Review* 35.3 (1986): 524–34.

Ruoff, A. Lavonne. "Ritual and Renewal: Keres Traditions in the Short Fiction of Leslie Silko." *MELUS* 5.4 (1978): 2–17.

Salyer, Greg. *Leslie Marmon Silko*. New York: Twayne, 1997.

Sando, Joe S. *Pueblo Nations: Eight Centuries of Pueblo Indian History*. Santa Fe: Clear Light, 1992.

Silko, Leslie Marmon. *Almanac of the Dead*. New York: Penguin Books, 1981.

———. *Ceremony*. New York: Penguin Books, 1977.

———. "A Conversation with Leslie Marmon Silko." By Lawrence Evers and Denny Carr. *Sun Tracks* 3.1 (1976): 28–33.

———. *The Delicacy and Strength of Lace: Letters between Leslie Marmon Silko and James Wright*. Ed. Anne Wright. St. Paul: Graywolf Press, 1985.

————. *Gardens in the Dunes*. New York: Scribner, 2000.

————. "From *Humaweepi, the Warrior Priest*." *The Man to Send Rain Clouds: Contemporary Stories by American Indians*. Ed. Kenneth Rosen. New York: Viking, 1974. 161–68.

————. "An Interview with Leslie Marmon Silko. By Thomas Irmer and Matthias Schmidt. *Conversations with Leslie Marmon Silko*. Ed. Ellen Arnold. Jackson: University of Mississippi Press, 2000. 146–61.

————. "Language and Literature from a Pueblo Indian Perspective." *Selected Papers from the English Institute*. Ed. Leslie Fiedler and Houston A. Baker Jr. Baltimore: Johns Hopkins University Press, 1981. 54–72.

————. "A Leslie Marmon Silko Interview." By Kim Barnes. *"Yellow Woman": Leslie Marmon Silko*. Ed. Melody Graulich. New Brunswick: Rutgers University Press, 1993. 47–65.

————. "Listening to the Spirits: An Interview with Leslie Marmon Silko." By Ellen Arnold. *Conversations with Leslie Marmon Silko*. Ed. Ellen Arnold. Jackson: University of Mississippi Press, 2000. 162–95.

————. "Narratives of Survival." By Linda Nieman. *Conversations with Leslie Marmon Silko*. Ed. Ellen Arnold. Jackson: University of Mississippi Press, 2000. 107–12.

————. "The Past Is Right Here and Now: An Interview with Leslie Marmon Silko." By Ray Gonzalez. *Conversations with Leslie Marmon Silko*. Ed. Ellen Arnold. Jackson: University of Mississippi Press, 2000. 97–106.

————. *Sacred Water: Narrative and Pictures*. Tucson: Flood Plain Press, 1993.

————. "Stories and Their Tellers—A Conversation with Leslie Marmon Silko." By Dexter Fisher. *The Third Woman: Minority Women Writers of the United States*. Ed. Dexter Fisher. Boston: Houghton Mifflin, 1980. 18–23.

————. *Storyteller*. New York: Seaver, 1981.

————. *Yellow Woman and a Beauty of the Spirit: Essays on Native American Life Today*. New York: Simon and Schuster, 1996.

Silverberg, Robert. *The Pueblo Revolt*. Lincoln: University of Nebraska Press, 1994.

Standing Bear, Luther. *My People the Sioux*. 1928. Lincoln: University of Nebraska Press, 1975.

St. Clair, Janet. "Death of Love/Love of Death: Leslie Marmon Silko's *Almanac of the Dead*." *MELUS* 21.2 (1996): 141–56.

————. "Uneasy Ethnocentrism: Recent Works of Allen, Silko, and Hogan." *S.A.I.L.* 6.1 (1994): 83–98.

Todorov, Tzvetan. *The Fantastic: A Structural Approach to a Literary Genre*. Trans. Richard Howard. Cleveland: Press of Case Western Reserve University, 1973.

Turner, Victor W. "Myth and Symbol." *International Encyclopedia of the Social Sciences*. Vol. 10. Ed. David L. Sill. New York: Macmillan, 1968. 576–82.

VanderWolk, William. "Gustave Flaubert." *The Johns Hopkins Guide to Literary Theory and Criticism*. Ed. Michael Groden and Martin Kreiswirth. Baltimore: Johns Hopkins University Press, 1994.

Witherspoon, Gary. *Language and Art in the Navajo Universe*. Ann Arbor: University of Michigan Press, 1977.

Young, Robert W., and William Morgan. *The Navajo Language: A Grammar and Colloquial Dictionary*. Albuquerque: University of New Mexico Press, 1980.

INDEX